Cosmopolitanism and the Development of the International Criminal Court

The Fairleigh Dickinson University Press Series in Communication Studies

General Editor:
Gary Radford, Department of Communication Studies, Fairleigh Dickinson University, Madison, New Jersey.

The Fairleigh Dickinson University Press Series in Communication Studies publishes scholarly works in communication theory, practice, history, and culture.

Recent Publications in Communication Studies

Jennifer Biedendorf, *Cosmopolitanism and the Development of the International Criminal Court: Non-Governmental Organizations' Advocacy and Transnational Human Rights* (2019)
Kate Dunsmore, *Discourse of Reciprocity* (2019)
Paul Matthew St. Pierre, *Cinematography of Carl Theodor Dreyer: Performative Camerawork, Transgressing the Frame* (2018)
Michelle Scollo and Trudy Milburn (eds.), *Engaging and Transforming Global Communication through Cultural Discourse Analysis: A Tribute to Donal Carbaugh* (2018)
Isaac E. Catt, *Embodiment in the Semiotic Matrix: Communicology in Peirce, Dewey, Bateson, and Bourdieu* (2017)
Craig T. Maier, *Communicating Catholicism: Rhetoric, Ecclesial Leadership, and the Future of the American Roman Catholic Diocese* (2016)
Paul Matthew St. Pierre, *Cinematography in the Weimar Republic: Lola-Lola, Dirty Singles, and the Men Who Shot Them* (2016)
Anastacia Kurylo and Tatyana Dumov (eds.), *Social Networking: Redefining Communication in the Digital Age* (2016)
Phil Rose, *Radiohead and the Global Movement for Change: "Pragmatism Not Idealism"* (2015)
Brent C. Sleasman, *Creating Albert Camus: Foundations and Explorations in His Philosophy of Communication* (2015)
Michael Warren Tumolo, *Just Remembering, Rhetorics of Genocide Remembrance and Sociopolitical Judgment* (2015))
Phil Rose, *Roger Waters and Pink Floyd* (2015)
Ronald C. Arnett and Pat Arneson (eds.), *Philosophy of Communication Ethics: Alterity and the Other* (2014)
Pat Arneson, *Communicative Engagement and Social Liberation: Justice Will Be Made* (2014)
Erik A. Garrett, *Why Do We Go to the Zoo?: Communication, Animals, and the Cultural-Historical Experience of Zoos*(2013)
Philip Dalton and Eric Kramer, *Coarseness in U.S. Public Communication* (2012)
Catherine Creede, Beth Fisher-Yoshida, and Placida Gallegos (eds.), *The Reflective, Facilitative, and Interpretive Practices of the Coordinated Management of Meaning* (2012)
Jolanta Aritz and Robyn C. Walker, *Discourse Perspectives on Organizational Communication* (2011)

On the Web at http://www.fdu.edu/fdupress

Cosmopolitanism and the Development of the International Criminal Court

Non-Governmental Organizations' Advocacy and Transnational Human Rights

Jennifer Biedendorf

FAIRLEIGH DICKINSON UNIVERSITY PRESS
Vancouver • Madison • Teaneck • Wroxton

Published by Fairleigh Dickinson University Press
Copublished by The Rowman & Littlefield Publishing Group, Inc.
4501 Forbes Boulevard, Suite 200, Lanham, Maryland 20706
www.rowman.com

6 Tinworth Street, London SE11 5AL

Fairleigh Dickinson University Press gratefully acknowledges the support received for scholarly publishing from the Friends of FDU Press.

British Library Cataloguing in Publication Information Available

Library of Congress Cataloging-in-Publication Data Available

ISBN 978-1-68393-179-9 (cloth)
ISBN 978-1-68393-180-5 (electronic)

Contents

Acknowledgments

This project benefited from the support of many people and institutions. It is the realization of a project that has been in the making since my doctoral graduate work at Pennsylvania State University. It was there that I developed an interest in the intersection of cosmopolitanism, memory, and human rights discourses. I thank my mentors for their intellectual generosity, thoughtful criticism, guidance, and support that helped refine the project and that helped me become a better scholar and teacher. I thank Tom Benson, to whom I am deeply indebted for having learned so much both as a scholar and as a teacher. I admire his pensive yet inspiring counsel, and I aspire to his model of intellectual generosity. I also thank him for deepening my knowledge of and love for the Eternal City. I thank J. Michael Hogan for his continued support and thoughtful criticism of my work. His dedicated pen has taught me to demand that I strive to put complex thoughts into clear writing without sacrificing depth. I would like to thank Janet Lyon and John Christman, who have supported me during the course of this project by offering their wealth of knowledge and by allowing me to learn from their extraordinary ability to communicate complex ideas that I am striving to acquire as a scholar and teacher. To sit in a lecture from these scholars is no less than to be a witness of the power and beauty of the history of ideas. I thank Stephen Browne, who served as the director of this project at Penn State. During this project, he respected me as an independent scholar yet generously offered valuable criticism, gentle guidance, and, when the first two weren't enough, much appreciated humor. His intellectual curiosity and depth of knowledge across multiple disciplines are both humbling and inspiring. In addition to these scholars' more direct involvement in this project, the work reflects the influence of several outstanding scholars that I had the opportunity to learn from over the years. In this particular project, I recognize the influence of Michael Bérubé,

Hubertus Buchstein, Winfried Fluck, Carol Greenhouse, Jane Juffer, Joan Landes, Sabine Lang, Nancy Love, Jeff Nealon, and Melissa Wright. I feel humbled to have studied under them and learned from them.

The project has also benefited from institutional support. At the Pennsylvania State University, I would like to thank the Institute for the Arts and Humanities for providing a dissertation fellowship and the Penn State Alumni Association for the Alumni Association Dissertation Award. Their generosity and support provided me with the much-needed time and resources to bring this project to fruition. At California State University, Stanislaus, I thank James Tuedio and the College of Arts and Humanities and Social Sciences for providing support in the final stages of this project that funded an on-site visit to the International Criminal Court in The Hague. An Undergraduate Assistantship Award from CSU, Stanislaus, also provided research support in the final stages of the project. In addition to inspiring me with their confidence in my work, the support of these institutions provided the time, space, and funding crucial in completing this project. I thank Reagan Swartz and Seth Allen for their help in preparing the manuscript for completion. I would like to thank Gary Radford at Fairleigh Dickinson University Press and Zachary Nycum, and Katherine Mullineaux at Rowman & Littlefield for their support.

I also owe gratitude to my friends and family. I would like to thank Sushmita Chatterjee for her thoughtful insights on my ideas and her friendship throughout our time at Penn State. I would like to thank Margaret Michels for being a mentor and friend—it would be hard to imagine someone that I would rather share a birthday with. I have learned much in conversations with Cindy Boes, Jeremy Engels, Brett Lunceford, Jennifer Ohs, and Jessica Sheffield, all of whom have helped me in some manner with this project.

I thank my parents and my family, to whom this journey must have, I am sure, seemed daunting. I am grateful for their unwavering support of my decisions in spite of it. My parents gave me and my siblings our first experiences with cosmopolitanism when they first took us abroad and later offered encouragement and support when I did so on my own. Those travels allowed me to become immersed in foreign lands with distinct cultures and traditions. These early experiences sparked my interest in languages, deepened my appreciation of different cultures, and, above all, invited me to think about how peoples might get along better across borders.

Lastly, I would like to thank my partner and children. Adele, Jasper, and Bennett have shown me that no matter what the larger questions might be that one is brooding over, sometimes it is more important to just go to the park, play, and be silly. I am grateful beyond words for the intellectual and emotional support of my partner, Michael Tumolo. His extraordinary ability to think with me and his inexhaustible willingness to discuss ideas, read drafts of my work, and conjure up meals (from scratch) to feed me when my mind was withdrawn from existential necessities has been invaluable during this process. I cannot thank him enough for it.

Chapter One

Memory Beyond Borders?

On July 17, 1998, Nelson Mandela offered the following remarks as South Africa became party to the Rome Statute, which is the treaty that created the International Criminal Court (ICC):

> We have sought to ensure that the ICC is guaranteed independence and bestowed with adequate powers. Our own continent has suffered enough horrors emanating from the inhumanity of human beings towards human beings. Who knows, many of these might not have occurred, or at least been minimized, had there been an effectively functioning International Criminal Court. [1]

Two decades later, on September 10, 2018, John Bolton, the U.S. national security advisor, delivered prepared remarks concerning the Trump administration's approach to the ICC and what it represents. Bolton surmised that

> the United States will use any means necessary to protect our citizens and those of our allies from unjust prosecution by this illegitimate court. We will not cooperate with the ICC. We will provide no assistance to the ICC. We will not join the ICC. We will let the ICC die on its own. After all, for intents and purposes, the ICC is already dead to us.

The gap between the panacea described by Mandela to the "illegitimate" institution decried by Bolton is the subject of this book.

The ICC is the first permanent juridical body designed to prosecute individuals who commit offenses including war crimes, crimes against humanity, and genocide. The adoption of the founding document, the Rome Statute, in 1998 was the crowning achievement of a decades-long movement to create a court that would hold individuals accountable for "universally condemned offences"[2] that are "the most serious crimes of concern to the international community as a whole."[3] Twenty years after the adoption of the Rome Statute, the court is serving as an important instrument in the protection of human rights, and many see the Rome Statute as one of the most important international treaties after the adoption of the UN Charter in 1945.

Due to a series of sociopolitical and cultural developments since the end of World War II, human rights discourses have become increasingly institutionalized and universalized. This can be seen in watershed events including the Nuremberg War Trials in 1946, the signing of the UN Charter in 1945, and the subsequent adoption of the Universal Declaration of Human Rights in 1948. These events mark attempts to both institutionalize international cooperation and offer a tacit acknowledgment that such cooperation was in service of idealistic visions of human rights. These principles were tested in the 1990s as the crimes committed in former Yugoslavia and Rwanda prompted a stronger enforcement of international law in an attempt to safeguard human rights. Consequently, the ICC emerged after a period of intensification of international cooperation to protect and promote human rights in response to the atrocities committed throughout the twentieth century.

Human rights discourses, and specifically questions about how to adjudicate human rights violations in international law, are closely connected to questions about collective memory. For instance, the Nuremberg War Trials were in part an attempt to influence the collective memory of the events or were later interpreted to fulfill that function.[4] In the case of the ICC, while the most obvious work of the court is to put people who have played instrumental roles in committing atrocities on trial, the court's larger function is symbolic. The court stands as a permanent memorial site that enshrines a commitment to memory beyond borders with the power to speak for a *transnational* community that is committed to particular rights and responsibilities that extend beyond geopolitical borders.

Cosmopolitanism and the Development of the International Criminal Court analyzes the development and implementation of the ICC to provide insight into how rhetorical action shaped the premier transnational juridical institution of our day. As an international juridical body designed to prosecute individuals for war crimes, crimes against humanity, and genocide, the ICC serves as a memory site for the institutionalization of human rights and as an illustration of a wider popular concern for international justice. As such, the ICC has the potential of shifting the production of memory and justice from primarily a national trajectory to a transnational one that also has the potential of strengthening our imagination of a transnational community. Central to this investigation is how and with what consequences advocates shaped the ICC as both a juridical institution and as a rhetorical figure representing a new vision of global community. An analysis of the rhetorical efforts to establish the court and the attempts to push for U.S. ratification will show that advocates for transnational human rights and increased international cooperation faced fierce and vocal opposition from state and nonstate actors.

This text examines how idioms of human rights, international law, and international juridical institutions function as sites of both transnational and national memory formation. The International Criminal Court, as an institution of international criminal law, has shaped the transnational memory of human rights and as such serves as a case in point to illustrate how such human rights discourses are employed. Rhetors draw on human rights discourses both for producing and challenging the constitution of trans/national subjectivities and communities. Specifically, *Cosmopolitanism and the Development of the International Criminal Court* shows that human rights discourses in the context of the establishment and workings of the ICC both aid in constituting new transnational memory discourses and transnational subjectivities and simultaneously serve as important sites for the articulation of nationalist discourses. That is, discourses that seem to be most explicitly directed toward trans/nationalism are also discourses that are heavily steeped in nationalist language and reproduce rhetorics of the nation-state.

The forward slash used here in the word "trans/nationalism" highlights one of the primary contributions of this project. On the one hand are advocates of cosmopolitanism to whom the creation of a transnational community is a "genuine" aspiration. On the other hand are advocates who favor traditional nation-state sovereignty and by implication oppose the creation of a transnational or cosmopolitan community. This project demonstrates how both draw on nationalist rhetoric to achieve their goals. While it comes as no surprise that opponents of cosmopolitanism frame their rhetoric around the nation-state, it seems to be paradoxical that advocates of cosmopolitanism or discourses that appear to be necessarily transnational are packaged and sold to national audiences in a language that privileges the nation-state. We will see that these rhetorics have severe consequences for the cultivation and maintenance of transnational or cosmopolitan subjectivities, communities, and memory.

The political and cultural transformations brought about by globalization processes have recently given rise to the thriving scholarship on the concept of cosmopolitanism. While a comprehensive account of the multiple facets of cosmopolitanism is outside the scope of this project, I will provide a brief overview of the main tenets pertinent to this project. Originating in ancient Greek thought, cosmopolitanism referred to the belief that humans are part of two communities: our closest kin and humanity as a whole. The concept was revivified by Immanuel Kant in his 1795 essay "Perpetual Peace," in which he envisioned cosmopolitan law as a structure of democratic republics guided by principles of mutual recognition and tolerance. Today, the concept of cosmopolitanism is being theorized in a host of disciplines with varying definitions and emphases that can roughly be divided into moral cosmopolitanism and legal/institutional cosmopolitanism.[5] The moral strand, predicated largely on Kant's notion of cosmopolitanism as a means to build solidarity, peace, and justice and the belief in a moral universalism, is concerned with issues of solidarity, feelings of belongingness, and ethical obligations that transcend national borders in a world community. It is committed to a global egalitarianism based on the notion that all humans have an equal moral status and thus a right to equal respect and concern regardless of nationality or citizenship.[6] The legal/political strand focuses on establishing institutions of global governance and legal institutions to guarantee and secure the protection of universal human rights. In the latter approach, cosmopolitanism refers to a "vision of a global political consciousness that is generated and sustained by institutional structures."[7] As a whole, cosmopolitanism is understood as an emancipatory political ideal concerned with democratizing processes in a global context.

The two primary relevant contexts for this study in which cosmopolitanism is invoked is the field of international law and cosmopolitanism endorsed through global civil society. Robert Fine has recently pointed out,

> Whilst international law has traditionally developed according to the principle that every state is sovereign within its own territory, cosmopolitanism endorses legal limitations on how rulers may behave towards the ruled; and whilst international law leaves it to states to protect the rights of individuals, cosmopolitanism looks also to the formation of international legal bodies above the level of nation-states to perform this function.[8]

Consequently, *Cosmopolitanism and the Development of the International Criminal Court* critiques how cosmopolitan ideals of a cosmopolitan community are advanced through the rhetorical discourses produced by and about international law and international judicial institutions, specifically the ICC. The second approach toward cosmopolitanism particularly relevant for this project is the argument that civil society and social movements occupy a significant role in the promotion of cosmopolitan ideals, partly due to their ability to create a global or transnational public sphere, which is seen by some as indicative of the formation of cosmopolitan citizenship.[9] Raising awareness about issues of human rights, global social justice, transnational solidarity, and global democracy, global civil society has become a prime agent in shaping alternative, cosmopolitan communities guided by cosmopolitan values and principles.

The underlying critical perspective guiding this work is the notion that communities are produced through discourse. This constitutive function of rhetoric, according to rhetorical scholar Michael Calvin McGee, is a "rhetorical fiction," an entity that comes into being only through the process of being addressed rhetorically as a collectivity in which individuals must be seduced into a collective identity by at least provisionally abandoning their individual identity. The concept of "the people," McGee argues, should be thought of more as a "process than [a] phenomenon," suggesting that "the people" is a transient construction.[10] "The people" exists only as long as the rhetorical discourse is effective in conjuring up a collective identity constructed of social and political beliefs or "myths" individuals are willing to accept. The entity of "the people" as a collective identity is thus always in the process of becoming and reconstitution while being on the verge of dissolution as discourse fails to constitute its subjectivity as a collective.

In addition to the constitutive function of rhetoric, this analysis is premised on the notion that international law plays a key role for the constitution of transnational communities and, more generally, the cultivation of a cosmopolitan consciousness. A key function in the development of transnational memory and cultivation of transnational communities is attributed to what sociologist David Hirsh calls "cosmopolitan law."[11] Cosmopolitan law emerged out of international law—which was concerned with protecting the rights of sovereign states—but seeks to "transcend" international law and limit state sovereignty by creating "minimum standards for the treatment of human beings by states."[12] The cosmopolitan criminal trial, then, fulfills a key function in the production of cosmopolitan law and, consequently, cosmopolitan memory. Hirsh argues that the "institutions of cosmopolitan law, as well as the body of law, rules and precedent on which they are based, are the mechanisms by which . . . cosmopolitan judgments may be arrived at."[13] Cosmopolitan law, and cosmopolitan criminal trials in particular, he argues, have the ability to produce "authoritative narratives of the crimes" and by doing so aid in the creation of "a global collective memory that can play a role in undermining myths of nationhood."[14] Applying international human rights standards and creating a transnational record of violations and jurisprudence, cosmopolitan law and its institutions have thus contributed to the forging of a "cosmopolitan social memory" and cosmopolitan consciousness.[15]

While memory discourses often emerge out of particular (that is, national or local) historic situations, the aim of this project is to contribute to the scholarship on the rhetoric of public memory by expanding the perspective of memory scholarship to include a stronger transnational focus. While memory discourses so far have been circumscribed by local or national contexts, the memory discourses produced by the ICC will contribute to a strengthening of transnational memory discourses and subjectivities. An analysis of the discourses emerging in the context of the creation, role, reach, and jurisdiction of the ICC demonstrates how such transnational trajectories are rhetorically employed, advanced, and resisted. Examining more closely the various ways in which the idea of transnationalism is invoked in these discourses will help chart the extent to which the formation of transnational subjectivities and thus the formation of a transnational community and sense of solidarity are possible.

While each of the chapters in this book focus on transnational memory discourses and discourses that constitute transnational communities, the focus of this project is on the residual challenges that the discursive framework of the nation-state poses to transnational or cosmopolitan memory. Thus, rather than solely illustrating the emergence of transnational memory discourses, the various moments in the development of the International Criminal Court that will be examined illustrate where the formation of an explicit move toward developing transnational subjectivities and transnational memory was rejected or obstructed. Taken together, an examination of these different moments in the development of the ICC demonstrate how the idea and practice of transnational memory and, by extension, the idea of the transnational or postnational subject or citizen, are alternatively cultivated and attacked.

The need for deepening our understandings of the constructions of postnational identities has become imperative in the context of economic and cultural globalization processes. As a consequence of these processes, political identities are becoming less clearly demarcated by territorial affiliations. Even though this may be perceived by the larger public as a rather intellectual discourse, these concerns have gained increasing relevance and have become a constitutive element of public discourse in the context of emerging discussions about the construction of a "European identity," an issue that has gained extraordinary momentum in response to the eastern territorial expansion of the European Union. These discussions attest to an emerging global consciousness about postnational subjectivities. This project thus engages questions about the contours and attitudes of such a transnational community through a consideration of transnational memory and addresses Kendall Phillips's and Mitchell Reyes's call to "explore more fully the intersection between public memory and globalization."[16]

Given that our loyalties are less and less circumscribed by nation-state boundaries, an overarching concern of this study is to explore how we might cultivate understanding and responsibility beyond individuals' immediate communities of solidarity. Overarching questions motivating this study include the following: What kind of rhetorical discourses are needed to produce such subjectivities? What is the ethos of such a rhetorically crafted transnational subject or community? What kinds of "memories" and values are being invoked transnationally? What kinds of political opportunities do transnational memory discourses enable and foreclose? What are the challenges to the construction of such a transnational community?

MEMORY, THE NATION, AND CONSEQUENTIAL MEMORY

This project's focus on transnational memory expands current memory scholarship that tends to examine the production of memory as tied to particularized local or national contexts. This focus is predicated on the foundational work in memory studies offered by the French sociologist Maurice Halbwachs at the beginning of the twentieth century. Halbwachs's sociological approach toward memory—rather than Durkheim's psychological approach—put forth the argument that "it is in society that people normally acquire their memories. It is also in society, that they recall, recognize, and localize their memories."[17] Memory, according to Halbwachs, is a social phenomenon; it is retrieved in social groups.

Moreover, Halbwachs's presentist account of memory—the notion that memory serves and is reconfigured to meet the concerns and needs of the present—conceptualizes memory as emerging out of bounded social contexts. In Halbwachs's analysis, social frameworks or the primary social groups through which collective memory is produced and transformed are the family, religion, and social class. Anne Whitehead notes that Halbwachs's conception of collective memory then relies heavily on the notion of place as collective memory "necessarily unfolds within a spatial framework."[18] The material spaces of the social frameworks (the home for the family, the space of the city, the church and its embodied and commemorative rituals and performances at holy or sacred locations) provide a sense of permanence and aid in retrieving memories and therefore become a "central feature of Halbwachs' conception of collective remembrance."[19]

The reliance on physical space evident in Halbwachs's conceptualization of collective memory has been emphasized in subsequent memory scholarship. While Halbwachs recognized the framework of the nation as a place that is memory generating—he considered the nation-state as too distant for individuals and thus less immediately relevant—subsequent scholarship employed the locus of the nation-state as the primary lens for the study of collective memory. From this perspective, the nation-state is configured as a primary site of identification, solidarity, and social organization. It thus comes as no surprise that the study of memory has been approached mainly within the territorial confines of the nation-state.[20] A classic example of this is the influential work of Pierre Nora, at the core of which is an assumption of continuity of national history and ethnicity within the boundaries of the nation-state. Nora and his contributors' seven volumes of the French edition of *Les Lieux de Mémoire*, compiled between 1984 and 1992, is an attempt to trace the "collective heritage" of French national culture by locating the various events, symbols, and rituals that mark French national culture and collective memory. Written against the backdrop of France's attempts to revisit and come to terms with its role during the Nazi regime in the 1940s and colonial legacies in Algeria and Indo-China and thus its attempt to redefine its national identity, Nora's project was concerned with "delineat[ing] the metamorphoses that French memory had undergone in recent times."[21] Acknowledging how a once unified French national history based on universal humanistic principles had turned into fragmented identities and memories, *Realms of Memory* traced how French national identity and its symbols had been reinterpreted and turned into new symbolic representations and how this fragmented, often politicized "memory process activate[s] a renewed sense of national self-consciousness."[22] In this sense, Lawrence Kritzman argues, Nora's project implicitly insists on the prominence of the nation-state in the forging of collective memory.

The connection between memory and nation has also been explored from a comparative perspective. James Young's *The Texture of Memory*, for instance, examines several countries' Holocaust memorials and memorial cultures and the "national myths, ideals, and political needs" out of which particular national memorial discourses emerge.[23] Examining the varying practices of commemorating the Holocaust in Germany, Austria, Poland, Israel, and the United States, Young illustrates how particular narratives of the Holocaust are rhetorically employed to uniquely serve each country's national identity formation. Focusing on how Holocaust memory is largely formed by national imperatives, Young's work is also implicitly reinforcing the conceptualization of a territorially confined notion of memory.[24]

The scholarly emphasis of tying the study of collective memory to the nation-state is not surprising given how memory discourses are providing the requisite narratives and myths that function as the ideological framework around which a transcendent national identity has been forged. Indeed, Phillips and Reyes conclude that "a strong connection can be observed between public remembrance and the nation-state evident in both theory and practice. Indeed, the very notion of a national identity can be said to have been largely constituted through practices of public remembrance that serve to forge a common origin as well as a sense of collective destiny."[25] The bulk of public memory scholarship remains focused on examinations of how memories are negotiated, contested, and appropriated by and for territorially bounded communities—that is, in local or national contexts. In short, such theorists and critics are examining how memory is made consequential, primarily within local contexts, and have only marginally explored how such memory discourses have transnational consequences.[26]

And yet, as Nora's work or that of James Bodnar in *Remaking America*, which analyzed vernacular forms of memory in the United States, have shown, the nation-state as the primary locus in the process of forging a sense of identity has been challenged. While few scholars have examined memory in international contexts, some inroads toward understanding memory production and contestation in a global context have been made. In addition to

Young's comparative work outlined above, some recent scholarship has taken a stronger focus on the transnationalization of memory practices—that is, the intersection of and relationships between local, national, and transnational memory production.[27]

One notable exception to the focus on memory as territorially bounded or parochial is the recent work of sociologists Daniel Levy and Natan Sznaider, which examines memory in a global or transnational context. Levy and Sznaider argue that "alongside nationally bounded memories a new form of memory"—what they call cosmopolitan memory—"has emerged."[28] Cosmopolitan memories, they write, are the "practices that shift attention away from the territorialized nation-state framework, which is commonly associated with the notion of collective memory. Rather than presuppose the congruity of nation, territory, and policy, cosmopolitan memories are based on and contribute to nation-transcending idioms, spanning territorial and national borders."[29] "Cosmopolitanism" here refers to the phenomenon that "global concerns become part of local experiences of an increasing number of people."[30] For Levy and Sznaider, this shift from "national to cosmopolitan memory cultures"[31] is primarily manifest in Holocaust remembrance in that it exhibits a simultaneous existence of global and local memory cultures.

Literary scholar Andreas Huyssen observes similarly that the Holocaust has taken on a "totalizing dimension," as the Holocaust has symbolically been rendered a "cipher for the twentieth century as a whole and for the failure of the project of enlightenment."[32] At the same time, the Holocaust as a "universal trope" has been appropriated to meet more particularistic or localized concerns and purposes in its remembrance.[33] That is, memories of the Holocaust serve as a universal resource that may then be articulated to highly localized concerns. Huyssen concludes from this that political struggles over memory are still primarily, and more importantly, most effectively carried out at local or nation-state levels but linked with each other:

> In the best-case scenario, the cultures of memory are intimately linked, in many parts of the world, to processes of democratization and struggles for human rights, to expanding and strengthening the public spheres of civil society. Slowing down rather than speeding up, expanding the nature of public debate, trying to heal the wounds inflicted in the past . . . those seem to be unmet cultural needs in a globalizing world, and local memories are intimately linked to their articulation.[34]

For the time being, Huyssen claims, we should be more concerned with how these discourses become manifest locally and how transnational memory supports or obstructs local memory practices.[35] However, as I show in this project, many memory discourses that are presented in a local idiom may have global consequences.

Levy and Sznaider draw slightly different conclusions from their claim about the proliferation of transnational memory discourses. They concur with Huyssen in that the Holocaust contributed to developing normative standards for moral debates about human rights and justice at a transnational scale, which made the Holocaust serve as the prime example of an emerging cosmopolitan memory. Having triggered the adoption of a series of legal instruments to codify human rights, memories of the Holocaust have "become the cultural foundation for global human rights politics."[36] This codification of human rights violations into international law calls attention to the constitutive function of international law, particularly international criminal law, as a vehicle for the formation of an institutionalized cosmopolitan memory.[37]

In addition to providing a general framework for international conduct, international criminal law serves a pedagogic function. Lawrence Douglas, for instance, has examined how the criminal trial as a specialized legal instrument has been used as a "tool of collective pedagogy."[38] The trials of the Holocaust, he argues, function as "dramas of didactic legality" designed to "teach history and shape collective memory."[39] Moreover, as we will see in the discourses over the establishment and ratification of the International Criminal Court, international criminal law has taken on and is widely recognized as an influential force in international policymaking. Legal scholar Ruti Teitel argues that newly established judicial institutions such as the ICC "make criminal justice the primary means of enforcing international rights law."[40] What has emerged is a new cosmopolitan criminal law that evolved "out of international humanitarian and human rights law" and that is not confined to the conduct of states but also includes nonstate organizations and individuals.[41] This kind of cosmopolitan law derives its authority not from state sovereignty but from "a set of supra-national principles, practices, and institutions."[42] This cosmopolitan law, sociologist David Hirsh argues, plays a key role in the cultivation of cosmopolitanism as it aids in constructing universal rather than particularistic narratives that represent a form of collective memory for an international community.[43]

GLOBALIZATION, COSMOPOLITANISM, AND TRANSNATIONAL MEMORY

Although the processes of globalization have been ongoing for centuries, the term "globalization" did not become widely used until the 1960s or 1970s. Since then, globalization has been studied by various disciplines, rendering "globalization" as a general descriptive term for a number of different developments and processes. In the broadest sense, globalization is conceived of as an "accelerating interdependence," or "global integration," which refers to the "enmeshment among national economies and societies such that events in one country impact directly on others."[44] Geographer David Harvey sees globalization as intricately linked to the postmodern condition and describes globalization as a "time-space compression" of social organization and interaction.[45] Arjun Appadurai has focused on the conditions a global and hybridized culture has produced through "global flows" of financial capital, commodities, communication, finances, and people.[46] While the subject of analysis and implications of globalization vary widely across disciplines, globalization is generally understood as an intensification of social interactions between people at a global scale. As such, globalization has brought about transformations at the economic, social-cultural, and political level, which raises questions about "the nature and scope of justice, democracy, and citizenship and their application beyond sovereign states."[47]

The social and political transformations in particular and their attendant concerns will also have profound implications for memory production and memory practices. One of the key issues relevant for the study of public memory is related to questions about identity formation. The degree of human migration has changed the composition of political communities and has established increasingly multicultural societies. Identity traditionally has been thought of as intricately tied to the nation—legally through formal citizenship and ideologically through participation in what Benedict Anderson called the "imagining" of a national culture and community.[48] During the nineteenth and twentieth centuries, citizenship was constructed in relation to nationality to such a degree that, as political theorist Etienne Balibar wrote, it "appears inseparable from belonging to a nation, whether through inheritance or naturalization."[49] The "enhanced and politicized awareness" of ethnic or cultural differences in increasingly multicultural societies, however, has called into question conventional assumptions about civic identity and its relationship to a particular political community.[50] As a result of increased recognition of such differences, "ethnic, cultural and national consciousness have brought about either the loosening or the actual fragmentation of polities hitherto thought of as nation-states."[51]

In addition to globalization processes having produced transformations with regard to cultural and political identity in the nation-state, they have brought on what is often referred to as a "crisis" for the sovereignty of the nation-state. At the level of the nation-state, globalization, and economic globalization in particular, have resulted in a degradation of democracy. With the rise of transnational actors such as international financial institutions, nation-state borders are increasingly eroded by multinational financial institutions and trade alliances, such as the International Monetary Fund, the World Bank, World Trade Organization, and the General Agreement on Tariffs and Trade. These supranational financial institutions are not subject to democratic electoral processes and therefore suffer from a democracy deficit or accountability deficit. Similar arguments are made about the increasing influence of global civil society operating outside of the formal decision-making process and influencing international conferences, treaties, and agendas. By circumventing democratic decision-making processes, these international actors curtail the sovereignty of the nation-state but traditionally do so in ways that are favorable to the aims of developed and powerful nations.

These developments have produced a series of conditions that play a significant role in the production of memory discourses and will require a rethinking of memory formation as primarily a national endeavor. The experience of increasingly overlapping identities that transform our loyalties and sense of allegiances originally associated with the nation-state is coupled with the fact that the locus of political power no longer resides principally in national governments, as "effective power is shared and bartered by diverse forces and agencies at national, regional and international levels."[52] As a result, we face a series of "new types of 'boundary problems,' which challenge the distinctions between domestic and foreign affairs, internal political issues and external questions, the sovereign concerns of the nation-state and international considerations."[53] States and governments are confronted with issues (such as epidemics, environmental issues, weapons of mass destruction, fundamentalist movements) that no longer fall into clear-cut categories of domestic or international affairs. In short, "the enmeshment of national political communities in regional and global processes involves [nation-states] in intensive issues of transboundary coordination and control," which results in the creation of what David Held refers to as "overlapping communities of fate."[54]

Globalization processes may also have a more direct effect on how collective memory is conceptualized and practiced. For instance, the proliferation of human rights discourses promoted by international organizations and institutions over the last seventy years has sparked a heightened concern with memory in general. This proliferation of memory discourses, Huyssen argues, must further be considered a response to decolonization processes and the emergence of new social movements in the 1960s and 1970s.[55]

At a more general level, globalization processes may have resulted in what Huyssen calls the "hypertrophy of memory" manifest in the abundance of archives and museums, in itself a response to changing notions of temporality and spatiality brought about by the globalization processes described above.[56] Against this background, Huyssen interprets the ever-increasing obsession with memory as evidence for a longing for stability and a sense of identity. Similar to Nora's argument put forth in his seminal essay "Between Memory and History: Les Lieux de Mémoire," he considers the urge to memorialize and archive a counter-reaction against rapid transformations in our lives that often seem beyond our control. The expansive growth of memory institutions (museums, archives, and monuments) is considered indicative of attempts to compensate for the loss of control by collecting, preserving, and stabilizing the past into a static entity. In this sense, memory discourses are not antithetical to globalization but rather emerge out of a will to counteract the amnesia produced by globalization processes.[57]

In short, the internationalizing or globalizing developments outlined above combined with an increased concern for human rights have contributed to a rise in transnational memory discourses. Hence, Halbwachs's territorially bounded approach toward the study of memory must be revised because it presumes relatively unchanging collective formations. Approaches that consider memory production primarily located in the nation-state no longer match the realities of how memory discourses are invoked and disseminated. Contemporary memory is characterized by fragmented memory politics of particular ethnic and social groups and is increasingly decentered. Memory practices are no longer territorially bounded but are increasingly part of a globalized system in which local, national, and transnational articulations of memory must be negotiated.

CHAPTER OVERVIEW

This book is structured thematically over five chapters. The book lays out the legal and theoretical issues framing the project and then progresses through key developmental phases of the International Criminal Court, including advocacy groups shaping the treaty during the negotiation phase, the court's coming into force, and the United States' unprecedented withdrawal of its signatory status.

This introductory chapter, "Memory Beyond Borders?" and chapter 2, "The International Criminal Court: History and Memory" outline the conceptual framework and historical background that provide the context in which the debates in the United States over the ICC emerged. The conceptual framework focuses on the relationship between international criminal law and transnational or cosmopolitan memory and the competing demands of national sovereignty and cosmopolitanism they bring to the fore. The historical account offers an overview of the development toward establishing a standing, rather than ad hoc, international criminal court and provides the historical background necessary to understand the roots of the debates over the establishment of the ICC.

Chapter 3, "The 'Distinctly American Internationalism:' The United States' Unsigning of the Rome Statute of the International Criminal Court," examines the larger U.S. public discourse relating to the ICC prior to its founding and then analyzes the United States' unprecedented act of "unsigning" an international treaty that it had previously signed so to submit it for ratification. This rhetorical act of unsigning—captured in the speech explaining the United States' decision to no longer be party to the Rome Statute—invites closer reflection on the competing demands of cosmopolitanism and national sovereignty in the rhetorical discourses concerning the ICC. This chapter consequently offers a framework to better understand subsequent decisions, for instance, the U.S. withdrawal from the Paris Agreement on climate change mitigation in 2017 and the U.S. call to openly oppose the ICC in 2018.

Chapter 4, "Remaking the ICC for the United States: Citizens for Global Solutions' Advocacy" analyzes the rhetorical strategies of nongovernmental organization (NGO) advocacy campaigns to influence the constitution and public support of the ICC. NGOs approached the ICC as more than a juridical institution, instead recognizing it as a vehicle for promoting a new version of an international community. This chapter pays specific attention to the conflicting rhetorical strategies between NGOs advocating for expanding cosmopolitanism and those who worked to frame the treaty to best represent U.S. interests.

Among many accomplishments, the ICC notably created the first international legal framework to protect gender-based rights with provisions on gender and sexual crimes. Consequently, chapter 5, "Gender, Sexual Violence, and International Community: The Fight for and against Gender Justice at the ICC," analyzes the competing rhetoric of NGOs working at the UN level. These discourses rendered the legal institution of the ICC into a public memorial that is understood as having the power to influence how and with what consequences women's rights and gender and sexual violence can and will be remembered. On one hand, this chapter details the work of a coalition of NGOs working to create a legal framework that acknowledges how gender and sexual violence are used as weapons of war. On the other hand, this chapter details the work of conservative state actors and organizations who collectively fought against the integration of a gender justice perspective into international law.

Chapter 6, "Sovereignty/Cosmopolitanism Revisited: The U.S. Military and the International Criminal Court," concludes the book by reflecting on the findings of the report *On Trial: The US Military and the International Criminal Court*, published by the Stimson Center in 2006. The report tracked the attitudes toward the ICC held by U.S. military personnel that were alternatively uninformed and well informed about the ICC. Contrary to the statements of United States–based anti–ICC advocates who argue that the ICC is at odds with the mission of the U.S. military, the report indicates that military personnel report levels of support that are analogous to their level of knowledge about the ICC. That is, military personnel who register as more knowledgeable about the aims and purpose of the ICC tend to support it, and those who are less knowledgeable reject it. Taking this report as a heuristic for my critical approach to the rhetoric of transnational public memory, I argue that the possibility for and character of cosmopolitan citizenship can be positively influenced by progressive advocates who work to better inform their audiences about cosmopolitanism rather than pander to them in nationalistic terms.

NOTES

1. Nelson Mandela, "Opening Address" (Second Conference of African National Institutions for the Promotion and Protection of Human Rights, Durban, July 1, 1998), http://www.mandela.gov.za/mandela_speeches/1998/980701_humanrights.htm.

2. Rosalyn Higgins, *Problems and Process, International Law and How We Use It* (New York: Oxford University Press, 1995), 72.

3. See Preamble of the Rome Statute. United Nations Diplomatic Conference of Plenipotentiaries on the Establishment of an International Criminal Court, *Rome Statute of the International Criminal Court*, UN document A/CONF. 183/9 (July 15–17, 1998), https://www.icc-cpi.int/nr/rdonlyres/ea9aeff7-5752-4f84-be94-0a655eb30e16/0/rome_statute_english.pdf.

4. Scholars are divided over the extent to which the Nuremberg trials functioned as a primary means to establish a collective memory of the crimes against humanity committed. Donald Bloxham, for instance, notes that the trials were themselves less significant and effective at documenting and creating a collective memory of the Nazi crimes than other "instructional media and propaganda forms." Donald Bloxham, "Genocide on Trial: Law and Collective Memory" in *The Nuremberg Trials: International Criminal Law since 1945*, edited by Herbert R. Reginbogin and Christoph J. M. Safferling (Munich: K. G. Saur Verlag, 2006), 74.

5. Patrick Hayden, *Cosmopolitan Global Politics, Ethics and Global Politics* (Burlington, VT: Ashgate, 2005), 3.

6. See Kok-Chor Tan, *Justice without Borders: Cosmopolitanism, Nationalism, and Patriotism, Contemporary Political Theory* (New York: Cambridge University Press, 2004), 10.

7. Pheng Cheah, "Cosmopolitanism," *Theory, Culture and Society* 23, no. 2–3 (2006): 486.

8. Robert Fine, *Cosmopolitanism* (New York: Routledge, 2007), 2–3.

9. See Nancy Fraser, "Transnationalizing the Public Sphere: On the Legitimacy and Efficacy of Public Opinion in a Post-Westphalian World," *Theory, Culture and Society* 24, no. 4–30 (2007); Jürgen Habermas, *Die Postnationale Konstellation: Politische Essays* (Frankfurt: Suhrkamp Verlag, 1998); Craig Calhoun, "Imagining Solidarity: Cosmopolitanism, Constitutional Patriotism, and the Public Sphere," *Public Culture* 14, no. 1 (2002); Margaret E. Keck and Kathryn Sikkink, *Activists Beyond Borders: Advocacy Networks in International Politics* (Ithaca, NY: Cornell University Press, 1998).

10. Michael Calvin McGee, "In Search of 'the People': A Rhetorical Alternative," *Quarterly Journal of Speech* 61, no. 3 (1975): 235–49.

11. See David Hirsh, *Law against Genocide: Cosmopolitan Trials* (London: GlassHouse Press, 2003), xii.

12. Ibid., 1.

13. Ibid., xix.

14. Ibid.

15. Ibid., 159.

16. Kendall R. Phillips and G. Mitchell Reyes, Introduction to *Global Memoryscapes: Contesting Remembrance in a Transnational Age* (Tuscaloosa: University of Alabama Press, 2011), 3.

17. See Maurice Halbwachs, *On Collective Memory*, translated by Lewis A. Coser (Chicago: University of Chicago Press, 1992), 38.

18. Anne Whitehead, *Memory* (New York: Routledge, 2009), 137.

19. Ibid.

20. For examples of scholars dealing with issues of memory at a national scale, see Robert Hariman and John Louis Lucaites, "Performing Civic Identity: The Iconic Photograph of the Flag Raising on Iwo Jima," *Quarterly Journal of Speech* 88, no. 4 (2002); Carole Blair, Marsha

S. Jeppeson, and Enrico Jr. Pucci, "Public Memorializing in Postmodernity: The Vietnam Veterans Memorial as Prototype," *Quarterly Journal of Speech* 77, no. 3 (1991); Stephen H. Browne, "Remembering Crispus Attucks: Race, Rhetoric, and the Politics of Commemoration," *Quarterly Journal of Speech* 85, no. 2 (1999); Stephen H. Browne, "Reading Public Memory in Daniel Webster's Plymouth Rock Oration," *Western Journal of Communication* 57, no. 4 (1993); Stephen H. Browne, "Reading, Rhetoric, and the Texture of Public Memory," *Quarterly Journal of Speech* 81, no. 2 (1995); John Louis Lucaites, "The Irony of 'Equality' in Black Abolitionist Discourse: The Case of Frederick Douglass's 'What to the Slave Is the Fourth of July?'" in *Rhetoric and Political Culture in Nineteenth-Century America*, edited by Thomas W. Benson (East Lansing: Michigan State University, 1997); John Louis Lucaites and Celeste Michelle Condit, "Reconstructing Equality : Culturetypal and Counter-Cultural Rhetorics in the Martyred Black Vision," *Communication Monographs* 57, no. 1 (1990); Charles E. Morris III, "My Old Kentucky Homo: Lincoln and the Politics of Queer Public Memory," in *Framing Public Memory*, edited by Kendall R. Phillips (Tuscaloosa: University of Alabama Press, 2004); Barbie Zelizer, "Reading the Past against the Grain: The Shape of Memory Studies," *Critical Studies in Mass Communication* 12, no. 2 (1995); Barbie Zelizer, *Remembering to Forget: Holocaust Memory through the Camera's Eye* (Chicago: University of Chicago Press, 1998). For comparative analyses, see for example Thomas McCarthy, "Vergangenheitsbewältigung in the USA: On the Politics of the Memory of Slavery," *Political Theory* 30, no. 5 (2002); Barry Schwartz and Horst-Alfred Heinrich, "Shadings of Regret: America and Germany," in *Framing Public Memory*, edited by Kendall R. Phillips (Tuscaloosa: University of Alabama Press, 2004). Nonetheless, even in these essays, memory cultures are understood as having a distinct national character.

21. Lawrence D. Kritzman, Foreword to *Realms of Memory: Rethinking the French Past Vol. 1—Conflicts and Divisions*, English language edition (New York: Columbia University Press, 1996), xi.

22. See Kritzman, xiii, xi.

23. James E. Young, *The Texture of Memory: Holocaust Memorials and Meaning* (New Haven, CT: Yale University Press, 1993), 2.

24. Ibid.

25. Phillips and Reyes, Introduction, 6.

26. See Pierre Nora, "Between Memory and History: Les Lieux de Mémoire," *Representations* 26 (Spring 1989).

27. See for instance Brian Conway, "Local Conditions, Global Environment and Transnational Discourses in Memory Work: The Case of Bloody Sunday (1972)," *Memory Studies* 1, no. 2 (2008); Christina Schwenkel, "Recombinant History: Transnational Practices of Memory and Knowledge Production in Contemporary Vietnam," *Cultural Anthropology* 21, no. 1 (2006); Geoffrey M. White, "Remembering Guadalcanal: National Identity and Transnational Memory-Making," *Public Culture* 7, no. 3 (1995); Thomas McCarthy, "Vergangenheitsbewältigung in the USA: On the Politics of the Memory of Slavery," *Political Theory* 30, no. 5 (2002); Lisa Yoneyama, "Traveling Memories, Contagious Justice: Americanization of Japanese War Crimes at the End of the Post-Cold War," *Journal of Asian American Studies* 6, no. 1 (2003).

28. Daniel Levy and Natan Sznaider, "Memory Unbound: The Holocaust and the Formation of Cosmopolitan Memory," *European Journal of Social Theory* 5, no. 1 (2002): 87.

29. Daniel Levy and Natan Sznaider, "Sovereignty Transformed: A Sociology of Human Rights," *The British Journal of Sociology* 57, no. 4 (2006): 660.

30. Levy and Sznaider, "Memory Unbound: The Holocaust and the Formation of Cosmopolitan Memory," 88.

31. Ibid.

32. Andreas Huyssen, *Present Pasts: Urban Palimpsests and the Politics of Memory* (Stanford, CA: Stanford University Press, 2003), 13.

33. Ibid., 13–14.

34. Ibid., 27.

35. Huyssen refers primarily to Holocaust memory as transnational memory in this context.

36. Levy and Sznaider, "Memory Unbound: The Holocaust and the Formation of Cosmopolitan Memory," 88.

37. See Levy and Sznaider, "Sovereignty Transformed: A Sociology of Human Rights," 662.

38. Lawrence Douglas, *The Memory of Judgment: Making Law and History in the Trials of the Holocaust* (New Haven, CT: Yale University Press, 2001), 2.

39. Ibid., 3.

40. Ruti G. Teitel, "Humanity's Law: Rule of Law for the New Global Politics," *Cornell International Law Journal* 35 (2002): 363. For Teitel, this is reason for concern as these developments give rise to a far-reaching legalism in foreign affairs, the appropriation of which is not clearly foreseeable.

41. Hirsh, *Law against Genocide: Cosmopolitan Trials*, xii–xiii.

42. Ibid., xiii.

43. Ibid., xii.

44. David Held and Anthony McGrew, "The Great Globalization Debate: An Introduction," in *The Global Transformations Reader: An Introduction to the Globalization Debate*, edited by David Held and Anthony G. McGrew (Malden, MA: Polity, 2000), 3.

45. David Harvey, *The Condition of Postmodernity: An Enquiry into the Origins of Cultural Change* (Malden, MA: Wiley-Blackwell, 1989).

46. Arjun Appadurai, "Disjuncture and Difference in the Global Cultural Economy," *Theory, Culture and Society* 7 (1990).

47. Niamh Reilly, "Cosmopolitan Feminism and Human Rights," *Hypatia* 22, no. 4 (2007): 180.

48. Benedict Anderson, *Imagined Communities: Reflections on the Origin and Spread of Nationalism*, revised and extended edition (London: Verso, 1991).

49. Etienne Balibar, "Propositions on Citizenship," *Ethics* 98, no. 4 (July 1988): 726.

50. Derek Benjamin Heater, *What Is Citizenship?* (Malden, MA: Polity, 1999), 2. Sociologist Yasemin Nuhoğlu Soysal for instance introduces a new model of citizenship that could account for the integration of noncitizen migrant populations, *guestworkers*, in Europe. Specfically, Soysal advances a model of "postnational citizenship," a model of citizenship in which the legitimation of membership is based on universal personhood rather than nationality or the concept of territorial citizenship. She argues, "In the postnational model, universal personhood replaces nationhood; and universal human rights replace national rights. . . . The rights and claims of individual are legitimated by ideologies grounded in a transnational community, through international codes, conventions and laws on human rights, independent of their citizenship in a nation-state. Hence, the individual transcends the citizen. This is the most elemental way that the postnational model differs from the national model." See Yasemin Nuhoglu Soysal, *Limits of Citizenship: Migrants and Postnational Membership in Europe* (Chicago: University of Chicago Press, 1994), 142.

51. Heater, *What Is Citizenship?*, 2.

52. David Held, "Regulating Globalization," in *The Global Transformations Reader: An Introduction to the Globalization Debate*, edited by David Held and Anthony McGrew (Malden, MA: Polity, 2000), 423.

53. Ibid., 423–24.

54. Ibid., 424.

55. Huyssen, *Present Pasts*, 12.

56. Ibid., 21.

57. See Ibid. See also Nora, "Between Memory and History: Les Lieux de Mémoire."

Chapter Two

The International Criminal Court

History and Memory

The preamble of the Rome Statute of the International Criminal Court (ICC) of 1998 lays out the motivations and objectives of the first permanent international juridical body to prosecute individuals responsible for mass violence, including war crimes, crimes against humanity, and genocide. Those states party to the Rome Statute—the legal foundation for the ICC—claim to be

> Conscious that all peoples are united by common bonds, their cultures pieced together in a shared heritage, and concerned that this delicate mosaic may be shattered at any time,
> Mindful that during this century millions of children, women, and men have been victims of unimaginable atrocities that deeply shock the conscience of humanity,
> Recognizing that such grave crimes threaten the peace, security, and well-being of the world, . . .
> Determined to put an end to impunity for the perpetrators of these crimes and thus to contribute to the prevention of such crimes, . . . [and]
> Resolved to guarantee lasting respect for and the enforcement of international justice.

Those party to the Rome Statute of the ICC attempt to "express a collective human conscience" premised on the notion that "human beings, as a race, a collectivity, have a kind of combined conscience that works in the same way, despite huge differences of culture, time, place, civilization and religion."[1] The ICC thus represents the crowning achievement for international human rights legislation.

This chapter serves to outline in more detail the conceptual framework for the book by first providing a historical perspective on the movement for the development of an international criminal court and serves to further illustrate the significance of the institution of the ICC. This chapter offers an introduction to the features and jurisdiction of the ICC. The remaining sections of the chapter provide a more detailed discussion of the intersections between international law, human rights, memory, and cosmopolitanism.

HISTORY AND FOUNDING OF THE INTERNATIONAL CRIMINAL COURT

The idea of a world court grew out of a lack of a permanent tribunal that could prosecute individuals for having committed the most serious crimes of international concern, such as war crimes, genocide, and crimes against humanity. Likely the earliest, though often forgotten, proposal of a permanent international criminal court dates back to Gustave Moynier, founding member and former president of the International Committee of the Red Cross. While Moynier had long favored the court of public opinion as sufficient for adjudicating violations of the First Geneva Convention relating to the treatment of sick and wounded soldiers from 1864, his proposal for a permanent international criminal court came as a response to the violations of humanitarian law during the Franco-Prussian war.[2] Moynier's proposal consisting of ten brief articles was introduced at a meeting of the International Committee of the Red Cross in 1872. Challenging dominant notions of international law and deemed ineffective by its critics at the time, the proposal never came to fruition.

Other efforts to try perpetrators for such grave offences can be traced back to the Hague Conventions and the League of Nations. The Hague Conventions for the Peaceful Settlement of International Disputes, a set of treaties from 1899 and 1907, were the first "international efforts to proscribe war crimes and to protect civilians during times of war."[3] While these conventions did not result in the establishment of an international court, they did provide "a solid body of humanitarian law" during World War I.[4] The violence that had occurred during World War I led to the establishment of the League of Nations' Permanent International Court of Justice to settle disputes between states. Steven Roach, scholar of government and international affairs, notes that despite the league's concern for "instituting the principle of international criminal accountability, most states rejected the inclusion of crimes against the laws of humanity,"[5] effectively leaving international law unprepared for the continued mass atrocities of the twentieth century.

This changed with the experiences of World War II, which played an important role in the development of the ICC. While human rights had received attention in the 1920s and 1930s when several legal scholars wrote proposals for an international criminal court, "most efforts toward international protection of rights were limited to jurisdiction at the national level."[6] The concern for human rights rose significantly following the end of World War II, when nations came face-to-face with modern atrocities. The adoption of the UN Charter in 1945 marked the "beginning of widespread human rights discourse."[7] It was followed by the establishment of the UN Commission on Human Rights in 1946 and the adoption of the Universal Declaration of Human Rights (UDHR) in 1948. On the fiftieth anniversary of the UDHR, Michael Ignatieff noted that "the Holocaust made the Declaration possible."[8] Together, these developments provided the path for human rights to become institutionalized at an international level.[9]

Despite advancements in international human rights legislation, the international community was not yet ready to create a permanent institution to prosecute international criminal law violations. Instead, the Nuremberg and Tokyo war tribunals were set up on an ad hoc basis. Subsequently, in popular memory and legal practice, the Nuremberg War Trials set the precedent for prosecuting individuals for "crimes against humanity." This new category of criminal offenses was created in response to the crimes committed during the Holocaust.

In 1948, the international community stepped further along the path toward internationalizing human rights legislation: The General Assembly of the United Nations adopted the Convention on the Prevention and Punishment of the Crime of Genocide. The document adopted by the General Assembly called for more international collaboration in the pursuit of this endeavor, recognizing that "at all periods of history genocide has inflicted great losses on humanity; and being convinced that, in order to liberate mankind from such an odious scourge, international co-operation is required."[10] In Resolution 260 B (III) of December 9, 1948, the General Assembly added that "in the course of development of the international community, there will be an increasing need of an international judicial organ," and hence asked the International Law Commission (ILC), a UN body in charge of developing and codifying international law, "to study the desirability and possibility of establishing an international judicial organ for the trial of persons charged with genocide."[11] Having established the benefits of the creation of an international court to prosecute individuals for genocide and similar crimes, ad hoc committees established by the General Assembly submitted a draft statute for a permanent international criminal tribunal in 1951 and a revised statute in 1953.

The political climate of the Cold War, however, resulted in the rejection of the statute as unfeasible. Despite the shelving of the proposals drafted in the early 1950s, the conviction that "international criminal trials could concurrently express outrage, affirm the moral and legal foundations of human society, tell the story of a crime as fully as it could be uncovered, determine those most responsible for it, and punish them" had remained "stubbornly alive" since the Nuremberg and Tokyo trials.[12] While scholars and legal experts periodically continued to work on proposals for a permanent international criminal court, more serious efforts to pursue these proposals were not made until 1989. Upon the request of the prime minister of Trinidad and Tobago in 1989, the General Assembly asked the ILC to draft a statute for a permanent international criminal court that would include jurisdiction over international drug trafficking. This, incidentally, was only one year after the United States had ratified the UN Convention on the Prevention and Punishment of the Crime of Genocide.

The movement toward an international criminal court regained urgency and momentum in the early 1990s in the context of the crimes committed in the former Yugoslavia and in Rwanda. The commission of such crimes in these crisis areas indicated that "military and political response to genocide, war crimes, and crimes against humanity were insufficient."[13] Lacking a permanent juridical body, the UN Security Council established ad hoc tribunals for the former Yugoslavia (ICTY) and the International Criminal Tribunal for Rwanda (ICTR) to adjudicate large-scale atrocities in 1993 and 1994. These tribunals presented an important development for the "concept of the international accountability of individuals" for severe crimes.[14] While these ad hoc tribunals had limited jurisdiction in terms of time and territoriality and were responsive to the specific situations for which they were set up, they also brought to light several shortcomings. For one, the establishment of ad hoc tribunals proved to be extremely costly. Furthermore, despite the high cost, ad hoc tribunals were unable to provide timely responses to prosecuting perpetrators, often extending over several years—circumstances that resulted in evidence being destroyed and perpetrators not being held accountable. Lastly, whereas those ad hoc tribunals were set up by powerful outsiders, a permanent criminal court would ensure a universal, "permanent commitment to punish these crimes consistently."[15]

Buttressed by the climate of urgency created by the crimes committed in the former Yugoslavia and Rwanda and the shortcomings of ad hoc tribunals, the ILC drafted an international criminal court statute in 1993 on the request from the General Assembly. The ILC submitted its final version in 1994. In 1995, the General Assembly established the UN Preparatory Committee on the Establishment of an International Criminal Court (PrepCom) to draft a treaty for the court. Their task was to prepare a "widely acceptable consolidated text of a convention, to be submitted to a diplomatic conference of plenipotentiaries."[16] The PrepCom was "supervised directly and exclusively by the General Assembly to achieve a court independent of (although closely related to) the UN."[17] Starting in 1996, the PrepCom held six sessions to draft the text of the statute before the statute was finalized at the Rome Conference in the summer of 1998.

The supranational institution envisioned by Moynier in 1872 was finally created during the intergovernmental conference held in Rome, Italy, from June 15 to July 17, 1998. The conference culminated in the adoption of what became formally known as the Rome Statute of the International Criminal Court, which is the document that laid the legal foundations for the establishment of an international criminal court. Based on the idea of universal human rights, the court is empowered to prosecute individuals responsible for genocide, war crimes, and crimes against humanity, such as torture, mass killings, political slaughter, mass rape, and ethnic cleansing, if their national judicial system is unable or unwilling to do so. The creation of the court not only establishes in international law "universal rules to protect human beings in principle" but also functions as "an instrument to punish individuals who gravely breach the rules," thereby addressing the previous lack of enforcement of international law.[18] Of the 160 countries attending the negotiations at the Rome Conference, 120 states voted yes on the approval of the statute, 21 abstained, and 7 states (United States, China, Iraq, Israel, Libya, Qatar, and Yemen) voted against the Rome Statute.[19]

Despite drafting members' estimations that it would take approximately ten years to gather the required sixty ratifications needed for the establishment of the court, the sixtieth state had ratified the treaty on April 11, 2002, only four years after the drafting of the treaty. That the drafting process and required ratifications moved along faster than originally anticipated is partly attributed to the events that had occurred in Rwanda and the former Yugoslavia. Moreover, Marc Weller suggests, the progress toward ratification must be seen in the context of the efforts of an "extraordinarily well coordinated global campaign of high quality NGOs in support of the Rome Conference" that imbued a sense of urgency to the creation of the court so that, in fact, "after half a century of abortive attempts, it seemed that the organized international community was almost eager to engage in an act of international constitutional law-making in this instance."[20] Located in The Hague, Netherlands, the ICC officially became operational on July 1, 2002. The first bench comprised of eighteen judges was elected by an Assembly of States Parties in February 2003. The first pretrial hearings were held in 2006. As of June 2019, 122 countries are states parties to the statute.[21]

STRUCTURE AND CHARACTERISTICS OF THE INTERNATIONAL CRIMINAL COURT

The creation of the ICC is based on the structure and principles of the United Nations but represents an independent institution and treaty body. The UN member states are not identical with the states supporting the ICC. Since each member state has a single vote in the Assembly of States Parties, the decision-making structure of the ICC differs in important ways from those of the UN, where the five permanent members of the Security Council (China, France, Great Britain, Russia, and the United States) have the power to veto decisions. Insofar as majority opinions need not cede to a powerful individual opposition, the ICC has a more democratic structure than the UN.

The ICC is designed to prosecute individuals responsible for the most serious crimes of international concern, such as genocide, crimes against humanity, and war crimes committed after July 1, 2002, when the court entered into force. It has no jurisdiction over crimes committed before this date. The ICC can exercise jurisdiction over nationals of a state party, individuals who are accused of having committed such crimes in the territory of a state party, and in situations where a state has specifically consented to the ICC's jurisdiction. Lastly, the ICC has jurisdiction over situations referred by the UN Security Council, provided that those situations constitute a threat or breach to international peace and security and in which case the jurisdictional requirements do not need to be fulfilled.

With regard to its jurisdiction, the ICC differs in important respects from the International Court of Justice and the aforementioned ad hoc tribunals in Nuremberg or the former Yugoslavia. Unlike the International Court of Justice, which deals primarily with disputes between states, the ICC has jurisdiction over *individuals*, not states or governments. Whereas the ad hoc tribunals such as the ICTY and the ICTR—created by the UN Security Council—are limited in their jurisdiction to the specific situation for which they were established, the ICC is designed to eventually have a global reach.[22]

In contrast to the ICTY and ICTR, the main justificatory principle for the ICC lies in its permanent status. While antecedent ad hoc tribunals were created as a response to previously committed atrocities, the ICC was established as an institution to deter future crimes on a continuous basis at a global level. With an emphasis on the goal of deterrence, the ICC, in large part, performs a *rhetorical function*. Cherif Bassiouni, chair of the Drafting Committee of the Diplomatic Conference on the Establishment of an International Criminal Court, explains that the ICC is meant to foster "public processes" that will "reinforce social values and expectations concerning international conduct that will then contribute to the individual internalization of these values."[23] In addition to serving as a rhetorical discourse useful for forging cosmopolitan values, the ICC is meant to stand as a persistent reminder to governments that the court could hold individuals and their governments accountable for war crimes and crimes against humanity. The persuasive discourses of the court serve as a type of rhetorical *threat* that may help prevent such crimes in the future.[24] The ICC serves as an "international social control mechanism in enforcing sanctions against these crimes as opposed to ad hoc processes in which norms apply only selectively."[25] For Bassiouni, what is at issue is not "the epistemological, ontological or ethical content of substantive norms prohibiting genocide, crimes against humanity and war crimes, but rather their effective instrumental function as a means of international social control."[26] In short, the court creates persuasive discourses that function as a mechanism to curtail particular practices of states. It's not just the proponents of the court that recognize this. As we will see, this theme is echoed in opponents' fears over the ICC crafting a world order based on cosmopolitanism rather than national sovereignty.

Once ratified by a state, the Rome Statute becomes part of the national law of the ratifying state. Consequently, the principle of complementarity is a central feature to the court. The principle, stipulated in Article 17 of the Rome Statute, specifies that the ICC's jurisdiction is "complementary" to national legal jurisdictions and is thus an international, not a supranational, institution.[27] The principle of complementarity further stipulates that the ICC adopts a case only if the accused person's state of primary jurisdiction is unwilling or unable to carry out the investigation or prosecution of the crime committed. When a state ratifies the treaty, it becomes part of the state's sovereign law, and ratifying states have the initial authority to investigate and prosecute crimes covered by the ICC. The court will hear only cases that the accused person's home government has refused to bring to court in a reasonable manner. In this sense, the ICC can be understood as a court of last resort.

The court itself is designed to reflect the diversity of its stakeholders. As stipulated in the Rome Statute, the ICC consists of eighteen judges, a chief prosecutor with one or more deputy prosecutors, and an administrative staff.[28] As is usual for international treaty organizations, the ICC's judges, prosecutor, and deputy prosecutors are elected by the states that ratified the statute—the Assembly of State Parties—with each national delegation having one vote. The eighteen judges, representing "the principal legal systems of the world" and displaying an "equitable geographical representation,"[29] are divided into several chambers: one chamber consisting of three judges exclusively dealing with indictments and pretrial matters; three trial chambers consisting of three judges each; an appellate chamber consisting of five judges; and one presiding judge. The Assembly of State Parties can remove any of the judges or prosecutors by a simple majority vote. The assembly's additional functions are to review and approve the budget and to approve amendments to the statute for possible ratification by the member states.[30] The court is financed by contributions from the states that are party to the Rome Statute, with each country's contributions being determined by the same mechanism used to determine contributions to the UN.

INTERNATIONAL LAW, MORALITY, AND MEMORY

International law both *influences* and is *influenced by* collective memory. The experience of World War II, and the Holocaust in particular with its subsequent trials adjudicating Nazi crimes, is widely considered to have played a key role in the process of creating international criminal law instruments. The evolution of the human rights regime and institutionalization of human rights norms are widely considered "a moral response" to the atrocities of WWII.[31] The Nuremberg trials, for instance, are considered a "turning point in conceptions of law" or a "vital contribution to the developing body of international law"[32] and led to "a period of unprecedented growth in the recognition of human rights and the fulmination of international criminal justice."[33]

It is widely recognized that the Holocaust, has become a moral reference point in human rights discourses and has provided one rationale for the establishment of a regime of global moral responsibility. Tracing the discursive construction of the Holocaust as a master symbol, sociologist Jeffrey Alexander demonstrates how the historical event of the Holocaust "has come over the last fifty years to be redefined as a traumatic event for all of humankind" and has "become transformed into a generalized symbol of human suffering and moral evil"[34] that serves as a gauge by which "new instances of grievous mass injury would be typified."[35] Sociologists Levy and Sznaider add that while "memories of the Holocaust do not directly cause the emergence of a global legal culture,"[36] the period following WWII is credited with what Martha Minow refers to as the unprecedented "invention of new and distinctive legal forms of response" to atrocities that distinguishes the post-Holocaust era from other periods and instances of atrocity.[37] It is in this sense that memories of the Holocaust "produce a continued negotiation process between 'international law' (i.e. finding the criteria for degrees of wrongdoing) and 'normative ethics' (based on questions of reason and morality),"[38] thereby creating a kind of "institutionalized cosmopolitanism."[39] This creation of a global legal culture, Levy and Sznaider argue, simultaneously leads to a shift from primarily "national to cosmopolitan memory cultures."[40] Some of the more recent outcomes of this development are observable in the demands for intervention in the Balkans, which "helped establish the link and thus the centrality of the Holocaust as a measure stick for international politics and a transnational value system."[41] More recently, memory of the Holocaust configured into a moral value system and principle of global responsibility has found expression in the concept of "responsibility to protect," the international community's commitment to intervene in or prevent humanitarian crises.[42]

Landmark developments in this process of an institutionalization of cosmopolitan memory created in the immediate aftermath of WWII, according to Levy and Sznaider, include the Universal Declaration of Human Rights, which set a new standard for human rights, and the UN Convention on the Prevention and Punishment of the Crime of Genocide, which codified genocide into an international crime.[43] The International Military Tribunal at Nuremberg is considered by many a turning point in international criminal law as it created legal precedents that limited nation-state sovereignty over citizens in the context of human rights violations.[44] Article 6c of the London Agreement—the charter that laid the foundation for the International Military Tribunal—codified "crimes against humanity" to include "murder, extermination, enslavement, deportation, and other inhumane acts committed against any civilian population, before or during the war, or persecutions on political, racial, or religious grounds . . . whether or not in violation of domestic law of the country where perpetrated."[45] In this sense, Levy and Sznaider argue, Article 6c represented a

> radical departure from existing international law by recognizing individual responsibility not just in wartime extending protection to one's own civilian population, granting supremacy to international law over domestic law, and internationalizing the persecution of minorities. On the one hand, the Nuremberg trials affirmed sovereignty, as crimes against Germany's own citizens could only be said to have occurred after Germany started its "aggressive war." War was still the major crime. On the other hand, Article 6c and the legacy of Nuremberg would over time become a formidable challenge to the hitherto sacrosanct sovereignty of nation-states.[46]

The Nuremberg trials, Levy and Sznaider argue, are thus "remembered for establishing the previously unknown legal notion of crimes against humanity, thus providing a legal precedent that has structured public and legal debate about genocide ever since."[47] It is in this sense that the collective memory of the Holocaust has influenced international law by creating a new human rights idiom and with it a new set of cosmopolitan values.

The law and rhetorical discourse go hand in hand. The principles established at the Nuremberg war crime tribunal and those established by the Universal Declaration of Human Rights adopted by the General Assembly of the UN on December 10, 1948, are "decisive for how contemporary human rights norms are limiting state sovereignty by providing international standards for how states can treat their own citizens."[48] Beyond creating legal stipulations, these documents have much to do with how we are invited to value universal rights of the individual within the context of an international community. Anne Cubilié calls special attention to the rhetorical dimension of the UDHR document for the constitution of an international subject. Cubilié notes that

> the role of the body as it is defined within the Declaration is crucial to the document's legal and cultural project of human rights. In order to lay claim to the right of governance over all bodies anywhere on the Earth, the Declaration must first construct an international subject that exists prior to its incorporation as subject/citizen within state and cultural systems. Such a subject is not just granted rights to which he or she is entitled regardless of national and cultural circumstance, but is also proscribed from behaving in certain ways toward the other members of the transnational community.[49]

Cubilié concludes that the UDHR "performatively enacts the subject of an international 'human' with internationally recognized rights and responsibilities who exists prior to entrance into any other structure of identity and regulation—national, ethnic, religious, gender, and so on."[50] Communication scholar Robert DeChaine expands on the importance of the UDHR as a "catalyst for a novel, publicly crafted rhetorical vision of an 'international community.'"[51] Central values undergirding the UDHR, DeChaine argues, are the principles of human dignity, universality, brotherhood, duty, and democracy, all of which have served as important ideographs in the rhetoric of the global human rights movement.[52] The principles and ideals laid out in the UDHR are powerfully articulated in contemporary human rights discourse from which the "ethos of the new international community" emerges.[53]

This emergence of an "ethos of a new international community" is both the product and the generator of cosmopolitan memory, which in turn can be generated by cosmopolitan trials. As sociologist Moshe Hirsch writes, the relationship between international law and collective memory is based on the premise that "collective memory and law, including international law, interact in both directions; law affects and is affected by collective memory."[54] Law influences the memory of "various social groups, including national, regional and global communities," for instance, by selecting particular events from a historical account as more or less significant for the purposes of a trial and by narrating these events in a particular way. Moreover, the judgments rendered by international tribunals are based on this selection of historical events and their particular interpretation by the tribunal.[55] International tribunals can thus serve as didactic trials that not only engage in the criminal prosecution—as "internationally sanctioned retribution"—of human rights violations but also serve as "tools of historical instruction."[56]

International trials' didactic function is manifold. Lawrence Douglas aptly labels international legal events that emerge in the context of atrocity as "perpetrator trials." Perpetrator trials serve as "normative demonstrations of the efficacy and legitimacy of the rule of law."[57] In the wake of systematic or arbitrary use of violence and cruelty, at its most basic level, perpetrator trials reestablish the legal norm that individuals are accountable for their actions and signify a public recommitment to international norms of conduct and thus "reintroduce norms of legality into a radically lawless space."[58]

Perpetrator trials also serve a didactic function in the sense of establishing a historical record and thereby reproducing a particular historical narrative. As a "specialized sub-breed of the criminal trial," perpetrator trials offer victims "a venue for expressing their pain, and by conferring public recognition upon the suppressed history of their victimization;" they aid in acknowledging the experiences and memories of the victims and can help forge a path toward reconciliation and social peace as well as a new form of (cosmopolitan) memory.[59] These struggles over the memory of human rights violations thus provide the opportunity for righting past wrongs in a juridical sense as well as an opportunity of shaping the memory for future generations by creating a record of the lived, traumatic experiences brought on by human rights violations.[60] As perpetrators, victims, and other actors have to negotiate the remembrance of such violations, what role remembrance of human rights violations should play generally, and to what extent it is silenced, encouraged, or even supported by state actors becomes a contested issue within any given society.[61] Consequently, such struggles over how human rights violations are narrated play an integral role for the constitution of communities.

More specifically, perpetrator trials, or what David Hirsh calls cosmopolitan trials, aid in creating or have the potential to forge a distinct form of memory—cosmopolitan memory. Cosmopolitan trials, Hirsh argues, "seek to produce a narrative free from national particularity."[62] He writes,

> The process that we can see happening in the emergence of cosmopolitan law is also in part a process of the development of a cosmopolitan social collective memory. Courts receive particular and contradictory testimony; they act upon this according to their own rules, and produce a single narrative. Cosmopolitan courts receive nationally particularistic narrative as testimony that they transform into an authoritative cosmopolitan social memory.[63]

The judgments or narratives produced by such cosmopolitan trials, Hirsh argues, carry "social power" with the potential to "shake the certainty of eternal myths of nationhood and ethnic superiority."[64] Thus, the narratives forged through cosmopolitan criminal trials aid in "undermining myths of nationhood," thereby contributing to the formation of a global collective memory.[65] Cosmopolitan trials, then, are creating new modalities of global or cosmopolitan citizenship through the creation of a cosmopolitan social memory.

COSMOPOLITAN MEMORY AND GLOBALIZATION

The legal documents and processes consolidating a human rights framework work in tandem with more general globalization processes that pave the way for the formation of cosmopolitan memories. As state authority and national decision-making processes have changed with processes of globalization, the nation-state no longer has a monopoly on the production of memory discourses. As a result, memory cultures and memory discourses have undergone transformations. Levy and Sznaider note that

> human rights are the new measure for a global politics, shaping the ways in which state authority is exercised. While the sovereignty of states remains intact, their authority to determine the scope of solidarities in purely national terms is diminished. New transnational solidarities have the potential to emerge. The decontextualized memory of the Holocaust facilitates this. In its 'universalized' and 'Americanized' form, it provides Europeans with a new sense of 'common memory.'[66]

While the monopoly of the nation-state in defining memory discourses seems to wither, other forces, such as migration, immigration, and the pervasiveness of electronic mass communication, are becoming increasingly important factors in the production of memory discourses that mitigate memory discourses sanctioned by the nation-state. For instance, frequent treatments of the Holocaust in media representations have brought forth a universalization of the Holocaust in the sense that the employment of the trope is no longer tied to a particular locale.

The transformation of memory cultures and discourses from a national to a transnational scale extend beyond Holocaust remembrance. Anthropologist Christina Schwenkel has shown in her case study on the memory of the war in Vietnam how commodification and "intensified global movements of people, knowledge, and capital" have prompted new articulations of Vietnamese memory of the war that is deeply affected by transnational forces, creating new transnational forms of memory.[67] Schwenkel argues that the "current production of historical memory in Vietnam is, in many respects, a transnational negotiated process that involves variously situated actors and their global engagements with memory."[68]

Similarly, Geoffrey White's study of the fiftieth Guadalcanal anniversary demonstrates the "construction of a national history that contends, on the one hand, with multiple local memories and, on the other, with powerful global forces of meaning."[69] In contrast to John Bodnar, who argues in *Remaking America* that vernacular memories that emerge at the subnational level compete with and resist memory production at the national level, White adds a further level of analysis by calling attention to the impact of supranational forces in the production of memory discourses. Demonstrated by the example of war remembrance in the Solomon Islands, White argues that "transnational practices of recalling war easily override or transform other, local meanings and histories, including dissonant memories within the dominant nations."[70] In this sense, transnational memory making does have homogenizing effects, even though, as Levy and Sznaider are careful to point out, cosmopolitan memory is not necessarily to be understood as merely a process of homogenization. Instead, they argue, "cosmopolitan memory" should be considered as emerging precisely from the encounter between global schemes of interpretations and local conditions and interpretive schemes.

White's analysis complicates this interplay of subnational and supranational forces in the production of memory, demonstrating that the production of war narratives typically falls under the auspices of world powers who have the authority to define and limit the appropriation of war memories by creating idealized representations of war—by invoking heroism, loyalty, and liberation rather than suffering—in an attempt to reconstruct their own national identity. This can have particularly adverse effects for the creation of a national history for young states who are "culturally, economically, and politically" closely tied to their former colonial powers. For these states, then, "representing world wars in global frameworks of meaning may easily deform stories that derive their significance from the more specific and longer sweep of colonial history"[71] or those stories that emerge from "a variety of local voices and recall the war in terms other than those of the Allied epic of liberation."[72] In short, there is a stronger need for recognizing the interdependent relationship between local and global memory discourses.

GLOBAL CIVIL SOCIETY AND COSMOPOLITAN MEMORY

In addition to the increasing codification of human rights at an institutional level that has led to the emergence of transnational memory cultures, some scholars suggest that transnational nonstate actors, or global civil society, will also play a crucial role in memory production across territorial borders. Sociologist Ulrich Beck argues that in future memory discourses the "fenced in" history and memory of the nation-state will increasingly be replaced by a "polycentric memory" promoted by transnational and nonstate actors, such as social movement organizations.[73] Global civil society actors, mostly comprised of nongovernmental organizations (NGOs), have been widely recognized as significant forces in the development and implementation of human rights norms and on issues of social justice.[74] As such, they are likely to play a formative role in the constitution of global communities and in defining the values, norms, and attitudes of those communities.

The definitions of global civil society vary among scholars. The term "global civil society" is often used synonymously with "international society," "transnational civil society," and "the global public."[75] In general terms, the label refers to a "global arena in which individuals and organizations other than sovereign states come together and engage in activities separate from those pursued by national governments."[76] Since the 1970s, the number of NGOs, the mainstay of global civil society, has steadily risen. David Chandler notes in *Constructing Global Civil Society* that

> today, as transnational questions of human rights, the environment and international terrorism dominate the international agenda, it appears as if non-state actors of various kinds are becoming increasingly important players in international policy-making. Not just playing a major role in United Nations' forums but also in the policy-making of international financial institutions and governments.[77]

Chandler summarizes that "both the need for and the existence of an international or global civil society has now gained a consensus."[78] While the growing role of global civil society and NGOs in particular is widely agreed on, the degree of influence these nonstate actors have or should have is a contested issue among scholars.

Though it is not necessary to quantify the influence of NGOs on cosmopolitan memory, it is increasingly important to gain an understanding of the role global civil society plays as an agent of social change. Located outside of formal political structures, civil society, and particularly nongovernmental institutions, global civil society primarily operates through creating public spheres, which, in turn, help promote alternative visions of the future. Patrick Hayden argues that global civil society has become "a force for good global governance through dissemination of information, formation of open forums for dialogue and debate, and advocacy of greater democracy, transparency, accountability in governmental and multilateral institutions."[79] In this sense, global civic engagement is a means to "restoring collective values and morality as a counterpoint to the narrow individualism or political apathy reflected in the institution of formal, state-based, politics."[80] The fascination with global civic activism seems to lie in the "construction of a new global space"[81] and in developing an "alternative way of doing politics" as well as a "new type of political discourse, one which is not based on states and rejects the formal political competition for power based on instrumental rationality."[82] Global civil society and the public sphere it creates, Craig Calhoun argues, may be thought of as the expression of a transformation of consciousness and as a space for new "social imaginaries" of transnational solidarity. As such, global civil society is "defined not by geographical or spatial limits but by ideological ones, by adherence to global values rather than the particularisms of place."[83] Drawing on the ICC as a case study, the following chapters will examine several nonstate actors' varying degrees of commitment to these ideals.

NOTES

1. John Washburn, "The International Criminal Court Arrives: Establishing an Ethic of Peace and Justice." Speech delivered at the Ethical Society of New York, AMICC (June 30, 2002), https://https://web.archive.org/web/20160814003230/http://www.amicc.org/docs/John_EthicalSoc.pdf

2. For a more thorough discussion of Moynier's proposal and its reception, see Christopher Keith Hall, "The First Proposal for a Permanent International Criminal Court," *International Review of the Red Cross* 38, no. 322 (31 March 1998), www.icrc.org/en/doc/resources/documents/article/other/57jp4m.htm.

3. Steven C. Roach, *Politicizing the International Criminal Court: The Convergence of Politics, Ethics, and Law* (Lanham, MD: Rowman and Littlefield, 2006), 20.

4. Marlies Glasius, *The International Criminal Court: A Global Civil Society Achievement*, Routledge Advances in International Relations and Global Politics (New York: Routledge, 2005), 7.

5. Roach, *Politicizing the International Criminal Court: The Convergence of Politics, Ethics, and Law*, 22.

6. D. Robert DeChaine, *Global Humanitarianism: NGOs and the Crafting of Community* (Lanham, MD: Lexington Books, 2005), 41.

7. Ibid., 46.

8. Michael Ignatieff, "Human Rights: The Midlife Crisis," *New York Review of Books*, May 20, 1999, p. 58.

9. DeChaine, *Global Humanitarianism: NGOs and the Crafting of Community*, 6.

10. UN General Assembly, *Convention on the Prevention and Punishment of the Crime of Genocide*, adopted December 9, 1948, entered into force January 12, 1951.

11. UN General Assembly, Resolution 260 B (III), December 9, 1948.

12. Fanny Benedetti and John L. Washburn, "Drafting the International Criminal Court Treaty: Two Years to Rome and an Afterword on the Rome Diplomatic Conference," *Global Governance* 5, no. 1 (1999): 3.

13. Ibid., 3.

14. Ibid.

15. Michael J. Struett, *The Politics of Constructing the International Criminal Court: NGOs, Discourse, and Agency* (New York: Palgrave Macmillan, 2008), 4.

16. UN General Assembly, Resolution 5216 (LII), fifty-second session, Official Records, Supplement 49 at 384, UN Doc A/5249 (1997). Cited in Benedetti and Washburn, "Drafting the International Criminal Court Treaty: Two Years to Rome and an Afterword on the Rome Diplomatic Conference," 3.

17. Ibid., 4. Benedetti and Washburn note that the General Assembly supervised the Prep-Com in their task to not "create new international criminal or human rights norms but rather to devise an institution to apply them to acts of individuals." Benedetti and Washburn, "Drafting the International Criminal Court Treaty: Two Years to Rome and an Afterword on the Rome Diplomatic Conference," 5.

18. Marlies Glasius, "Expertise in the Cause of Justice: Global Civil Society Influence on the Statute for an International Criminal Court," in *Global Civil Society 2002*, edited by Marlies Glasius, Mary Kaldor, and Helmut Anheier (Oxford: Oxford University Press, 2002), 137.

19. Interestingly, several of these are countries that the United States has labeled "rogue" states. Israel has since then signed the treaty.

20. Marc Weller, "Undoing the Global Constitution: UN Security Council Action on the International Criminal Court," *International Affairs* 78, no. 4 (2002): 697.

21. See "The States Parties to the Rome Statute" on the ICC's official website, https://asp.icc-cpi.int/en_menus/asp/states%20parties/pages/the%20states%20parties%20to%20the%20rome%20statute.aspx.

22. It should be noted here that despite the United States' strong opposition to the ICC, the United States is showing relatively strong support for the ICTY and ICTR as well as for the Special Court for Sierra Leone. Due to the limited range of these courts with regard to "territories, time periods, crimes, and categories of suspects," Scheffer, Cooper, and Voinov Kohler

argue, they pose "minimal or no judicial risk to American nationals." See David Scheffer, Richard Cooper, and Juliette Voinov Kohler, "The End of Exceptionalism in War Crimes: The International Criminal Court and America's Credibility in the World," *Harvard International Review* (2007), https://web.archive.org/web/20090306061211/http://www.harvardir.org:80/articles/1647/.

23. Cherif Bassiouni, "Policy Perspective Favoring the Establishment of the International Criminal Court," *Journal of International Affairs* 52, no. 2 (Spring 1999): 801.

24. Philippe Kirsch, former chair of the Preparatory Commission for the International Criminal Court and current president of the ICC, is slightly more specific with respect to the argument about the ICC being a deterrent of crimes. He argues that "no one expects the ICC, on its own, to deter all crimes. The ICC must be part of a framework of measures to sustain a culture of accountability, including increased domestic prosecution of such crimes, greater use of universal jurisdiction, and greater international cooperation in suppressing international crimes. The United Nations, and in particular the Security Council, have an important role to play in this regard." See Philippe Kirsch, "The International Criminal Court: Current Issues and Perspectives," *Law and Contemporary Problems* 64, no. 1 (2001): 4–5.

25. Bassiouni, "Policy Perspective," 801.

26. Ibid.

27. Ibid., 797.

28. The current chief prosecutor, the Gambian lawyer Fatou Bensouda, took office in June 2012.

29. United Nations Diplomatic Conference of Plenipotentiaries on the Establishment of an International Criminal Court, *Rome Statute of the International Criminal Court*, Article 36.

30. Ibid.

31. Daniel Levy and Natan Sznaider, "The Institutionalization of Cosmopolitan Morality: The Holocaust and Human Rights," *Journal of Human Rights* 3, no. 2 (2004): 154.

32. Lawrence Douglas, "History and Memory in the Courtroom: Reflections on Perpetrator Trials," in *The Nuremberg Trials: International Criminal Law since 1945*, edited by Herbert R. Reginbogin and Christoph J.M. Safferling (Munich: K. G. Saur Verlag, 2006), 104.

33. Mary J. Gallant and Harry M. Rhea, "Collective Memory, International Law, and Restorative Social Processes after Conflagration: The Holocaust," *International Criminal Justice Review* 20 no. 3 (2010): 269. See also Gary Jonathan Bass, *Stay the Hand of Vengeance : Politics of War Crimes Tribunals* (Princeton, NJ: Princeton University Press, 2000), chapter 5, for a similar discussion of the legacy of the Nuremberg trials. Scholars are somewhat divided over the legacy of the Nuremberg trials with regard to prosecuting human rights violations as for some of the Allies, the overriding concern was with the crime of war of aggression rather than crimes against humanity.

34. Jeffrey C. Alexander, "On the Social Construction of Moral Universals: The 'Holocaust' from War Crime to Trauma Drama," *European Journal of Social Theory* 5, no. 1 (2002): 6.

35. Ibid., 49.

36. Levy and Sznaider, "The Institutionalization of Cosmopolitan Morality," 144.

37. Martha Minow, *Between Vengeance and Forgiveness: Facing History after Genocide and Mass Violence* (Boston: Beacon, 1998), 1. Cited in Alexander, "On the Social Construction," 50.

38. Levy and Sznaider, "The Institutionalization of Cosmopolitan Morality," 144.

39. Ibid., 155.

40. Daniel Levy and Natan Sznaider, "Memory Unbound: The Holocaust and the Formation of Cosmopolitan Memory," *European Journal of Social Theory* 5, no. 1 (2002), 88.

41. Ibid., 98.

42. See http://www.responsibilitytoprotect.org/.

43. Levy and Sznaider, "The Institutionalization of Cosmopolitan Morality," 143.

44. Ibid., 147. See also Bass, *Stay the Hand of Vengeance*, 147–205.

45. *Charter of the International Military Tribunal, Nuremberg Trial Proceedings*, Vol 1, section II, http://avalon.law.yale.edu/imt/imtconst.asp.

46. Levy and Sznaider, "The Institutionalization of Cosmopolitan Morality," 149.

47. Ibid. In fact, the term originated in the preamble to the 1907 Hague Convention and was used in the context of the Armenian genocide in 1915. However, it was the Nuremberg Charter that first established crimes against humanity in positive international law.

48. Ibid., 150.

49. Anne Cubilié, *Women Witnessing Terror: Testimony and the Cultural Politics of Human Rights* (New York: Fordham University Press, 2005), 20–21.

50. Ibid., 18.

51. DeChaine, *Global Humanitarianism: NGOs and the Crafting of Community*, 39.

52. Ibid., 46–49.

53. Ibid., 49.

54. Moshe Hirsch, "Collective Memory and International Law," *ESIL Reflections* 3, no. 7 (September 2014): 1. For two case studies of how collective memory influenced international law, see Moshe Hirsch, "Collective Memory and International Law," in *Invitation to the Sociology of International Law* (New York: Oxford University Press, 2016), 46–90.

55. Hirsch, "Collective Memory," 1.

56. Douglas, "History and Memory," 95.

57. Ibid.

58. Ibid., 96.

59. Ibid., 95.

60. Elizabeth Jelin, "The Politics of Memory: The Human Rights Movement and the Construction of Democracy in Argentina," *Latin American Perspectives* 21, no. 2 (Spring 1994): 39.

61. Ibid., 52–53. Jelin provides an interesting discussion of this tension between memory of trauma and forgetting in the context of Argentina's struggle for democracy. Similar examples include truth and reconciliation efforts in South Africa in the aftermath of the apartheid regime and other Latin American countries' shift to democratic forms of government.

62. David Hirsh, *Law against Genocide: Cosmopolitan Trials* (London: GlassHouse, 2003), 148. Specifically, Hirsh discusses the legal cases of *Irving*, *Sawoniuk*, *Eichmann* and *Demjanjuk*.

63. Ibid., 142.

64. Ibid., 146, 50. This is particularly significant, Hirsh argues, since the very substance of crimes against humanity is "the most extreme ethnic and national conflict" and "coloured by national social memories." See p. xix.

65. Ibid., xix.

66. Levy and Sznaider, "Memory Unbound," 100. For a discussion of whether the invocation of the Holocaust as a symbol for a "post-Holocaust morality" is primarily a Western phenomenon, see Alexander, "On the Social Construction," 58–60.

67. Christina Schwenkel, "Recombinant History: Transnational Practices of Memory and Knowledge Production in Contemporary Vietnam," *Cultural Anthropology* 21, no. 1 (2006): 5.

68. Ibid., 20.

69. Geoffrey M. White, "Remembering Guadalcanal: National Identity and Transnational Memory-Making," *Public Culture* 7, no. 3 (1995): 530.

70. Ibid., 552.

71. Ibid.

72. Ibid., 553.

73. Ulrich Beck, "Wie Versöhnung Möglich Werden Kann," *Die Zeit*, July 16, 2003. More specifically, Beck anticipates that one of the key questions in the politics of memory will be how reconciliation can become possible. The exemplary function of South Africa's Truth and Reconciliation Commission serves as one such example of the intersection between reconciliation and the role of transnational actors.

74. For an overview, see for instance William Korey, *NGOs and the Universal Declaration of Human Rights: A Curious Grapevine* (New York: St. Martin's, 1998). See also Margaret E. Keck and Kathryn Sikkink, *Activists Beyond Borders: Advocacy Networks in International Politics* (Ithaca, NY: Cornell University Press, 1998).

75. Akira Iriye, *Global Community: The Role of International Organizations in the Making of the Contemporary World* (Berkeley: University of California Press, 2002), 7.

76. Ibid.
77. David Chandler, *Constructing Global Civil Society: Morality and Power in International Relations* (New York: Palgrave Macmillan, 2004), 5.
78. Ibid., 9.
79. Hayden, *Cosmopolitan Global Politics , Ethics and Global Politics* (Farnham, UK: Ashgate, 2005), 7.
80. Chandler, *Constructing Global Civil Society: Morality and Power in International Relations*, 7.
81. Ibid., 113–14.
82. Ibid., 112.
83. Craig Calhoun, "Imagining Solidarity: Cosmopolitanism, Constitutional Patriotism, and the Public Sphere," *Public Culture* 14, no. 1 (2002): 114.

Chapter Three

The "Distinctly American Internationalism"

The United States' Unsigning of the Rome Statute of the International Criminal Court

Since World War II, there have been "some 250 international and regional armed conflicts" that have produced an estimated 170 million casualties.[1] That these atrocities were committed, Cherif Bassiouni, former chair of the Drafting Committee of the Diplomatic Conference of the Establishment of an International Criminal Court, noted in 1999, was in part due to the lack of a permanent international criminal system that could address such gross human rights violations and breaches of the Geneva Conventions.[2] Before the twentieth century, perpetrators of mass violence were mostly able to act with impunity as no system of accountability for such acts of violence was in place. The atrocities of the early part of the twentieth century sparked a growing realization that a system of accountability needed to be in place and triggered the emergence of what the *New York Times* labeled the "dawn of a world conscience."[3] Despite the growing recognition of the need for such a system of accountability in the wake of World War II, however, establishing a permanent international juridical body to adjudicate war crimes, crimes against humanity, and genocide was a tedious process.

The path to the creation of the ICC was forged by an international movement for the global enforcement of human rights that gained strength especially in the aftermath of World War II. Some landmark developments in the creation of international human rights instruments include the signing of the UN Charter in 1945, the Nuremberg War Trials in 1946, and the adoption of the Universal Declaration of Human Rights in 1948. In the mid- to late

1980s, the movement for international human rights law regained momentum with the establishment of the 1984 United Nations Convention Against Torture and Other Cruel, Inhuman, or Degrading Treatment or Punishment—the so-called Torture Convention—and a proposal to prosecute individuals for international drug trafficking in 1989. During the early 1990s, the end of the Cold War and the mass violence in former Yugoslavia and Rwanda urged the international community to develop mechanisms for stronger enforcement of international law to safeguard human rights and prompted the establishment of ad hoc war crime tribunals to prosecute those responsible for the atrocities. The experiences with these tribunals helped catalyze the most recent efforts to codify international human rights law through a permanent international court that would be authorized to prosecute individuals (rather than states) for the most heinous crimes of international concern—the International Criminal Court (ICC).

After half a century of drafting the legal foundations of an international criminal court, the court became a reality. A UN diplomatic conference held in Rome, Italy, in the summer of 1998 concluded its drafting process with the adoption of the Rome Statute of the International Criminal Court, the legal treaty founding the ICC, and opened the court for signature and ratification. As laid out in the preamble of the Rome Statute, the ICC is designed to "put an end to impunity" of those who perpetrate the "most serious crimes of concern to the international community as a whole."[4] Having entered into force on July 1, 2002, the ICC was hailed by former UN secretary general Kofi Annan as the "missing link" in the international legal system because it creates the legal framework for individual accountability for crimes such as genocide, crimes against humanity, and war crimes.[5] As such, the court is considered "the culmination of international law-making of the twentieth century."[6] With its potential to try cases involving perpetrators who have committed some of the gravest crimes of mass violence, the founding of the ICC has been "compared in significance to the founding of the United Nations itself."[7]

U.S. DIS/ENGAGEMENT

Keeping with the historical centrality of the United States in establishing judicial bodies to enforce human rights on a global level since World War II, the United States played an instrumental role in developing the ICC. U.S. support eventually wavered despite its deep involvement in the drafting process and the historical record that repeatedly proves that a criminal court operating at the international level is necessary for a more effective enforcement of human rights. At the end of the five-week Rome Conference during which the United States played a pivotal role in the statute's drafting process, the United States voted against the adoption of the Rome Statute. This vote against the adoption of the ICC was cast in response to treaty stipulations that did not grant the UN Security Council veto power over the court.[8] On this point, it should be noted that the ICC was designed to be a democratic institution that wouldn't grant any individual states parties more power and influence over any other states parties. The U.S. request would thus have undercut the democratic structure of the court.

Even so, two and a half years later, President Clinton signed the Rome Statute on the last day it was open for signature (December 31, 2000). This last-minute action made the United States a signatory to the treaty in an attempt to ensure the United States' future influence on the court. While U.S. public discourse about the court had been intense during the drafting process, Clinton's signature—signaling a commitment to the idea of the court—served as a catalyst for even fiercer debates in U.S. domestic and foreign policy centering on issues of the court's jurisdiction and procedural safeguards.

The promise of U.S. engagement with and support of the court that was secured by Clinton's signature was fundamentally altered on May 6, 2002, just two months before the scheduled date of the ICC entering into force. On that date, the Bush administration engaged in a heretofore unprecedented act in the international community—it "unsigned" an international treaty. The Bush administration had sent a notice to the United Nations, the depositary of the Rome Statute, informing the international community of its decision to withdraw the U.S. signature from and to not recognize any obligations toward the statute. Although the United States had been outspoken about its objections to the ICC, renouncing its previously delivered signature was significant in so far as the signature only required the United States to not actively work *against* the purpose of the ICC. By implication, the rhetorical act of withdrawing its signature from the treaty represented the United States' intent to actively oppose the ICC.[9]

The act of unsigning the treaty had far-reaching consequences in the United States and abroad. At the domestic level, it resulted in the Bush administration launching a campaign aimed at further undermining the ICC, which has become manifest in a series of legislative acts ostensibly designed to protect U.S. citizens from being prosecuted by the ICC. While the Bush administration and Congress were engaged in developing safeguards to exempt U.S. personnel from the court's reach, proponents of the court were caught worrying about the withering of the United States' credibility as a supreme enforcer of human rights. At the international level, responses to the act of unsigning ranged from incomprehension to sheer indignation. Among supporters of the ICC in the international community, the Bush administration's decision to unsign the treaty has been portrayed as a destructive move on the part of the United States. Given the nature of the crimes the court is supposed to adjudicate, the United States' repudiation of the institution seems counterintuitive and raised the question if, in the words of political scientist Marlene Wind, the United States is "fighting 'Global Justice'?"[10]

Moreover, given the unsigning's highly symbolic value, the United States' official stance toward the ICC prompted a heated debate about the possible legal implications of such a course of action for future international treaties. Most prominently, the international community expressed fears that the act of unsigning would set a dangerous precedent soon to be followed by other countries that no longer saw the need or desire to ratify certain international treaties or uphold treaty obligations. David Scheffer, who was ambassador at large for war crimes and who headed the U.S. delegation during the ICC negotiations in Rome for the Clinton administration, cautioned that "if we 'unsign' the ICC, we give a signal that a new practice is acceptable, and we lay the groundwork for undermining a whole range of treaties."[11]

This chapter focuses on the rhetorical discourses of the Bush administration and its surrogates announcing and explaining the heretofore unprecedented act of unsigning an international treaty—namely, the unsigning of the Rome Statute of the International Criminal Court. The creation of the Rome Statute, and by extension the ICC, marks a new type of international commitment to the preservation and protection of human rights on a global level. Conversely, I argue, the act of *unsigning* the Rome Statute represents an undoing of that commitment. As such, it serves as a crucial moment for the United States to reconstitute its identity and position in the international community.

The ICC is both an artifact of transnational public memory and at the same time a site of transnational public memory production. The ICC is an *artifact* of transnational public memory as the institution evolved out of several decades of concerted efforts to prosecute perpetrators for having committed war crimes, crimes against humanity, and genocide. It stands as empirical proof of the triumph of international cooperation to create a system of accountability for acts of genocide, war crimes, and crimes against humanity. The ICC is a *producer* of transnational public memory discourses as the cases it will hear will hold perpetrators accountable, will help restore justice in war-ravaged communities, and will help rebuild a sense of community. Furthermore, the cases it will hear will create greater awareness of human rights and will continue to shape how people are invited to remember human rights and mass violence at an international scale. Given this context, to the international community, the unsigning serves as a type of memorial to how discourses of national sovereignty remain dominant in an era when transnational interdependency and the need for transnational cooperation are becoming ever more important and inescapable. As such, the act of unsigning functions as a site of global memory production as it inaugurated a distinct foreign policy agenda that John Bolton labeled "American internationalism."

The rhetorical act of unsigning the international ICC treaty—a symbolic act with very real consequences—became manifest in the speech "American Foreign Policy and the International Criminal Court" delivered on May 6, 2002, by Under Secretary of State for Political Affairs Marc Grossman before the Center for Strategic and International Studies (CSIS).[12] The speech explains the United States' stance on the ICC and the decision to withdraw its signature from the Rome Statute as communicated in an official letter to the UN earlier that day and serves as an illuminating and rich supplement to the official declaration sent to the UN. Drawing on Grossman's speech and public discourse discussing the moment of unsigning, I examine the rhetorical strategies employed by the Bush administration to present its concerns and decisions regarding the ICC in an attempt to explain the political and ideological assumptions that have shaped the controversy about the court and to reveal the United States' implied vision of its role as a member of the international community.

My analysis is informed by Philip Wander's call for an ideological turn in criticism that "reflects the existence of crisis, acknowledges the influence of established interests and reality of alternative world-views, and commends rhetorical analysis not only of the actions implied but also of the interests represented."[13] By analyzing the principal U.S. objections to the ICC, I show how notions of sovereignty and community figure in U.S. public discourse about the ICC. I conclude by analyzing how this discourse impedes or creates the possibility of forging a transnational imaginary informed by cosmopolitan values. The chapter begins with an outline of the U.S. role in the movement for the establishment of a permanent international criminal court and details U.S. objections to the court. This is followed by an analysis of the rhetorical strategies at work in the speech "American Foreign Policy and the International Criminal Court" examining the U.S. self-image and particular understanding of sovereignty that is promoted through the speech and ancillary texts.

THE "DISTINCTLY AMERICAN INTERNATIONALISM"— U.S. OBJECTIONS TO THE ICC

Historically, the United States has played a seminal role in creating documents and institutions that would lead to the establishment of an international human rights system. With its influence on the (eventually unsuccessful) attempts to create a League of Nations, the founding of the United Nations and its attending documents, its leadership in creating major war crimes tribunals over the last seventy years, and its participation in drafting international human rights treaties, the United States has crafted its legacy for significant "contributions to the contours of human rights practice, policy, and action worldwide."[14] What is more, legal scholar Helen Stacy notes, is that the United States' "funding of post-Cold War Rule of Law programs and support for domestic human rights systems . . . has further entrenched the international community's perception of the United States as a human rights beacon."[15] Thus, the United States' human rights legacy is not limited to the procedural aspects of international human rights legislation but also serves an important rhetorical function.

Despite the United States' dominant role in human rights legislation and efforts to build institutions of global governance, attempts at building an international criminal court in the early 1990s were tainted by U.S. policy makers' distrust of international courts and specifically their distrust of such courts' ability to neutrally apply international law, both of which were concerns that had been evolving against the backdrop of Cold War international relations.[16] The principal argument supplied against an international criminal court from the United States in the early 1990s was that such a court would have jurisdiction over U.S. citizens and could be used for politically motivated prosecutions.[17] These widely held beliefs created substantial obstacles for proponents arguing for the creation of an international criminal court.

In the mid-1990s, a confluence of factors created a context that contributed to the United States becoming more supportive of the creation of an international criminal court. These factors included the outbreak of the conflict in Yugoslavia and the growing realization that an institution that could hold *individuals* (rather than states) responsible could provide strategic advantages.[18] In 1993, the Security Council created an international criminal tribunal for the former Yugoslavia. Coupled with the already ongoing process of drafting a statute pursued by the International Law Commission, a UN body in charge of developing and codifying international law, and the influence of NGOs who had played an important role in raising public awareness about the necessity of an international criminal court, these developments provided a window of opportunity for the United States to change its view on the desirability and feasibility of an international criminal court.[19]

By 1993, the United States had decided to support the creation of an international criminal court. Having played a seminal role in establishing the kinds of institutions that would render justice at an international scale, the United States was also at the forefront in drafting the ICC. Representatives of the Clinton administration were actively involved in the negotiations establishing the ICC. However, as political scientist Marlies Glasius points out, the United States was at the same time "working very hard to create the kind of Court that the United States wanted."[20] The final statute included several issues the United States would not agree to, which has subsequently resulted in strong U.S. opposition to the ICC. While several countries have expressed their objections to the treaty, the United States has done so more forcefully than others. Glasius notes that most countries that oppose the ICC "have been satisfied merely not to ratify the treaty and to stay away from further negotiations," whereas the United States is the "only state to date that has pursued an active policy of opposing the Court."[21] The fierce rejection of the ICC is evidenced by impassioned commentaries on this issue in U.S. public discourse about the ICC and by legislation enacted immediately following the United States' unsigning of the Rome Statute.

The public opposition to the ICC was spearheaded by former senator Jesse Helms, Republican of North Carolina and chair of the Senate Committee on Foreign Relations. His views were published in an op-ed in the London daily *Financial Times* shortly after the United States voted against the Rome Statute in July 1998. Alleging that the ICC poses a "threat to US national interests," Helms exhorted his audience to "slay" the "monster"—that is, to destroy the ICC and what it represents. Rather than standing out as particularly polarizing, Helms's views reflected U.S. public discourse (and eventual policy maneuvers) about the ICC more generally. Helms argued that "rejecting the Rome treaty is not enough. The US must fight the treaty . . . even if the US never joins the court, the Rome treaty will have serious implications for US foreign policy."[22] Calling the Rome treaty an "irreparably flawed and dangerous document," he concluded that the United States "cannot treat it with the 'benign neglect' Mr. Axworthy [the Canadian foreign minister] is hoping for. As a Dutch delegate put it at the conclusion: 'I won't say we gave birth to a monster, but the baby has some defects.' He is wrong. The ICC is indeed a monster—and it is our responsibility to slay it before it grows to devour us."[23]

Foreshadowing fierce opposition to come, Helms vowed, "And so long as there is breath in me, the US will never—I repeat, never—allow its national security decisions to be judged by an International Criminal Court."[24] Helms would later be responsible for introducing the American Service-Members' Protection Act that became law in August 2002.[25] As we will see, Helms was not alone in thinking that abstention or even withdrawal from the treaty would be insufficient to incapacitate it and that opponents must vigorously work against the court if they desired to dismantle it. In fact, Helms's op-ed echoed a statement made by Senator Rod Grams of Minnesota at the Senate Foreign Relations Committee hearings held on July 23, 1998, in the immediate aftermath of the adoption of the Rome Statute. In his opening statement, Grams said, "I hope that now the administration will actively oppose this court to make sure that it shares the same fate as the League of Nations and collapses without U.S. support for this court truly I believe is the monster and it is the monster that we need to slay."[26]

Beyond this kind of commentary that refers to the ICC in devil terms (i.e., the monster), the U.S. administration provided a host of specific arguments against the ICC with regard to the court's authority and structural characteristics. The United States' principal objections to the ICC include the court's jurisdiction over states that have not ratified the treaty, the court's interference with state sovereignty, its allegedly weak procedural safeguards, and its perceived potential for allowing politically motivated prosecutions. One of the primary concerns advanced by the Bush administration against the ICC is the court's jurisdiction over individuals from states that have not ratified the treaty. As such, the treaty is regarded as "[threatening] the sovereignty of the United States."[27] But the concern over the potential loss of U.S. sovereignty is often articulated more explicitly in terms of the ICC subjecting the United States to supranational law and institutions. An editorial in the *Wall Street Journal*, for instance, argued that the enforcement of human rights and global justice is "best achieved by U.S. leadership and military strength."[28] These objectives, critics of the ICC argued, would be threatened by globally operating juridical institutions that oversee the application of U.S. rule and military force. The editorial drew from a comment made by Harold Koh—former assistant secretary of state for democracy, human rights, and labor in the Clinton administration and professor of law at Yale University arguing in favor of the ICC—who had likened the creation of the ICC to "an international Marbury versus Madison moment."[29] Contrary to how Koh presumably employed this comparison, the editorial characterized the 1803 decision as giving "a fledgling U.S. Supreme Court authority over the other branches of government."[30] Just as the federal Supreme Court had gained power over state jurisdiction with the *Marbury v. Madison* decision, the ICC as a "world court" would have "similar powers over America's democratic decisions and global leadership"[31] by providing the grounds for international law superseding national law and effectively being subject to judicial oversight by the ICC.

Concerns over the shifting locus of power occupy the heart of the controversy over the ICC and spill over into scholarly circles as well. David Davenport, research fellow at the conservative Hoover Institution, raises fears about the potentially waning status of U.S. leadership in the international community. Tracing the increasing influence of nongovernmental institutions in global politics, for instance in the creation of the ICC, Davenport decries the emergence of such actors and their tactics as manifesting a "new diplomacy."[32] The globalist agenda of this "new diplomacy," he argues, undermines nation-state interests and sovereignty. Accordingly, the "most powerful tool of the new diplomacy," and thus the most alarming, is that it "is replacing the leadership of the U.S. and other world powers with that of nongovernmental organizations and smaller states."[33] Davenport's article reveals a deep mistrust of the influence of both international institutions and NGOs that have become increasingly important players in global politics.

Such commentary reinforces how the influence of international institutions, like the ICC and globally operating NGOs, figures prominently as a threat to U.S. leadership and to the concept of sovereignty in the U.S. debates over the ICC. At the root of these arguments is the fear over a loss of the Westphalian model of the nation-state. According to this model, nation-states had complete sovereignty over their own territory. The desire to preserve this notion of the nation-state and with it the uncompromising pursuit of national interests takes priority over benefits of the ICC for the larger global community, such as the ability to guarantee the enforcement of human rights norms at a global scale.

Anxieties over declining nation-state sovereignty brought about by the ICC were articulated boldly by John Bolton during his tenure as assistant secretary of state for international organization affairs.[34] In a passionate article published in the *Washington Post* in January 2001, Bolton, labelled by the British newspaper *Guardian* as the "intellectual leader of opposition to the ICC,"[35] urged the future administration to "unsign" the treaty as the "Rome Statute may risk great harm to our national interests."[36] Bolton maintained that the Rome Statute of the ICC "is, in fact, a stealth approach to eroding our constitutionalism and undermining the independence and flexibility that our military forces need to defend our interests around the world."[37] In his article, Bolton cast the supporters of the ICC as ill-informed and misled, guided by a hidden, conspiratorial plan designed to undermine the power of the United States or as a "thinly disguised effort to block passage" of an act stipulating the immunity of U.S. peace forces. Denouncing the ICC as "an object of international ridicule and politicized futility," Bolton echoed Davenport's suspicion of international organizations and institutions usurping national institutions' power and decried ICC supporters as having an "unstated agenda, resting, at bottom, on the desire to assert the primacy of international institutions over nation-states."[38]

Bolton had put forth a similar argument about the ICC's reach during the hearings before the United States House Committee on International Relations in July 2000. There he suggested that the true but hidden motive of ICC supporters is to create a system that would handcuff the United States:

> Support for the International Criminal Court concept is based largely on emotional appeals to an abstract ideal of an international judicial system, unsupported by any meaningful evidence, and running contrary to sound principles of international crisis resolution. Moreover, for some, faith in the ICC rests largely on an unstated agenda of creating ever-more comprehensive international structures to bind nation states in general, and one state in particular.[39]

Bolton's charge that the ICC "binds" nation-states must be understood as synonymous with the fear of no longer having impunity. Bolton made no attempts at addressing why an international community might want to bind one nation-state in particular to international oversight. The act of "binding," instead, serves to instill fear of the proscription of U.S. national sovereignty without attempting to reconcile the contrary notion that his (Bolton's) opposition to the ICC implies a desire for the United States to be able to impose its sovereign will on other sovereign nation-states without the possibility of being held accountable for such impositions. Bolton's rhetoric combines invoking fear of the ever-encroaching power of international organizations onto the sovereignty of nation-states with an attack against President Clinton by casting the Clinton administration's support of the ICC as "naïve"[40] and characterizing Clinton's "last-minute decision" to sign the Rome Statute as "injurious" and "disingenuous."[41] With these portrayals of the ICC and his accusations that the Clinton administration never "understood that the ICC's problems are inherent in its concept," Bolton not only discredited the ICC as an institution but also publicly undermined Clinton's ethos as a competent decision maker.[42]

To legitimize his argument and, presumably, to position himself as being on the right side of history, Bolton worked to associate himself with the U.S. legacy of assuming a leadership role in the protection of human rights, claiming that "no one disputes that the barbarous actions under discussion are unacceptable to civilized peoples."[43] Bolton proceeded by distinguishing between ICC opponents and ICC supporters regarding their views about the appropriate *means* through which the enforcement of human rights should be achieved—that is, by creating a distinction between privileging "international power" over "international law." Bolton concluded that

> the real issue is how and when to deal with these acts, and this is not simply or even primarily a legal exercise. The ICC's advocates make a fundamental error by trying to transform matters of international power into matters of law. Misunderstanding the appropriate role of force, diplomacy and power in the world is not just bad analysis, but bad and potentially dangerous policy for the United States.[44]

His position suggests that international law would put unnecessary and undesirable restrictions on the ways in which U.S. power could be expressed internationally. Bolton's conceptualization of proper internationalism suggests that power (represented by powerful nation-states) may authorize itself to "do justice" when the need arises without the need or desire to create laws or institutions that would bind nations together. By contrast, Bolton sees the ICC being the opposite of a proper internationalism because it limits the selective application of force and enforces a consistent application of the rule of law when standing in judgment of and punishing those responsible for genocide, war crimes, and other crimes against humanity.

Drawing this argument to its logical conclusion, Bolton proposes that the United States withdraw from the treaty, urging the incoming administration to unsign the Rome Statute. Foreshadowing President Bush's actions that would follow in May 2002, Bolton asserted that "what one president may legitimately (if unwisely) do, another may legitimately (and prudently) undo.

The incoming administration seems prepared to take similar actions in domestic policy, and it should not hesitate to do so internationally as well."[45] Acknowledging the potential slippery slope that such an action could inaugurate, Bolton frames the act of unsigning an international treaty as a defining feature of "American internationalism."[46] Bolton explains that "not only would an unsigning decision make the U.S. position on the ICC clear beyond dispute, it would also open the possibility of subsequently unsigning numerous other unratified treaties. It would be a strong signal of a distinctly American internationalism."[47] Ironically, the distinct "American" dimension of the internationalism that Bolton envisions is precisely the retreat from and repudiation of notions and practices of "internationalism" (here understood as a kind of cosmopolitanism). Hence, the U.S. brand of internationalism previewed in Bolton's remarks would amount to a unilateralism rather than an embracement of internationalism. Not only does it ignore the fact that the kinds of crimes the ICC has been designed to adjudicate cannot be dealt with by one country alone; it also reveals a lack of concern for a more democratic world order.[48]

In addition to these reservations about the institution of the ICC as a source of a potential loss of sovereignty, the United States objects to several specific stipulations in the Rome Statute. Several of these objections refer to what the United States considers weak procedural safeguards in the overall design of the court,[49] some of which were amended during the drafting process of the Rome Statute.[50] Despite concessions to U.S. interests during this process, however, the alleged unchecked power of the prosecutor in initiating prosecutions remains major grounds for U.S. opposition to the court. ICC opponents consider the way in which prosecutions can be initiated as posing the risk that the United States would become the target of politically motivated accusations, which makes the office of the prosecutor one of the most cited contentious issues and a target of ridicule. Echoing a language similar to Helms's and Bolton's commentaries, Lester Munson, former spokesperson of the Senate Foreign Relations Committee, spoke of the office of the prosecutor as containing "enormous potential for abuse," warning that "it doesn't look so bad on paper, but then Dr. Frankenstein never intended for his monster to run amok."[51] In an attempt to eliminate this alleged flaw or "Frankenstein factor" in the structure of the court, the United States proposed to have the UN Security Council grant the exclusive authority to initiate prosecutions but ultimately did not succeed. The United States was outwardly concerned about a possible abuse of power by the office of the prosecutor and sought to limit its power through granting veto power over prosecutions to the UN Security Council. However, as noted earlier, the choice to not heed the request was a deliberate decision during the drafting process. As political theorist Jason Ralph points out, "in order to gain sufficient political support, the Court had to be seen to be impartial. The Court's basic principles, therefore, had to be applied equally to all states."[52] Had the proposition been accepted, members of the Security Council would have been granted more power, thereby reproducing existing hierarchies among states and eliminating the democratizing element of this provision.

An examination of the public discourse about the impending establishment of the ICC illustrates that implicit in most of these claims advanced by the United States is the anxiety about the loss of power and sovereignty of the United States. Moreover, the fear is that the ICC could render "false" justice due to politicized prosecutions and investigations of U.S. personnel. The final set of objections raised in the public discourse about the ICC comprises a presumed lack of due process protections. While some of the objections address the typical problems and "usual inadequacies of UN majority rule,"[53] such as how to ensure that the best lawyers are chosen, how the court will be financed, or how to recruit the court's investigating force, supporters of the ICC consider these objections as unwarranted and exaggerated, if not displaying a willful ignorance that veils more deep-seated concerns regarding the leadership role of the United States. Legal scholar Bruce Broomhall notes,

> The United States' legal argument is widely thought to be weak, but arises from deeper concerns emanating in different forms from the U.S. Congress and the Executive. . . . These concerns are relatively widespread among conservative commentators, but are not well supported among even sympathetic U.S. academics, who typically recognize that the Rome Statute offers significant safeguards (many based on U.S. proposals) and that constitutional concerns are misplaced.[54]

The eventual unsigning thus must be interpreted as founded on partisan grounds, lacking substantial support, even from partisan scholars, and based on a perceived lack of safeguards, many of which, ironically, were drafted by the United States. While the U.S. objections are presented as arguments against the structure of the court, its legality, and its potential threat to the Constitution of the United States, these objections reveal a more deep-seated anxiety over the loss of U.S. sovereignty in an age where one must be naïve or cynical to deny the status of international interdependency.

UNSIGNING THE ROME STATUTE

The United States played an important role in promoting and developing antecedents to the ICC that sought to enforce human rights on a global level, such as the Nuremberg War Crimes Trials and the international tribunals for the former Yugoslavia and Rwanda. The Clinton administration upheld U.S. involvement in such bodies by aiding in the drafting of the Rome Statute.

Specifically, the U.S. government was "one of the keenest advocates of the application of the advanced definitions of crimes against humanity and war crimes."[55] In fact, legal scholar Marc Weller notes, the United States was "one of the most effective and technically competent delegations in this process, both before the Rome conference, at Rome, and even afterwards, when the elements of crimes were being defined."[56] When the time came to approve the Rome Statute, the United States cast a negative vote on the grounds of particular stipulations in the treaty. Two and a half years later, despite several points of contention with the treaty, President Clinton signed the Rome Statute on December 31, 2000, joining 138 other countries that had signed the Rome Statute by then.[57] The date of Clinton's signature is significant for two reasons: First, Clinton signed the treaty in the waning days of his term of office—to be precise, eighteen days prior to his administration leaving the White House. Second, the date marked the end of the period during which the Rome Statute was open for signature, as the deadline to sign the document closed on December 31, 2000.[58] In the weeks prior to Clinton's decision to sign the Rome Statute, there had been vigorous debates about the approaching deadline. While Secretary of State Madeleine Albright and legal advocacy organizations, such as the American Bar Association and the Lawyers Committee for Human Rights, had urged Clinton to sign the treaty, the Pentagon was strongly opposed.[59]

Still, one should not be too quick in praising Clinton's move toward joining the ICC as it was not delivered without reservations. Although Clinton did provide his signature to the international treaty, an act that according to diplomatic conventions typically signals a state's intention to ratify a treaty, he simultaneously qualified his signature by reiterating his administration's objections to the treaty, declaring that the United States is not "abandoning our concerns about significant flaws in the treaty."[60] What is more, Clinton concluded his statement by urging his successor to hold off ratifying the treaty until the United States' concerns about the court's weaknesses would be addressed. He stated, "I will not, and do not recommend that my successor submit the treaty to the Senate for advice and consent until our fundamental concerns are satisfied."[61] Although an ambiguous diplomatic maneuver as a whole, Clinton's last-minute decision is considered to express a desire for an "ongoing policy of 'constructive engagement'" in the negotiations of the ICC.[62] Clinton's rationale was that, at the very least, the signature would allow the United States to "remain engaged in making the I.C.C. an instrument of impartial and effective justice in the years to come," whereas the refusal to sign the Rome Statute would exclude the United States from engaging in the evolution of the court in the future.[63] Despite Clinton's cautious handling of the signature, Senator Jesse Helms quickly reinserted himself in the public debate, claiming that the main U.S. objections have not been resolved since the vote on the Rome Statute in July 1998. Foreshadowing his efforts to weaken the required consent of the Senate for ratification of the treaty, Helms pledged that "nothing—I repeat, nothing—has changed since then to justify U.S. signature. . . . This decision will not stand."[64]

In contrast to the prevailing message sent by the Clinton administration—that is, one of a hesitant commitment to the institution of the ICC but one that foresees a probable future engagement with it—the Bush administration's actions have been interpreted as representing a clearly antagonistic posture. This assessment is owing to its official repudiation of the ICC in May 2002, which was most explicitly manifest in the act of unsigning the Rome Statute. Leading up to this act was a gradual move to pull out of the revision process of the Rome Statute. Whereas the Clinton administration had taken a lead role in the legal drafting process, the Bush administration's initial stance "over the early course of 2001, was one of withdrawal from the ICC-related PrepCom process and of slow stocktaking, as the administration worked to develop a policy distinct from its predecessor."[65] As it became clear that the required number of ratifications would be met, which in turn would result in the entering into force of the ICC on July 1, 2002, the United States submitted a formal letter to United Nations secretary general Kofi Annan on May 6, 2002, renouncing its signature. The letter, signed by Under Secretary of State John Bolton, stated that the United States "does not intend to become a party to the treaty" and that consequently "the United States has no legal obligations arising from its signature on December 31, 2000."[66] Secretary of Defense Donald Rumsfeld declared in a press statement released on May 6, 2002, that the action "effectively reverses the previous U.S. Government decision to become a signatory."[67] What the Clinton administration had signed, the Bush administration proceeded to *unsign*. On the same day, May 6, 2002, Under Secretary of State for Political Affairs Marc Grossman delivered a speech at an event hosted by the Center for Strategic and International Studies in which he explained why the United States would renounce its involvement in a treaty creating an international criminal tribunal.

Grossman's announcement of the United States' official repudiation of the Rome Statute constituted a novelty in international law, though it did not come as a complete surprise. Following Bolton's call to rescind the ICC signature in 2001, several commentators had discussed the possibility of the United States withdrawing its signature from the Rome Statute several months before it was officially announced.[68] At the end of March 2002, Pierre-Richard Prosper, the State Department's ambassador at large for war crimes issues, had declared that the unsigning of the treaty was "one of several options being considered by Washington as an indication that it was not bound by the treaty."[69] With the decision to unsign the treaty, the Bush administration chose the most public and most rhetorically significant of its available options. The rhetorical dimensions of this act are highlighted by the fact that, as *Boston Globe* reporter Elizabeth Neuffer points out, it is not unusual for countries to sign a treaty and then not to submit it for ratification by lawmakers or to take a long time to ratify it. This was the case, for instance, with the Genocide Convention the United States had signed in 1948 but did not actually ratify until 1988. It is unusual, however, for a country to remove its signature altogether.[70] No president has ever revoked his predecessor's signature to a treaty. William Aceves, professor of international law, notes that the act of unsigning an international treaty is "unique in the history of international law, and U.N. officials indicate that no such precedent exists."[71] Scheffer, the ambassador at large for war crimes during the Clinton administration, has argued that retracting the signature "exceeded even the actions of the Reagan administration."[72] The Reagan administration decided in 1987 to not seek ratification of an amendment to the Geneva Conventions known as Protocol 1 that the Carter administration had signed as the document would have given protections to soldiers of insurgent movements.[73]

Due to its exceptionality, the act of unsigning created some debate among legal scholars about its significance and constitutionality.[74] Specifically, it raised questions about the role of the United States in the international community and the negative legal precedent this symbolic and legal act of unsigning an international treaty would set for the future. The unsigning marks the culmination of the fierce debates over the ICC that themselves were in violation of the spirit, if not the letter, of Article 18 of the Vienna Convention on the Law of Treaties. This 1969 treaty stipulating the obligations of nations to obey other international treaties requires signatory nations to "refrain from acts which would defeat the object and purpose of a treaty . . . until it shall have made its intention clear not to become a party to the treaty."[75] This would mean that Clinton's signature legally bound the United States to assuming, at minimum, a more detached and neutral stance toward the court.

MARC GROSSMAN: "AMERICAN FOREIGN POLICY AND THE INTERNATIONAL CRIMINAL COURT"

Accompanying the official announcement of the unsigning of the Rome Statute was Grossman's address delivered at the Center for Strategic and International Studies. The speech warrants a close examination as it elucidates U.S. foreign policy regarding the ICC. Moreover, the speech provides insight into the implicit understanding of the concept of sovereignty that is used to dismiss the ICC. As such, the speech provides further insight into the United States' self-concept and vision of its role in the international community. Drawing loosely on the rhetorical conventions of the manifestic genre, I contend that the act of unsigning functions as a constitutive moment for the production of a political subjectivity that eschews global responsibility in an effort to protect U.S. sovereignty. Grossman's speech accomplishes this by gradually narrowing the way of being offered by his speech while purportedly speaking from and for an inclusive, unified "American" voice.

Divided into six sections, the speech "American Foreign Policy and the International Criminal Court" comprises several formal elements characteristic of the manifestic genre. In her book *Manifestoes: Provocations of the Modern*, Janet Lyon identifies several distinct argumentative strategies typically found in manifestoes. First, the manifesto displays an oversimplified, highly selective history that outlines the development of oppression until the present. This selective history "functions more like myth than like empirical historiography" and is usually given in a passionate tone.[76] Second, the manifesto typically employs the form of an enumeration of grievances or demands to create the impression of one group being oppressed by another. The characteristic paratactical structure of numbered lists serves as a means to create a heightened sense of urgency of these grievances. The third recurring feature Lyon identifies may be the "only uniform convention among manifestoes" and refers to its particular "hortatory rhetorical style."[77] This rhetorical device of calling for a course of action is coupled with the manifestic genre's concern with the act of "truth-telling." The fourth commonality found among most manifestoes is then an "epigrammatic, declarative rhetoric which directly challenges the named oppressor . . . while uniting its audience in an exhortation to action."[78] The general function of the manifesto has thus been to offer "revised historical perspectives" and "new hierarchies of power" by creating a rupture in the dominant political order.[79]

The speech begins with Grossman listing a set of "American" beliefs and values that evoke common U.S. ideographs, or foundational values, such as justice, the rule of law, and freedom. Following his opening remarks, Grossman abruptly proclaims the following "American" beliefs:

> Here is what America believes in:
>
> - We believe in justice and the promotion of the rule of law.
> - We believe those who commit the most serious crimes of concern to the international community should be punished.
> - We believe that states, not international institutions are primarily responsible for ensuring justice in the international system.
> - We believe that the best way to combat these serious offenses is to build domestic judicial systems, strengthen political will and promote human freedom.[80]

Grossman's proclamation of a set of beliefs and values—emphasized by the anaphoric use of "we believe"—is particularly noteworthy because he favors the connotative term "America" over the more denotative term "United States," which is preferred in diplomatic circles. Declaring "America's beliefs" rather than U.S. beliefs, Grossman invokes "America" as an ideograph, associating it with foundational values such as "justice" and "human freedom" and thus appealing to an idealized or nostalgic version of U.S. political culture rather than a realist approach to international relations. Following Michael Calvin McGee, an ideograph is an ordinary language-term, words, or phrases primarily used in political discourse that function as abstractions or what he calls "one-term sums"[81] of an ideological "collective commitment to a particular but equivocal and ill-defined normative goal."[82] The ideograph "America" is used here to invoke a series of unquestioned ideals and political values the United States has historically been associated with and is cast as the guarantor of these morally virtuous principles.

The use of the ideograph "America" also sets the stage for a gradual narrowing of agents throughout the speech and instructs audiences how to read the act of unsigning. Given the exigency of the speech situation—the unsigning of the Rome Statute with far-reaching consequences in U.S. diplomatic relations—Grossman's preference of the label "America" over the label "United States" seems unusual. As an official document detailing the U.S. position on the withdrawal of the U.S. signature from an international treaty, the speech addresses not only a U.S. audience but also, if not primarily, an international audience, and specifically an international audience consisting of experts, such as policy makers, diplomats, and other officials working in the administration. Considering the high-profile positions of the audience members, the use of the label "America" rather than "United States" constitutes a break with the proper naming conventions, one that heads of states and ambassadors would be highly attuned to. The lack of regard for the proper naming practices in the company of representatives of the international community parallels the lack of concern for the rules of conduct as a member of the international community expressed in the act of nullifying the signature to an international treaty. Translated into the realm of foreign relations, the United States–centered attitude latent in the opening paragraphs of the speech replicates the act of unsigning as an exceptionalist approach in foreign policy.

Grossman's use of the label "America" rather than "United States" serves another important function. Employing "America" as an ideograph that evokes associations with the rule of justice, the rule of law, and national sovereignty, Grossman simultaneously invokes the universal voice of the American people. The personification of "America" subsumes a myriad of voices into one unified position, suggesting that essentially all Americans share these beliefs. The use of the manifestic pronoun "we" in the series of "we believe" statements serves to anchor them as the widely held beliefs of the American people as a whole rather than the deliberate choice of foreign policy makers. The repetition of "we believe" proclamations subsumed under one unified "American" voice then serves to redirect attention away from the more contentious statements cast as "beliefs" (such as the focus on domestic institutions) as they are conflated with an ideographic and thus uncontested and unchallenged understanding of "American" beliefs. As a whole, Grossman's rhetorical choices in the opening of the speech suggest that the address was not delivered primarily for an international audience but rather functions as a rhetorical performance for a U.S. audience.

I have suggested so far that Grossman speaks from the position of a general audience of Americans to a general audience of Americans. As the speech proceeds, however, the text gradually invites the audience into a way of being or subject position that is consistent with and affirms the Bush administration's approach to foreign policy.[83] The main purpose of the speech is to communicate the United States' conviction that it is the responsibility of "states" or, by implication, domestic institutions rather than international institutions to "[ensure] justice in the international system." To accomplish this task, Grossman establishes high moral ground for the United States representing a repertoire of noble ideals and principles. Consequently, "American foreign policy" is initially positioned as affirming or upholding core values that provide the basis for the ICC.

After laying out what "America believes in," Grossman continues by bluntly announcing that "we have concluded that the International Criminal Court does not advance these principles." This context of the ICC allegedly not meeting the high standards of principles that "America" upholds will serve as the backdrop for the specific charges against the ICC laid out in the course of the speech. Having established a case pitting the United States—generally recognized as the champion of international justice—against the ICC as a "false" attempt at international justice, Grossman provides a second and structurally similar list of beliefs to the one outlined in his opening remarks, this time by outlining how these principles purportedly clash with the institution of the ICC:

- We believe the ICC undermines the role of the United Nations Security Council in maintaining international peace and security.
- We believe in checks and balances. The Rome Statute creates a prosecutorial system that is an unchecked power.
- We believe that in order to be bound by a treaty, a state must be party to that treaty. The ICC asserts jurisdiction over citizens of states that have not ratified the treaty. This threatens U.S. sovereignty.
- We believe that the ICC is built on a flawed foundation. These flaws leave it open for exploitation and politically motivated prosecutions.[84]

The list of U.S. objections to the current status of the statute is reminiscent of the manifesto's tendency to present a selective historical narrative and a list of grievances condemning the opponent. The inherent logic of the speech suggests the conclusion that the United States must renounce the ICC because the court fails to advance "American" principles.

The enumeration of beliefs in the opening section of the speech implied a "we" consisting of an abstract, yet unified, "America" sharing and upholding a set of foundational values. By contrast, the referent of the pronoun "we" in this declaration of beliefs represents a different community. The "we" that is speaking and being addressed in this section advances specific criticisms of the ICC that derive from specialist knowledge about the alleged flaws of the institution. Since a general audience is unlikely to have the expertise to make such arguments, this section marks the narrowing of the "we" from the nation as a whole to a "we" comprised of policy makers. Coupled with the statement "we have concluded," which suggests a process of deliberation about this issue, this section suggests that the "we" persona used in this section refers to a speaking subject and audience addressed of experts rather than an all-American "we." The implied audience has shifted from an all-inclusive "we" of the American people as a whole to one consisting of policy makers familiar with the intricacies of the International Criminal Court and responsible for making decisions such as unsigning a treaty.

This shift in personae from an inclusive national "we" to a "we" consisting of policy makers reveals an attitude of technocratic rationality underpinning the speech. Originating in the Progressive Era, the rhetoric of technocratic realism, Philip Wander argues, reemerged during the Kennedy administration and was based on the assumption that matters in foreign policy had become too sophisticated or "complex" to be discussed and decided on by ordinary citizens. Instead, foreign policy required level-headed, analytical, "dispassionate, informed and pragmatic expertise" of informed elites.[85] The underlying endorsement of a technocratic notion of reason is rendered more explicit as the speech unfolds, specifically in the gradual transformation of personae invoked in the speech.

In the third paragraph, the speaking persona and implied audience no longer represent the American public writ large. Grossman is now speaking on behalf of President Bush: "President Bush has come to the conclusion that the United States can no longer be a party to this process." One individual has replaced both the abstract and universal voice of an American "we" and the multiple voices of policy makers invoked earlier in the speech, collapsing agency into one locus of power. The will of the people has been rendered irrelevant. While maintaining that the signature withdrawal was a communal decision—evidenced by the claim that it was "*our* intention not to become a party to the Rome Statute" (my emphasis)—the agent in this drama has morphed from the American people into President Bush as the sole arbiter of such a decision.

We have now seen several shifts in the construction of the speech's first and second persona. Edwin Black developed the concept of the "second persona" as a way of opening texts up to critical judgment based on implied audiences in the text.[86] As the second persona undergoes several transformations over the course of the speech, so too does the rhetorical agency and way of being produced by the speech. The implied audience is initially invoked as a group who possesses the virtue of democratic decision-making. By the end of the speech, this virtue is demonstrated by agreeing with the Bush administration's rejection of the ICC. Thus, Grossman gradually narrows the scope of rhetorical agency, ending on the will and authority of the president to reign over matters foreign and domestic.[87]

This narrowing of rhetorical agency betrays a crucial element of the doctrine of a new "American internationalism" repeatedly invoked by Bolton. That is, while the speech invites U.S. audiences to see the unsigning as protecting their ("Americans'") rightful lead in all affairs domestic and international, the decision was made by and for the presidential administration. Conversely, the people in whose voice the speech purports to speak initially are gradually written out of the decision-making process. At the same time, the people/Americans are invited to think of the unsigning *as if* they were part of this discourse and decision-making process. Thomas W. Benson argues that rhetoric as a way of being is "ideally a collaboration between speaker and listener to find a mutually satisfactory notion of themselves as interacting agents."[88] In this speech, this is achieved in the opening remarks where Grossman appeals to values shared by all Americans. Addressed as a community of Americans that share foundational "American" principles embraced by an all-inclusive American "we," the speech offers a way of being the audience is readily willing to accept. As the speech unfolds, however, the argumentative structure is based on the presumption that the initial endorsement of those values that provide the grounds for the rejection of the ICC is still valid. The argumentative arc relies on the audience's initial tacit endorsement of "American" principles, even though, over the course of the speech, the principles that are cited as being violated by the ICC are of a different character than those referred to as "American" principles in the opening of the speech. Cast in a language of well-reasoned arguments, the positions justifying the unsigning of the Rome Statute reveal positions predominantly emanating from the conservative side of the political spectrum. The narrowing of rhetorical agency, then, works through two competing movements in this speech. On one hand, it effaces the narrowing of rhetorical agency by inviting the audience to think of itself as an agent. On the other hand, it subtly but gradually limits the number of those who can legitimately claim agency. What seems particularly insidious about this rhetoric is that the audience is invited to feel empowered while the speech disguises its own efforts to preserve the power of the few over both Americans and the international community under the banner of preserving national sovereignty.

The subtle narrowing of rhetorical agency is further accomplished through the use of technocratic notions of reason. Coupled with the narrowing of rhetorical agency via the gradual reduction of personae and their agency in the speech, the rhetoric of technocratic reason assists in further justifying and solidifying the act of unsigning rather than opening it up for debate. As Grossman moves into detailing the motivating factors for the United States' repudiation of the Rome Statute, he primarily appeals to reason by employing "factual" arguments about the defective institution of the ICC. These arguments are not presented in a fashion that would invite the "discussion" Grossman envisioned in the beginning of the speech but rather are asserted as if they were uncontested. For instance, Grossman states, "the current structure of the International Criminal Court undermines the democratic rights of our people and could erode the fundamental elements of the United Nations Charter, specifically the right to self defense." Grossman appeals to a vague and unspecified concept of American citizens' "democratic rights" and associates these with the necessity to use military force. Grossman continues by outlining the reasons why the United States repudiates the ICC:

> With the ICC prosecutor and judges presuming to sit in judgment of the security decisions of States without their assent, the ICC could have a chilling effect on the willingness of States to project power in defense of their moral and security interests. This power must sometimes be projected. The principled projection of force by the world's democracies is critical to protecting human rights—to stopping genocide or changing regimes like the Taliban, which abuse their people and promote terror against the world.[89]

Again, Grossman presents these arguments as if they were empirical facts. Using the passive construction that "power must sometimes be projected," he deemphasizes that the use of military force is a political decision made by human agents. The mode of argumentation presented by Grossman is strikingly similar to Bolton's rhetoric against the ICC. Bolton's main argument against the United States joining the Rome Statute is that the "ICC's failing stems from its purported authority to operate outside (and on a plane superior to) the U.S. Constitution."[90] For Bolton, the ICC is a "stealth approach to erode our constitutionalism."[91] Discussing the elements of executive power, Bolton reveals what appears to be at the core of U.S. objections to the ICC: "Never before has the United States been asked to place any of that power outside the complete control of our national government."[92] Bolton's and Grossman's statements reveal an implicit understanding of the "U.S. Constitution" and "American democracy" as the highest goods conceivable, the supreme achievements of their kind.

What is at work here is a particular belief in the exceptionalism of U.S. institutions that is coupled with or emerges out of a particular understanding of sovereignty. Mansell and Haslam explain that U.S. opposition to the ICC is partially rooted in the belief in the superiority of U.S. institutions. According to this view, "the USA must be free to act in ways which its citizens democratically determine. Every attempt to constrain through external agreement moves authority away from the Constitution to the international community whose interest may not coincide with those of the USA. Why fetter future governments and, arguably, unconstitutionally hand power to outsiders? Implicit in this argument is the exalted and elevated status of the US Constitution, than which no greater authority apparently exists."[93]

This belief in the exceptional status of U.S. political institutions is coupled with a particular understanding of sovereignty that neoconservatives have embraced. At the heart of it is the assumption that, as Ralph notes, "all of America's significant foreign policy traditions (including the Wilsonian tradition) have assumed that world society is naturally divided into nation-states" and that these have generally "supported democracy promotion" in the international system.[94] The powers and status of the independent, sovereign nation-state, however, are thrown into question in the context of international law seeking to create universal codes of conduct in the international system and thereby democratizing global politics. Marlene Wind notes that neoconservatives, such as Bolton, question the legitimacy of international law altogether. International law consists of a set of rules and codes of conduct that states voluntarily subscribe to and agree to comply with. As a set of voluntary agreements between governments, international law is not accountable to a higher authority and therefore lacks the ability to sanction noncompliance. Bolton's statements belie a positivist interpretation of law, which is, in the field of international law, considered an outdated interpretation that is contrary to the very premise of the principle that agreements are made through freely consenting states and that these agreements are to be respected even in the absence of direct sanctions. Drawing on the strict positivist legal interpretation, so-called international law is, in Bolton's view, not considered law and thus not binding.[95]

Wind notes that natural rights influences reemerged in the post WWII era in global politics, which resulted in the human rights–related conventions. In fact, she notes, "respect for human rights has become part and parcel of what it means to be a legitimate democratic state today" and has become a "prerequisite for *avoiding* external challenges to sovereignty."[96] Wind points out that in spite of this general movement toward a natural rights focus, embodied in contemporary human rights law, the Bush administration "maintained a classical positivist approach to international law and international relations."[97] This particular understanding poses a certain dilemma since the United States has been at the forefront of enforcing human rights globally and democratizing the international system. What stands in opposition to this is the conviction that international institutions are not authorized to "directly promote democracy because, according to this view, there is not a single and identifiable community that can hold them accountable."[98] The outgrowth of these ideologies is what we repeatedly see in Grossman's and Bolton's remarks about the ICC.

Drawing on the implicit assumption that U.S. democratic institutions are unparalleled, Grossman continues by depicting President Bush's decision to unsign the treaty as the only logical conclusion to the United States' failed efforts to shape the institution according to U.S. standards and expectations. Grossman crafts the Bush administration's decision to withdraw its signature as the only reasonable response to agonizing struggles over questions of how to respond to the creation of the institution, assuring his audience that "the President did not take his decision lightly."[99] The Bush administration is depicted as having proceeded methodologically and prudently in its decision. Grossman asserts that the United States studied and analyzed the ICC systematically, and, when this comprehensive analysis showed shortcomings in the institution of the ICC, the United States did everything in its power to amend those flaws and participate in the revision process of the Rome Statute. Grossman's assertions present the United States as having carefully considered the implications of the Rome Statute and thoroughly weighed arguments for and against the decision to unsign. Adding to this characterization is Grossman's emphasis on the virtuousness of President Bush's decision by contrasting the United States' prudent and far-sighted approach toward drafting the ICC with the hasty and careless approach of the international community: "But in the rush to create a powerful and independent court in Rome, there was a refusal to constrain the Court's powers in any meaningful way."[100] Having crafted this image of the United States, the motif of the rational, level-headed, and cooperative global player finds its logical and sensible solution in the U.S. renunciation of the Rome Statute. Grossman states, "But after years of working to fix this flawed statute, and having our constructive proposals rebuffed, it is our only alternative."[101]

As noted earlier, the United States has built a reputation for distancing itself from international treaties that it signed. As with the UN Convention on the Prevention and Punishment of the Crime of Genocide, the United States could have retained its signatory status while holding off the process of ratification indefinitely. That such an alternative to unsigning is well documented suggests that the sense of inevitability for the unprecedented act of unsigning projected by Grossman was a strategic move. That is, it was a political decision packaged as a necessary outcome to retroactively justify the action performed by the Bush administration.

Grossman casts the U.S. withdrawal from the treaty as a quasi-natural yet well-reasoned response to the fact that not all of the United States' objections were removed. In connection with the invocation of U.S. founding principles, the act to unsign is legitimate and needs no further justification. Grossman announces in an overtly patronizing manner that "in the end, despite the best efforts of the U.S. delegation, the final treaty had so many defects that the

United States simply could not vote for it."[102] But the conclusion to withdraw the signature is not just a reasonable reaction. Rather, the logic underlying Grossman's argument is that when the United States' "serious" engagement in the revision process turned out not to be fruitful, the United States saw it as its *moral duty* to renounce the Rome Statute. The United States is presented as a righteous and benevolent player merely seeking to act in accordance with its own long-established, sensible principles, such as the concept of checks and balances that ostensibly stand in opposition to the principles of the ICC: "First, we believe the ICC is an institution of unchecked power. In the United States, our system of government is founded on the principle that, in the words of John Adams, 'power must never be trusted without a check.' Unchecked power, our founders understood, is open to abuse, even with the good intentions of those who establish it. But in the rush to create a powerful and independent court in Rome, there was a refusal to constrain the Court's powers in any meaningful way."[103] Although asserted as transparent "facts" that need no further explanation, the U.S. objections against the ICC are contested. The appearance of transparency is enhanced by a presentation of the arguments in a manner that transforms the five criticisms of the ICC into a violation of foundational principles of the United States. Conversely, U.S. democratic principles are cast as subject to the unpredictable forces of the ICC (as a system of global governance) that must be tamed and countered.

The presentation of self-evident "facts" is designed to quell the need for further examination, above all because the United States' conclusion to unsign the Rome Statute is to be thought of as the outcome of having the merits and shortcomings of the ICC already subjected to careful scrutiny. The primary implied audience or second persona in the speech, policy makers, is no longer invited to pursue intellectual inquiry or to have a "discussion" with the American public. Rather, it is asked to merely reproduce a presidential dictate. As such, I argue, the rhetoric employed in this speech is one that constructs the second persona as a disciplined subject. The site for mutual satisfaction of speaker and audience is the construction of a "disciplined" subject position that upholds prefabricated political views. Moreover, the effacement of arguments and their ideological underpinnings under the guise of self-evident "facts" creates the illusion of this being a "rhetoric-free" text. The rhetoric at work here is then a rhetoric of containment that fosters a desire for security and control rather than deliberation and democracy.

While the speech as a whole is premised on and works to reproduce a binary between those countries that are party to the statute and the United States, the last two sections of the speech, entitled "Our Philosophy" and "We Will Continue to Lead," attempt to create identification with advocates of the ICC by reinforcing U.S. principles and the requirements the ICC would have to meet in order for the United States to accept the statute. The final section outlines the future role of the United States in the international community, stressing a continuing commitment to bringing those who violate international humanitarian law to justice, despite the unsigning of the Rome Statute. The speech lists twelve points of what "we will" do in the future. Consisting of an amorphous enumeration of broad U.S. objectives, including to "support creative ad-hoc mechanisms" like those in Sierra Leone, to "work with countries to avoid any disruptions caused by the Treaty," to "continue to discipline our own when appropriate," to continue the United States' "longstanding role as an advocate for the principle that there must be accountability for war crimes," and to "seek to mobilize the private sector to see how and where they can contribute," the referent of the pronoun "we" expands once again from signifying a previously select group of ICC experts to policy makers in general. The seemingly optimistic, future-oriented content of these objectives is reflected in the section's hortatory style reminiscent of the introductory remarks of the speech. Grossman calls for "working together," despite advocates' contradictory views on the ICC. Characterizing the disagreements between the supporters and the opponents of the ICC as "differences" in their "approach and philosophy," Grossman attempts to establish commonalities by calling for a joint objective: "While we oppose the ICC we share a common goal with its supporters—the promotion of the rule of law."[104]

The "rule of law" and the promotion of "justice" serve as two important factors around which the Bush administration's approach to the ICC would be built. Grossman declares, "So despite this difference, we must work together to promote real justice after July 1."[105] Here, in typically manifestic tradition, the text announces a break with history. The fulcrum of history and future is demarcated by the date the ICC comes into effect. What is at stake is nothing short of the concept of justice itself. More specifically, July 1, 2002, the date the ICC will enter into force, marks the ending date of a period during which "real justice" and the "rule of law" prevailed. The date is cast as inaugurating a period in which "real justice" will be severely compromised by a competing notion of justice—that is, justice promoted and adjudicated by the ICC. Lincoln P. Bloomfield Jr., assistant secretary for political-military affairs, echoed this view in a speech to the United Nations in September 2003 in which he declared that "across the political aisle in Washington, there was and is a consensus view that the Rome Statute is incompatible with U.S. standards of justice."[106] By implication, "real justice" would have reigned had the Rome Statute been modified according to the United States' demands. Assuming control over the definition of the term "justice," the United States is constructed once again as the sole legitimate arbiter of justice, whose wise admonitions and foresight were neglected by supporters of the ICC.

Rather than presenting the role of the ICC in terms of its function—namely, to adjudicate the most serious international crimes under circumstances where nation-states are unable or unwilling to do so—Grossman casts the ICC as a counterproductive instrument that would encourage nation-states to shirk on their responsibilities for mending their violent pasts and undermine the principle of the law. He argues that, "in order for the rule of law to have true meaning, societies must accept their responsibilities and be able to direct their future and come to terms with their past."[107] The ICC, as an "unchecked international body," must be hindered from intruding into this "delicate process" of forming a national collective memory of a nation-state's past. At this point, Grossman turns U.S. concerns over a loss of U.S. sovereignty into a matter of nation-state responsibility—namely, an issue of a sense of duty for nation-states to deal with their own, domestic, issues: "International practice should promote domestic accountability and encourage sovereign states to seek reconciliation where feasible."[108] Casting U.S. particularistic (national) interests in a language of quasi-universal concern for the sovereignty of other countries, Grossman announces that "a world of self-governing democracies is our best hope for a world without inhumanity."[109] Grossman's statement suggests that justice can ultimately be rendered only at a national or subnational level and that the United States will therefore require nonintervention concerning domestic issues. The conclusion thus casts the United States' act of unsigning as the path from the false justice of internationalism to the true justice of so-called American internationalism.

CONCLUDING REMARKS: IMPLICATIONS OF THE "UNSIGNING"

The purposeful opposition to the operations of the International Criminal Court did not end with the U.S. unsigning the Rome Statute. Rather, the United States engaged in what Weller calls an "aggressive diplomatic campaign to undermine the core concepts that underpin the ICC."[110] Carried out at both the administrative and the congressional level, the campaign aimed at undermining the ICC "ranged from the deployment of national legislation against the Court, to the obstruction of crucial decisions of the UN Security Council and to pressure directed against individual states to contract out of the ICC regime they had just joined."[111]

Specifically, U.S. efforts to weaken the ICC have included various measures to protect U.S. nationals from the reach of the court, including the enactment of legislation such as the Nethercutt Amendment, which includes provisions to cut off economic support funds to nations who are party to the ICC and who have not entered into bilateral immunity agreements that protect U.S. nationals from the jurisdiction of the ICC.[112] The campaigns to weaken the ICC were driven into the realm of the absurd when the U.S. Congress passed the American Service-Members' Protection Act (ASPA) in August 2002. This law, passed in the Senate by a margin of seventy-eight to twenty-one votes, serves to protect the members of U.S. Armed Forces "against criminal prosecutions carried out by the International Criminal Court" and obliges countries that have signed the bilateral agreement to not surrender American citizens to the ICC.[113] Section 2008 of the ASPA authorizes the president "to use all means necessary and appropriate to bring about the release" of any U.S. national or allied personnel "who is being detained or imprisoned by, on behalf of, or at the request of the International Criminal Court."[114] Highlighting that, per the act, the United States is authorized to use military force to release nationals that are detained by the ICC in The Hague, critics have aptly nicknamed this provision "The Hague Invasion Clause" or "The Hague Invasion Act."

Another incident that sparked a considerable debate about the United States' claimed special status was the U.S. threat to veto all future peacekeeping operations unless the UN Security Council provided immunity from prosecution through the ICC for its peacekeeping forces. The UN Security Council granted the United States immunity for a period of twelve months in 2002 and extended the immunity period for an additional year in 2003.[115] In addition to these ICC-related decisions, the Bush administration rejected the Kyoto Protocol and the Anti-Ballistic Missile Treaty within the first eight months after taking office.[116] Although not directly linked to the debates surrounding the ICC, the sum of these decisions in association with ICC-related legislation is considered to be evidence for the "Bush administration's inclination to steer away from multinational obligations."[117]

The unprecedented maneuver of unsigning an international treaty has been interpreted as a sign of an increasingly unilateralist approach in U.S. foreign policy. Several commentators noted the potentially negative effects of the unsigning for international treaties, contending that it could result in a larger trend of countries pulling out of international treaties. Critics commenting on the potential effects for the United States suggested that this "rash action" could result in undermining U.S. "leadership and credibility."[118] One month before the official statement was delivered by Grossman, Scheffer, who acted as ambassador at large for war crimes and who signed the treaty for the Clinton administration, had noted in the *New York Times* that "a Bush 'unsigning' would be a decisive repudiation that would not only devastate America's credibility as the champion of international justice but reveal an American denial of reality."[119] Others argued that the unsigning of the treaty would have doubly detrimental consequences as the United States would be even more subject to the will of the signatories to the Rome Statute because the United States would have less influence on the development of the ICC. Others viewed the U.S. withdrawal as an "empty gesture that will further estrange Washington from its allies."[120] The *San Francisco Chronicle* anticipated the impending decision about the unsigning of the treaty to be an indicator of a recent trend toward unilateralism: "But the symbolism of the U.S. decision will be clear—the administration can either support the movement for global justice and human rights, or it can further its reputation as an arrogant Lone Ranger."[121]

Perhaps more importantly than the legal consequences and ramifications for the United States' reputation among world leaders, the act of unsigning is imbued with symbolic implications. Given the context of the United States' human rights legacy, the act of unsigning rhetorically functioned as a rejection of principles of global responsibility, democracy, justice, and universal human rights. Recognizing the impact of the criticism of the U.S. position on the ICC, Lincoln Bloomfield, assistant secretary for political-military affairs, conceded in 2003 that the United States had come up short in addressing its concerns regarding the ICC. Bloomfield argues that the Bush administration "lowered its public level of rhetoric" when it took up negotiations seeking bilateral immunity agreements in 2002 that would exclude U.S. citizens and military personnel from the jurisdiction of the ICC.[122] Looking back on how the United States publicized these developments, he admits that the Bush administration

> probably could have made a more public display of its change in approach, because in fact this also represented a significant policy evolution as well. As we explained to foreign governments in our diplomatic discussions, but did not particularly advertise to the international press and foreign public opinion, the Administration decided to set aside the U.S. objections to the ICC and accept the reality of the Rome Statute and the Court. We informed governments the U.S. does not seek to undermine the ICC, and asked in return that our decision not to become a party be similarly respected.[123]

In short, the administration worked behind the scenes to mend fences and change its policy course while not correcting the specter of monstrosity that it sold to its people and the world.

While U.S. rhetoric regarding the opposition to the ICC may have softened over time, the symbolic effect of the act of unsigning the treaty endures. Jacques Derrida's discussion of the symbolic meaning of the signature is illustrative in this context. Derrida argues that the "we" of the American people did not exist as an entity before its declaration in the Declaration of Independence and was constituted only through the act of the signature. In this sense, the "we" that comes into being "gives birth to itself, as free and independent subject, as possible signer, this can hold only in the act of the signature. The signature invents the signer."[124] If the signature invents the signer, what type of signer is invented by an unsigning?

According to rhetorical scholar Maurice Charland, constitutive rhetoric constitutes the subject from preexisting ideologies or narratives that audiences enter into and from which they understand the world. At the moment we enter language, we have always already entered a subject position within the context of narratives, ideologies, or inherent logics. "Constitutive rhetorics of new subject positions can be understood, therefore, as working upon previous discourses, upon previous constitutive rhetorics."[125] For Charland, then, "the process by which an audience member enters into a new subject position is therefore not one of persuasion. It is akin more to one of conversion that ultimately results in an act of recognition of the 'rightness' of a discourse and of one's identity with its reconfigured subject position."[126] It is in this sense that to overcome the force of the unsigning one would need to reconstitute an "American" public.

The novelty of the subject position configured by the unsigning rests in the ramifications that it has on the modern international community. It is not, however, a wholly new phenomenon. Rather, it is marked by the American exceptionalist tradition, which is rooted in the Puritan vision of the United States as imbued with uniqueness. This vision has enjoyed a stronghold in the United States' dominant understanding of itself as a "city upon a hill" that serves as the shining (moral) example for the rest of the world. In the realm of foreign policy, the belief in the superiority and invariability of U.S. institutions and the conviction that "US law was not to be trumped by any international law" function as reminders and manifestations of this exceptionalist tradition.[127] The documented relationship between the United States and international law attests to the simple fact that the administration has alternatives at its disposal for ignoring or otherwise freeing itself from the responsibilities of the international treaties that it signs.

In unsigning the treaty, the Bush administration did maintain a tradition of holding itself outside of the reach of international law. At the same time, however, it opened up a new chapter of open disregard for the international community under the banner of a "new American internationalism." Grossman's speech, the official announcement of the unsigning, made extensive use of the manifestic genre because the unsinging was not an explanation of differing legal or juridical models. Rather, it was the performance of a new political subjectivity, the "new American internationalism" that Americans were to identify with.

The act of unsigning the Rome Statute, then, served primarily a rhetorical function. The "unsigning" of the Rome Statute has "undone" the United States as an agent in the international community. The act of unsigning communicates publicly that the United States distances itself from and, in fact, has consigned itself outside of the international community. If the signature invents the signer, the unsigning "uninvents" the original signer committed to the enforcement of international human rights. Thus, the United States, previously a signer committed to the codification of international human rights law, has relinquished its status as a full member of the international community for, practically, it is no longer in the position of having an impact on issues concerning the ICC, and symbolically, it no longer considers itself commensurate with that identity. As political scientist Jason Ralph notes, the Bush administration's foreign policy leads to "prioritiz[ing] the interests of strong states rather than the victims of core crimes."[128] As a result, he notes, "America's commitment to global democracy is quite clearly limited by its commitment to statehood."[129] The concern with statehood or classical understanding of sovereignty in this interpretation is primary and will always override international justice efforts.

The moment of unsigning rhetorically functions to break the United States' commitment to international justice and as such operates as a constitutive moment of a new kind of subject that creates and invites a new kind of memory of itself. Philosopher Ed Casey argues in *Remembering: A Phenomenological Study* that "we are what we remember ourselves to be."[130] The act of unsigning manifests the departure from and undoing of one kind of political subjectivity. The unsigning invents a new "we"—a "we" that is the conduit of unilateral U.S. foreign policy that precludes public deliberation and instead "domesticates" discourses of international justice. At the same time, the speech that officially announced the unsigning of the Rome Statute constructed a discourse that effaced its own rhetorical constitution of subjects and with it the United States' joint responsibility to enforce accountability for war crimes and crimes against humanity at a transnational level.

The remaining chapters will trace rhetorical discourses that variously attempt to challenge and promote this political subjectivity of an "American internationalism." We will see that, while the political subjectivity performed by Grossman poses a significant challenge, advocates for a more cosmopolitan subjectivity are learning to use the resources of public memory effectively to bring about changes in how U.S. citizens see their role as members of an international community.

NOTES

1. M. Cherif Bassiouni, "Policy Perspective Favoring the Establishment of the International Criminal Court," *Journal of International Affairs* 52, no. 2 (Spring 1999): 795. Bassiouni is a professor of international law and former chair of the UN committee that drafted the Rome Statute of the International Criminal Court.
2. Ibid., 796.
3. *New York Times*, "The Coming War Trials," October 9, 1945, p. 20.
4. See preamble of the Rome Statute. United Nations Diplomatic Conference of Plenipotentiaries on the Establishment of an International Criminal Court, *Rome Statute of the International Criminal Court*, UN document A/CONF. 183/9 (July 15–17, 1998), https://www.icc-cpi.int/nr/rdonlyres/ea9aeff7-5752-4f84-be94-0a655eb30e16/0/rome_statute_english.pdf.

5. United Nations, "Press Conference on International Criminal Court," April 11, 2002, https://www.un.org/press/en/2002/ICCrome.pc.doc.htm. William Pace and Jennifer Schense note that the creation of the Rome Statute "reflects the increasing centrality of the individual in international law, and in particular an international consensus about the accountability of individuals as perpetrators and the need to address the suffering of individual victims." See William Pace and Jennifer Schense, "The Role of Non-Governmental Organizations," in *The Rome Statute of the International Criminal Court: A Commentary*, edited by Antonio Cassese, Paola Gaeta, and John R. W. D. Jones (New York: Oxford University Press, 2002).

6. Marc Weller, "Undoing the Global Constitution: UN Security Council Action on the International Criminal Court," *International Affairs* 78, no. 4 (2002): 693.

7. Brian Farrell, "An Isolationist View of the International Criminal Court," *America* 187, no. 17 (2002): 19.

8. Paul Kahn "The International Criminal Court (ICC)—The End of Impunity: Why the United States Is So Opposed," *Crimes of War Magazine*, December 2003, https://web.archive.org/web/20110509102940/http://www.crimesofwar.org/print/icc/icc-kahn-print.html.

9. See "Advocacy Center" on AMICC's website at https://web.archive.org/web/20121123013925/.

10. Marlene Wind, "Challenging Sovereignty? The USA and the Establishment of the International Criminal Court," *Ethics and Global Politics* 2, no. 2 (2009): 89.

11. Steven Mufson and Alan Sipress, "U.N. Funds in Crossfire over Court: Exemption Sought for U.S. Troops," *Washington Post*, August 16, 2001, p. A01.

12. According to the CSIS's website, the center is an "independent, nonpartisan public policy research organization." Most of the CSIS publications carry titles including references to "homeland security," "transnational threats," "National Missile Defense," and "weapons of mass destruction." In the press release of the CSIS announcing Grossman's speech, Grossman's position is described as being "the department's chief crisis manager [who] is responsible for integrating political, economic, global and security issues into U.S. bilateral relationships." See http://www.csis.org/press/ma_2002_0506.htm.

13. Philip Wander, "The Ideological Turn in Modern Criticism," in *Readings in Rhetorical Criticism*, edited by Carl R. Burgchardt (State College, PA: Strata, 2000), 122.

14. Helen Stacy, "Relational Sovereignty," *Stanford Law Review* 55 (May 2003): 2052.

15. Ibid., 2053.

16. Michael J. Struett, *The Politics of Constructing the International Criminal Court: NGOs, Discourse, and Agency* (New York: Palgrave Macmillan, 2008), 69–70.

17. Ibid., 68. As we will see, similar arguments were made in the context of the adoption of the Rome Statute in 1998 and the ICC's entering into force in 2002.

18. Ibid., 74.

19. Ibid., 71–75.

20. Marlies Glasius, *The International Criminal Court: A Global Civil Society Achievement* (Routledge Advances in International Relations and Global Politics) (New York: Routledge, 2005), 16.

21. Ibid., 17.

22. Jesse Helms, "We Must Slay This Monster," *Financial Times*, July 31, 1998, p. 18.

23. Ibid.

24. Ibid.

25. Helms's bill of the American Service-Members' Protection Act was adopted by an overwhelming majority in the Senate in December 2001. The bill became law in August 2002.

26. United States Senate Subcommittee on International Operations of the Committee on Foreign Relations, *Is a U.N. International Criminal Court in the National Interest?* 105th Congress, second session, July 23, 1998, Senate hearing (Washington, DC: US Government Printing Office, 1998), 105–724. Statement by Senator Rod Grams. The hearings were held to "determine why the United States voted against the International Criminal Court and to ascertain future U.S. policy with respect to the Court." See Michael P. Scharf, "Results of the Rome Conference for an International Criminal Court," *ASIL Insights* 3, no. 10 (August 1998), web.archive.org/web/20120716203934/http://www.asil.org/insigh23.cfm.

27. Marc Grossman, "American Foreign Policy and the International Criminal Court," Remarks to the Center for Strategic and International Studies, Washington, DC, U.S. Department of State (May 6, 2002), https://2001-2009.state.gov/p/us/rm/9949.htm.

28. *Wall Street Journal*, "A Global Special Prosecutor?" May 7, 2002, p. A26.

29. Ibid.

30. Ibid.

31. Ibid.

32. David Davenport, "The New Diplomacy," *Policy Review*, no. 116 (December 2002–January 2003).

33. Ibid., 22.

34. John Bolton is serving as a national security adviser in the current Trump administration in which he continues to challenge the ICC. This was most notably demonstrated in his speech "Protecting American Constitutionalism and Sovereignty from International Threats" to the Federalist Society in September 2018. Video and searchable transcript are available at https://www.c-span.org/video/?451213-1/national-security-adviser-john-bolton-addresses-federalist-society.

35. Matthew Engel, "Rift with Us: Distaste for 'International Entanglements' Runs Deep," *Guardian*, July 2, 2002, p. 4.

36. John R. Bolton, "Unsign That Treaty," *Washington Post*, January 4, 2001, p. A21.

37. Ibid.

38. Ibid.

39. United States House of Representatives Committee on International Relations, *The International Criminal Court*, 106th Congress, second session, July 25–26, 2000 (No. 106–176). (Washington, DC: US Government Printing Office, 2000). Statement by John R. Bolton.

40. Ibid.

41. Bolton, "Unsign That Treaty."

42. Ibid.

43. United States House of Representatives Committee on International Relations, *The International Criminal Court*. Statement by John R. Bolton.

44. Ibid.

45. Bolton, "Unsign That Treaty."

46. Ibid.

47. Ibid. The term was introduced in the speech "A Distinctly American Internationalism" by Governor George W. Bush at the Ronald Reagan Presidential Library, Simi Valley, California, on November 19, 1999.

48. Michael Scharf characterized the debate over the ICC in response to the United States voting against the court in Rome as "the beginnings of an isolationist movement." See United States Senate Subcommittee on International Operations of the Committee on Foreign Relations, *Is a U.N. International Criminal Court in the National Interest?* Statement by Michael Scharf.

49. Critics of the ICC have argued that the ICC lacks an appropriate system of checks and balances and thus could be used to launch political attacks. The Rome Statute does include, however, several stipulations designed to ward off the potential instrumentalization of the court for political reasons. For instance, an investigation initiated by the prosecutor will require the approval of a pretrial chamber of three judges that screens the evidence the prosecutor has collected. This pretrial chamber must give their approval to proceed with the investigation. In addition, the pretrial chamber must confirm any warrant requests. Furthermore, an accused person or any involved country has the chance to challenge the indictment during confirmation hearings before the pretrial chamber. See United Nations Diplomatic Conference of Plenipotentiaries on the Establishment of an International Criminal Court, *Rome Statute of the International Criminal Court*, Article 15.

50. Even though the United States did not succeed in achieving its goals at the Rome Conference on all points, the Rome Statute adopted in July 1998 does include a number of provisions that reflected U.S. lobbying efforts. See for instance Phillippe Kirsch, former president of the ICC, who noted that many safeguards were included specifically to meet U.S.

demands. Philippe Kirsch, "The International Criminal Court: Current Issues and Perspectives," *Law and Contemporary Problems* 64, no. 1 (Winter 2001): 11. Similarly, Michael Scharf noted that "early on the United States correctly decided to engage, to make a major effort to try to turn this court into something that we could live with. And David Scheffer should be applauded; because, really, the United States bullied its way into getting the U.S. stamp on almost every single provision in the International Criminal Court statute. It is really a U.S. statute with just a couple of exceptions, a couple of things that we did not get." See United States Senate Subcommittee on International Operations of the Committee on Foreign Relations, *Is a U.N. International Criminal Court in the National Interest?* Statement by Michael Scharf.

51. Elizabeth Neuffer, "US Pushes to Keep Its Troops Exempt from World Court," *Boston Globe*, May 23, 2002, p. A1.

52. Jason Ralph, "Between Cosmopolitan and American Democracy: Understanding US Opposition to the International Criminal Court," *International Relations* 17, no. 2 (2003): 197.

53. Hugo Young, "We Can't Allow US Tantrums to Scupper Global Justice," *Guardian*, July 2, 2002, p. 14.

54. Bruce Broomhall, *International Justice and the International Criminal Court: Between Sovereignty and the Rule of Law, Oxford Monographs in International Law* (New York: Oxford University Press, 2003), 165.

55. Weller, "Undoing the Global Constitution: UN Security Council Action on the International Criminal Court," 701.

56. Ibid.

57. Bill Nichols, "Clinton Backs a World Criminal Court Treaty Faces Opposition from Many Republicans in Senate," *USA Today*, January 2, 2001, p. 9A.

58. Sean D. Murphy, "U.S. Notification of Intent Not to Become a Party to the Rome Statute," *The American Journal of International Law* 96, no. 3 (2002): 724.

59. Steven Lee Myers, "U.S. Signs Treaty for World Court to Try Atrocities," *New York Times*, January 1, 2001, p. A1.

60. *New York Times*, "Clinton's Words: 'the Right Action,'" January 1, 2001, p. A6. This is the full-text transcript of Clinton's statement delivered at Camp David regarding the addition of the United States' signature to the Rome Statute. I used the *New York Times* transcript due to its accessibility.

61. Murphy, "U.S. Notification," 724.

62. Coalition for the International Criminal Court, "Overview of the United States' Opposition to the International Criminal Court," (2006), http://www.iccnow.org/documents/CICCFS_US_Opposition_to_ICC_11Dec06_final.pdf.

63. *New York Times*, "Clinton's Words: 'the Right Action.'"

64. Thomas E. Ricks, "U.S. Signs Treaty on War Crimes Tribunal; Pentagon, Republicans Object to Clinton Move," *Washington Post*, January 1, 2001, p. A1.

65. Broomhall, *International Justice and the International Criminal Court: Between Sovereignty and the Rule of Law*, 178.

66. John R. Bolton, "International Criminal Court: Letter to UN Secretary General Kofi Annan," U.S. Department of State (May 6, 2002), https://web.archive.org/web/20040630100111/. This is the official letter sent to the United Nations. According to Sean Murphy in his article "U.S. Notification of Intent Not to Become a Party to the Rome Statute," there was no formal response from the United Nations to the United States letter except for a notification to the parties that indicated the receipt of the letter. See Murphy, "U.S. Notification."

67. See Donald Rumsfeld, "Secretary Rumsfeld Statement on the ICC Treaty," U.S. Department of Defense (May 6, 2002), https://web.archive.org/web/20061229224351/.

68. The *Washington Post* reported in August 2001 that the Bush administration is "considering how to 'unsign' the treaty" without running the risk of having "its hands tied by the anti-ICC legislation" or "infuriating" ICC allies. See Mufson and Sipress, "U.N. Funds in Crossfire over Court: Exemption Sought for U.S. Troops." Although the possibility of unsigning the treaty by sending a letter to the UN to unsign the treaty at the time was only one alternative, one senior official administrator stated that "such a letter would arguably just be stating the truth, "

indicating that such a statement would be in keeping with the United States' strong oppositional stance toward the court. See Mufson and Sipress, "U.N. Funds in Crossfire over Court: Exemption Sought for U.S. Troops."

69. Elizabeth Neuffer, "US to Back out of World Court Plan Envoy: Bush Team May 'Unsign' Treaty," *Boston Globe*, March 29, 2002, p. A22.

70. Ibid.

71. William J. Aceves, "The President's Roman Holiday," *San Diego Union-Tribune*, September 5, 2002. It should be noted here that there seemed to be consensus among international law experts and commentators that the act of unsigning an international treaty *per se* was unprecedented, as a country's signature indicates the intent to ratify. See, for instance Michael Kelly, "Ignoring Criminal Treaty Harms U.S. Legacy," *USA Today*, April 16, 2002, p. 12A.The legality and ramifications of such an act, however, were more contentiously debated issues among scholars. Some commentators speculated whether or not unsigning does not represent a more sincere approach in the context of the U.S. opposition than a signature that would not lead to ratification or whose ratification would be delayed indefinitely. Commentators noted, for instance, the practice of the United States to sign but not ratify or to only partially subscribe to international treaties, especially international human rights treaties. Such treaties include the Convention on the Elimination of All Forms of Discrimination Against Women, International Labor Organization Conventions, and the Convention on the Rights of the Child. Of 193 sovereign states, the United States, together with Somalia, are the only two countries that have not ratified the Convention on the Rights of the Child. Interestingly, some of the United States' arguments against ratification echo those of U.S. opposition against the ICC—namely, the issue of sovereignty. For a more detailed discussion of the failed ratification process of the Convention on the Rights of the Child in the United States, see Julie Mertus, *Bait and Switch: Human Rights and U.S. Foreign Policy* (New York: Routledge, 2004), 155–59. For a more thorough discussion of this topic see also Edward T. Swaine, "Unsigning," *Stanford Law Review* 55, no. 5 (May 2003). That the U.S. unsigning may have set a precedent was recently evidenced by Burundi's and the Philippines' withdrawal from the Rome Statute in 2017 and 2019 respectively.

72. Neil A. Lewis, "U.S. to Renounce International Crime Tribunal," *Pittsburgh Post-Gazette*, May 5, 2002, p. A19.

73. Ibid.

74. Luke A. McLaurin, "Can the President 'Unsign' a Treaty? A Constitutional Inquiry,"*Washington University Law Review* 84, no. 7 (2006): 1941.

75. United Nations, *Vienna Convention on the Law of Treaties*, United Nations Treaty Series Volume 1155 (May 23, 1969). See Article 18. https://treaties.un.org/doc/publication/unts/volume%201155/volume-1155-i-18232-english.pdf. There is some ambiguity about the status of Article 18 as well as the recognition of Article 18 by the United States. While the United States has not actually ratified the Vienna Convention, Bolton's statements in his article "Unsign That Treaty" at least implicitly recognizes Article 18 of the Vienna Convention, while simultaneously arguing for disregarding it. Bolton writes: "The president is undoubtedly thinking of Article 18 of the Vienna Convention, which requires signatories to a treaty, before ratification, not to undertake any actions that would frustrate its objectives." Shortly thereafter, he continues, "Relying on Article 18, which cannot sensibly apply to our government of separated powers, is wrong in many respects, not least that the United States has never even ratified this Vienna convention." See Bolton, "Unsign That Treaty."

76. Janet Lyon, *Manifestoes: Provocations of the Modern* (Ithaca, NY: Cornell University Press, 1999), 15.

77. Ibid., 13. Lyon argues that the manifesto derives this style that urges some course of action from its "constitutive discourses of religious prophecy, and chiliasm (or millennialism), the martial language of war or siege; and the forensic mode of persuasive rhetoric" (13).

78. Ibid., 15.

79. Ibid.

80. Ibid.

81. Michael Calvin McGee, "The 'Ideograph': A Link between Rhetoric and Ideology," *Quarterly Journal of Speech* 66, no. 1 (1980): 7.

82. Ibid., 15.
83. See Thomas W. Benson, "Rhetoric as a Way of Being," in *American Rhetoric: Context and Criticism* (Carbondale: Southern Illinois University Press, 1989).
84. Grossman, "American Foreign Policy."
85. Philip Wander, "The Rhetoric of American Foreign Policy," *Quarterly Journal of Speech* 70, no. 4 (1984): 350. See also Murphy's discussion of technocratic realism in the context of the Kennedy administration. John M. Murphy, "The Language of the Liberal Consensus: John F. Kennedy, Technical Reason, and the 'New Economics' at Yale University," *Quarterly Journal of Speech* 90, no. 2 (2004).
86. See Edwin Black, "The Second Persona," *Quarterly Journal of Speech* 56, no. 2 (1970).
87. Ibid.
88. Benson, "Rhetoric as a Way of Being," 318.
89. Grossman, "American Foreign Policy."
90. John R. Bolton, "The Risks and Weaknesses of the International Criminal Court from America's Perspective," *Law and Contemporary Problems* 64, no. 1 (2001): 169.
91. Ibid.
92. Ibid.,173.
93. Wade Mansell and Emily Haslam, "John Bolton and the United States' Retreat from International Law," *Social and Legal Studies* 14, no. 4 (2005): 465.
94. Ralph, "Between Cosmopolitan," 196.
95. Wind, "Challenging Sovereignty?," 96–97. See also Mansell and Haslam, "John Bolton," 470–471.
96. Wind, "Challenging Sovereignty?," 98. Emphasis in original.
97. Wind, "Challenging Sovereignty?," 99.
98. Ralph, "Between Cosmopolitan," 209.
99. Grossman, "American Foreign Policy."
100. Ibid.
101. Although the pronoun "our" also refers not only to the Bush administration but also the previous Clinton administration, Grossman is consistent in that he refers to presumable knowledgeable experts making these decisions.
102. Grossman, "American Foreign Policy."
103. Ibid.
104. Ibid.
105. Ibid.
106. Lincoln Bloomfield, "Bloomfield Defends U.S. Course on International Criminal Court: Lincoln Bloomfield Remarks in New York to Parliamentarians for Global Action," Bureau of International Information Programs, U.S. Department of State (September 17, 2003), https://web.archive.org/web/20061001231803/http://usinfo.state.gov/xarchives/display.html?p=washfile-english&y=2003&m=September&x=20030917172946samohtj0.8693201.
107. Grossman, "American Foreign Policy."
108. Ibid.
109. Ibid.
110. Weller, "Undoing the Global Constitution: UN Security Council Action on the International Criminal Court," 694.
111. Ibid.
112. The Bilaterial Immunity Agreements (BIA) would exclude several groups of U.S. personnel (military personnel, former and current government officials, U.S. nationals as well as foreign contractors working for the United States) from jurisdiction of the court and would prohibit their surrender to the ICC. Hence, the BIAs are alternatively referred to as Article 98 agreements, impunity agreements or bilateral nonsurrender agreements. While the United States argues that the BIAs conform to Article 98 of the Rome Statute, the legality of such agreements is highly contested among legal experts.
113. See "American Service-Members' Protection Act of 2003," U.S. Department of State, https://web.archive.org/web/20130310112048/http://www.state.gov/t/pm/rls/othr/misc/23425.htm.

114. Ibid., Section 2008.
115. United Nations Security Council Resolution 1422. See UN Security Council Press Release SC/7450, "Security Council Requests International Criminal Court Not to Bring Cases against Peacekeeping Personnel from States Not Party to Statute," United Nations (July 12, 2002), http://www.un.org/News/Press/docs/2002/sc7450.doc.htm.
116. John Keane, *Global Civil Society?* (Cambridge: Cambridge University Press, 2003), 119.
117. Neil A. Lewis, "U.S. Will 'Unsign' Global Court Treaty: White House Fears Capricious Charges," *Chicago Tribune*, May 5, 2002, p. 4.
118. *Wall Street Journal* , "A Global Special Prosecutor?"
119. David Scheffer, "A Treaty Bush Shouldn't 'Unsign,'" *New York Times*, April 6, 2002, p. A15.
120. *Wall Street Journal*, "A Global Special Prosecutor?"
121. *San Francisco Chronicle*, "No Way to Lead the World," April 23, 2002, p. A16.
122. Bloomfield, "Bloomfield Defends U.S. Course on International Criminal Court: Lincoln Bloomfield Remarks in New York to Parliamentarians for Global Action."
123. Ibid.
124. Jacques Derrida, "Declarations of Independence," *New Political Science* 7, no. 1 (1986): 10.
125. Maurice Charland, "Constitutive Rhetoric: The Case of the Peuple Québécois," *Quarterly Journal of Speech* 73, no. 2 (1987): 142.
126. Ibid.
127. See Forsythe for a brief discussion on this issue. David P. Forsythe, "The United States and International Criminal Justice," *Human Rights Quarterly* 24, no. 4 (2002): 975. For an analysis of how President Bush's rhetoric associates human rights with the myth of American exceptionalism, see Mary E. Stuckey and Joshua R. Ritter, "George Bush, [Human Rights], and American Democracy," Presidential Studies Quarterly 37, no. 4 (2007).
128. Ibid., 209.
129. Edward S. Casey, Remembering: A Phenomenological Study (Bloomington: Indiana University Press, 1987), 290.
130. Edward S. Casey, *Remembering: A Phenomenological Study* (Bloomington: Indiana University Press, 1987), 290.

Chapter Four

Remaking the ICC for the United States

Citizens for Global Solutions' Advocacy

The International Criminal Court (ICC) marks the culmination of the post–World War II movement for the global enforcement of human rights. Though there are antecedents, the concern for establishing a permanent international criminal court became more seriously pursued with the series of events including the signing of the UN Charter in 1945, the Nuremberg War Trials in 1945 and 1946, and the adoption of the Universal Declaration of Human Rights in 1948. The experience of the Holocaust in particular made it increasingly apparent that promises of "never again" required vigilance and action. The international community's attempts to establish an international criminal court failed in the early 1950s, and, although efforts to develop an international criminal court stagnated during the Cold War, the concern with international human rights did not. The 1970s saw an increasing interest in international human rights with civil society organizations maturing in the West, partly in response to threats issued during the Cold War.[1] Their presence helped reinvigorate a movement toward an international criminal court, which became a more realistic possibility as the Cold War ended.[2]

During the early 1990s, the atrocities committed in the former Yugoslavia and Rwanda provided the impetus for a renewed effort to establish a permanent international judicial body that would punish the perpetrators of mass atrocities. These crimes again highlighted the need for a court with global reach that would be able to prosecute war crimes, genocide, and crimes against humanity. Philippe Kirsch, former chair of the Preparatory Commission for the International Criminal Court, explained that the main objective of the establishment of an international criminal court was to "replace a culture of impunity for the commission of very serious crimes, which has existed and still exists to a large extent, with a culture of accountability."[3] Out of these considerations, the International Law Commission was charged with drafting a statute for a future international criminal court. In 1994, the International Law Commission submitted its final draft to the UN, which subsequently led to the establishment of UN committees to review and revise the draft statute. After a four-year process of drafting and negotiating a statute, the legal document for the establishment of an international criminal court was finalized at the UN Conference of Plenipotentiaries on the Establishment of an International Criminal Court in Rome, Italy, in July 1998; hence the treaty is referred to as the Rome Statute. The ICC became operational on July 1, 2002, after sixty states had ratified the treaty.

The previous chapter traced the path from the United States' tumultuous encounter with the ICC to the Bush administration's unprecedented unsigning of an international treaty. I have argued that this act represented the United States' abdication of a commitment to its human rights legacy and as such an erasure of a kind of transnational memory with consequences for the future formation of transnational memory discourses. Chapters 4 and 5 extend this discussion of transnational memory by examining the rhetorical discourses of global civil society organizations in the adoption and ratification process of the Rome Statute of the ICC. Since the drafting of the Universal Declaration of Human Rights, global civil society, specifically nongovernmental organizations (NGOs), has played a significant role in shaping the agendas and discourses of contemporary humanitarian politics.[4] Accordingly, NGOs were also instrumental in the creation of the ICC. Scholars who have studied the role of civil society actors in the creation of the ICC have even gone so far as to argue that the "input of global civil society in the process which led to the adoption of this Statute has been almost unprecedented in international treaty negotiations."[5] The involvement of global civil society actors (or, more precisely, NGOs) illustrates that NGOs are on the front lines in engaging in the kind of advocacy that contributes to the formation of transnational memory and community. Inquiring into the rhetorical work of these organizations is instrumental to understanding how memory discourses operate and their potential impact at a transnational scale. Furthermore, it showcases the oft-unseen work of advocacy organizations operating independent of and/or in concert with states to achieve policy ideas in international law.

This chapter examines the rhetorical discourse of nongovernmental organizations' efforts to create a "global public sphere" in support of the ICC, focusing on the implicit understanding of transnational memory and community operating in the rhetorical discourses of NGOs working to promote ratification of the ICC. In these discourses, we see how advocates influenced international politics within the constraints of national audiences. Through this analysis, we will gain a better understanding of how nonstate actors worked to shape international policy and how such advocacy and its object—namely, international policy—invites us to remember ourselves as citizens and actors in a trans/national context.

The chapter begins with an overview of the emergence of NGO involvement and their modes of mobilization in an effort to create an ICC in the 1990s. The focus here is on the Coalition for the International Criminal Court (CICC), a network now consisting of over 2,500 NGOs advocating for the establishment of a fair and independent international criminal court.[6] Founded in the context of the UN Ad Hoc Committee meetings for the ICC in 1995, the coalition's goals were to raise awareness and disseminate information about the court, promote ratification of the Rome Statute, and support the work of the ICC. This alliance of a diverse set of organizations has been "hailed as a model of collaboration among civil-society actors and between civil society, governments and international organizations."[7] The following section hones in on advocacy materials produced by one NGO member of the CICC, Citizens for Global Solutions, whose goal was to promote ratification of the ICC after the Rome Statute was adopted. My analysis of the group's rhetoric details how the NGO packages a cosmopolitan (or transnational) notion of citizenship—manifest in U.S. support of the ICC—in language that Americans can readily identify with as Americans and accept.

NGO INVOLVEMENT IN THE ICC NEGOTIATIONS

After failed attempts to establish an international criminal court in the 1950s,[8] the political climate of the early 1990s provided the context for NGOs to reinsert themselves into the reemerging ICC negotiations and to launch a campaign that would culminate in the participation of a broad spectrum of NGOs at the Rome Conference in 1998. Several NGOs and legal experts had followed the UN deliberations about an international criminal court in the early 1990s and the negotiations about the ad hoc tribunals in the former Yugoslavia and Rwanda in 1993 and 1994.[9]

At the same time, William Pace of the World Federalist Movement had been establishing contacts with NGOs interested in ICC advocacy. In March 1994, the World Federalist Movement arranged a conference call with a set of NGOs to discuss NGO strategies for the meeting of the UN General Assembly's Sixth Committee that was scheduled for fall 1994 to discuss the International Law Commission's draft statute.[10] During the UN meeting, Pace organized a meeting with several NGOs to further discuss NGO strategies. The NGO meeting was partly prompted by the UN General Assembly's decision to not send the draft statute to a treaty-drafting conference but rather to discuss the potential creation of a court further in an ad hoc committee.[11]

On February 10, 1995, twenty-five NGOs joined together to form the NGO CICC to observe the Ad Hoc Committee meeting called for by the UN General Assembly's Sixth Committee and that was to start its work in April 1995.[12] The newly founded coalition's objectives were to "advocate for the creation of an effective, just, and independent International Criminal Court" and to serve as a forum for information exchange between NGOs and state delegates and as a "resource for coordination between NGOs."[13] The Ad Hoc Committee's purpose was to determine whether or not to hold formal negotiations and a diplomatic conference on an international criminal court and the feasibility of such endeavors. To that end, during the two ten-day meetings of the Ad Hoc Committee, the coalition worked closely with a small group of so-called like-minded governments who supported the creation of the ICC in order to secure the creation of a preparatory committee by the UN General Assembly. The coalition's principal forms of advocacy included "NGO-government consultations and the conduct of expert dialogue between NGOs and governments," raising global awareness by building civil society networks as well as "documentation and distribution of information related to the ICC."[14]

The Ad Hoc Committee concluded with a report that emphasized the broad consensus over the necessity of an international criminal court,[15] and the Ad Hoc Committee was converted into the preparatory committee (PrepCom) with the mandate to create a draft statute that could serve as the basis for negotiation at a diplomatic conference. During the six PrepCom meetings held between March 1996 and April 1998, leading up to the Rome Conference in July 1998, the CICC's main strategies for mobilization were to raise awareness about the court both for the general public and state delegations. The coalition members met with state delegates involved in the negotiations, wrote position papers, provided reports from NGOs on relevant issues to delegates, publicized materials on the ICC electronically, and published articles in legal journals.[16] International relations scholar Marlies Glasius notes that the CICC provided "specialist documentation," which served primarily to inform and influence "a specialist public of NGOs, academics, and state representatives on specific sub-themes, promoting certain alternatives over others with reference to precedent, legal argument, or political realities."[17] In the years prior to the Rome Conference, NGOs also organized conferences around the world, "contributing substantially to a global specialist debate on the court and international justice"[18] involving "academics, NGO advocates, practicing lawyers, and state officials."[19]

From the 25 organizations that founded the CICC in 1995, the coalition grew to include over 800 organizations by the time the Rome Conference began. Of these, 236 were accredited to participate in the Rome Conference, providing 450 representatives in the Rome negotiations.[20] Representing a multitude of issues and interests, not all coalition members necessarily agreed on all the specific details of the proposed court. Political scientist Michael Struett notes that while the members of the CICC had a variety of focal areas, their overall unity was established through their fundamental agreement that "some sort of international criminal court was the best way to deal with the impunity that perpetrators of international law crimes have historically enjoyed."[21] Moreover, the coalition secretariat aided in building consensus among the various coalition members by "identify[ing] and expand[ing] areas of commonality" and by encouraging them to "develop joint positions and strategies where possible."[22] Similarly, Borroughs and Cabasso note that the coalition "typically did not expressly take positions on specific contested issues, but there was agreement and advocacy as to broad principles."[23] The diversity of backgrounds and interests brought to the table by the multitude of NGO members, then, created a certain set of limitations and benefits for how the NGOs could shape their rhetorical discourse. Borroughs and Cabasso, for instance, note that "there was no thorough discussion, still less any formal collective decision-making, among all participating NGOs. Partly this was for practical reasons, because of the number of NGOs, the cumbersome internal decision-making procedures of some NGOs, and the onslaught of events, and partly because it was deemed too divisive to get into controversial matters."[24] Perhaps out of a recognition that consensus over specific rhetorical positions would be hard to establish let alone communicate with such a diverse group of advocates, William Pace, as convener of the CICC, emphasized the value of the coalition's pluralism, insisting that it is "vital to maintain the plurality of ideas and objectives represented by the Coalition's loosely bound constituents."[25]

While Pace's statement may primarily reflect a rhetorically crafted image to divert attention from the coalition's difficulty in building broad-based consensus on specific issues, the fact that NGO participants came from a variety of backgrounds with different focal points did indeed prove advantageous for their advocacy campaign. Based on their thematic interests, NGOs split into regional, thematic, and faith-based caucuses, which allowed for more focused advocacy work on the part of NGO participants.[26] The CICC formed twelve working groups, each consisting of four to eight members, to follow different thematic areas in the negotiation process and to publicize the results in daily reports to NGOs and state delegations.[27] NGOs also provided valuable information and documentation about the rationale for certain provisions and how they had developed during the earlier stages of the negotiations.[28] This was crucial, since only about sixty states were represented at the PrepCom negotiations held from 1996 to 1998, whereas representatives from over 160 countries attended the Rome Conference.[29]

Besides providing research and publicizing such documentation to state delegations and the wider public, other forms of NGO advocacy during the Rome Conference included holding regular meetings with NGOs and state delegations and seeking funding to bring more NGOs from the Global South to the Rome Conference. The NGO No Peace without Justice provided a technical assistance program that offered legal experts to state delegations. This way, several state delegations, particularly from developing countries, were able to increase their size and influence.[30]

News of the conference was disseminated to a wider public by the coalition's newspaper *ICC Monitor* and the UN daily news bulletin *Terraviva*. The NGO Advocacy Project produced daily newsletters about the proceedings of the negotiations for interested advocates.[31] In an effort to create more public awareness of the ICC, some organizations engaged in street activism. Amnesty International organized the performance of a "human carpet" symbolizing the victims of war crimes and crimes against humanity during the Rome Conference in July 1998, while No Peace without Justice orchestrated a vigil the day before the outcome of the Rome Conference. Prior to the Rome Conference, some organizations had made efforts to create widespread public support of the court by publishing petitions for the establishment of an international criminal court, including signatures from celebrities, in international newspapers such as *Le Monde* and *The International Herald Tribune*.[32] The significance of the coalition's broad-based advocacy work is succinctly summarized by one state delegate who claimed that the CICC was "the world's principal source of information on the ICC."[33]

Although it is difficult to trace NGO involvement in the treaty negotiations in the final outcome, there is a consensus that NGOs were particularly successful with regard to shaping the role of the prosecutor. While the prosecutor was originally not supposed to be able to initiate proceedings, NGO efforts aided in redefining the role into that of an independent prosecutor who is able to do so. Furthermore, the inclusion of certain provisions regarding the psychological and financial support of victims and witnesses and the financing of the court are areas in which civil society actors have left at least some imprint. Lastly, the unprecedented recognition of gender and sexual violence as among the most serious violations of international human rights and humanitarian law and their inclusion in the Rome Statute is largely attributed to NGO advocacy campaigns, an issue that will be discussed in the next chapter. In addition to these thematic provisions included in the Rome Statute that are beneficial outcomes of the NGO involvement in the ICC negotiations, Glasius points to the democratic implications of civil society activism in international law making. She concludes that one of the primary outcomes of the unprecedented NGO involvement in the drafting of an international treaty was the enhancement of transparency in the negotiation process. She writes,

> Traditionally, international law-making has occurred in complete secrecy; all that became available to the public was the final product—and sometimes, there were also secret treaties. It is unlikely that international negotiations will ever be entirely open, but the Coalition for an International Criminal Court took the potential for making international negotiations transparent to its limits.[34]

NGO involvement in the drafting and negotiation process thus set the precedent for a more democratic process of international law making.[35] The coalition continues to work on promoting awareness of the ICC, supporting ratification and implementation, encouraging civil society participation with the ICC, and "mainstreaming accountability for grave crimes" into the agendas of international organizations.[36]

CITIZENS FOR GLOBAL SOLUTIONS

Having traced the emergence of NGO involvement in the ICC negotiations in the early 1990s and the general rhetorical strategies employed by NGOs in putting the ICC on the international agenda, we now turn our attention to the U.S. ratification campaign of the ICC after the Rome Statute was adopted in the summer of 1998. Specifically, this section examines a set of texts produced by the prominent NGO member of the Coalition for an International Criminal Court, Citizens for Global Solutions. Citizens for Global Solutions works on issues including U.S. global engagement, peace and security, international institutions, health and environment, and international law and justice. The NGO promotes U.S. cooperation at a global level, recognizing that "in today's interconnected world, our lives, our jobs and our families are increasingly affected by global problems."[37]

Citizens for Global Solutions emerged out of the movement for world federalism founded in the 1930s in an attempt to work toward ensuring international peace. Today, the organization is part of the larger World Federalist Movement–Institute for Global Policy, an alliance of organizations working toward a global federalist system of "democratic global structures that are accountable to the citizens of the world."[38] Citizens for Global Solutions seeks to "build political will" for finding global solutions by "educating Americans about our global interdependence, communicating global concerns to public officials, and developing proposals to create, reform, and strengthen international institutions such as the United Nations."[39] Since it is committed to "[strengthening] laws and institutions that protect human rights," one of Citizens for Global Solutions' focal points is the promotion of U.S. cooperation with the ICC. Hence, the group also serves as a member of the steering committee for the American NGO Coalition for the International Criminal Court. Specifically, Citizens for Global Solutions' campaign focuses on offering advocates communication strategies to garner support of the ICC.

Citizens for Global Solutions' campaign for support of the ICC was set against the backdrop of U.S. opposition to the court, which made the United States the primary audience the organization sought to address with its advocacy campaign. Emphasizing the crucial role the United States played in the promotion of human rights in the past, Citizens for Global Solutions expressly drew from a transnational public memory discourse of human rights and invoked the legacy of human rights promotion so often summoned in U.S. public address. On its website informing about issues of "international law and justice," Citizens for Global Solutions stated,

> Ever since the Nuremberg war crimes trials after World War II, the United States has championed international law as a means to end impunity for war crimes and genocide while promoting American principles like due process, equality before the law and the protection of basic human rights. The United States was instrumental in creating tribunals to prosecute the individuals responsible for genocide and ethnic cleansing in Yugoslavia and Rwanda, and actively participated in the process that created the International Criminal Court (ICC).[40]

Citizens for Global Solutions' campaign for support of the ICC is informed by a memory of the United States' formative role in the global movement for the enforcement of human rights. Moreover, the organization's rhetoric invokes a transnational memory of atrocities, listing the names of political leaders who bear responsibility for atrocities that now fall under the jurisdiction of the ICC. In doing so, Citizens for Global Solutions implicitly endorses cosmopolitan commitments to international justice and law. Highlighting that the United States' past commitment to the promotion of human rights has been weakened by the Bush administration that has "turned its back on this legacy,"[41] Citizens for Global Solutions claims that the Bush administration's attitude toward the ICC is "inconsistent with our traditional role as the leading proponent of human rights, the rule of law, and justice."[42] The rhetoric of transnational memory is coupled with an exceptionalist discourse that is used to legitimize the United States' continued engagement in human rights promotion. Appealing to advocates' sense of ethical obligation to get involved in the support of the ICC, the organization claims that "it is our duty to ensure that the Hitlers and Pol Pots of the future face justice for their crimes."[43] Invoking a community guided by cosmopolitan values, Citizens for Global Solutions exhorts its audience to "continue to work with our allies to uphold our legacy of championing international law and human rights."[44] While occasionally drawing from national memory discourses and invoking national interests, the overall mission of the organization documented publicly is geared toward forging a cosmopolitan community. However, this commitment to cosmopolitanism is not so obvious in the organization's rhetorical campaign in support of ratification of the ICC. In this regard, I argue, the organization misses an important opportunity to create a vision of a cosmopolitan community by resorting to a language that invokes primarily a national (meaning U.S.) collective memory.

We have seen in the previous chapter that U.S. opposition to the court—culminating in the unsigning of the Rome Statute—has been vigilant and has proven to be difficult to overcome. Citizens for Global Solutions has addressed this issue by drafting documents that attend to the particular challenges the ICC poses for garnering support from various audiences. The difficulty of building support for the ICC rests on two grounds: First, the ICC functions as an international justice institution, and second, the U.S. discourse is deeply steeped in arguments about national concerns. The following sections discuss how Citizens for Global Solutions addresses these challenges in its advocacy materials. The analysis draws on two of the organization's central documents. The first document, entitled "Communications Strategies for International Justice Institutions: The Third Vancouver Dialogue," explains the characteristics of international justice institutions that tend to impede broad-based public support. The second, entitled the "New ICC Communications Guide: . . . And Justice for All: How to Talk about the ICC in the U.S.," addresses the specific rhetorical constraints that the ICC poses for *U.S.* audiences.

The "Communications Strategies for International Justice Institutions: The Third Vancouver Dialogue" report is the outcome of a conference held at the Liu Institute for Global Issues at the University of British Columbia in December 2004. The conference was convened to provide a forum for "educational and outreach events that can mainstream international justice into the public consciousness."[45] Recognizing that "collective international action to end impunity for mass crimes is still relatively new," the authors of the report argue that an overarching goal of international justice institutions (IJIs) will be to "build support globally for international justice."[46] In this discourse, building support for IJIs is roughly synonymous with instilling them into the public consciousness, which suggests that the group is cognizant that its work is primarily engaging in the rhetoric of public memory.[47] That is, the organization is using rhetorical devices to create and shape consciousness favorable toward IJIs and the principles they stand for, thereby creating one of the foundations from which transnational memory discourses can be developed.

The report begins by establishing the relatively new and difficult position IJIs are occupying with regard to communicating their objectives and work. Independent IJIs are, by definition, not affiliated with other organizations, which creates a particular set of problems for institutions that should be impartial and independent. Having their own "communications strategy" to promote their work and objectives on the one hand, and guaranteeing their commitment to operating as an independent institution on the other hand, is "a very complex and relatively new task" such judicial institutions are encountering.[48] The report explains,

> International justice institutions (IJIs) are among the most recent members of the community of international institutional actors. Both their newness and uniqueness has meant that they are undergoing the basic developmental processes that nation-states, other international organizations, and even most types of non-governmental organizations, now take for granted. In this evolution and rapid acceleration of their role in international affairs, learning to communicate effectively has proved to be among the most pressing challenges for IJIs.[49]

The report emphasizes how IJIs find themselves in a peculiar conundrum between upholding neutrality as judicial institutions while at the same time having to raise public consciousness and garner public support for their work as judicial institutions. Whereas NGOs, governments, and civil society have relatively few limitations for how they communicate about issues regarding international justice, and are "*expected* to take a stand" and advocate a particular position, IJIs are "constrained by the customs of legal process and independence," while working in highly "politicized environments."[50] As a result, the competing trajectories of IJIs often create a "communications policy nightmare."[51] Furthermore, IJIs often do not have access to communication experts or the "resources to create the strategies and tools."[52] These circumstances are exacerbated by the commonly held perspective that IJIs are "not supposed [to] engage in strategic communications" to begin with.[53] Justice, as we are taught to believe, is to be blind, outside the realm of the political and the ideological and "above the fray."[54] This unfortunate learned belief places justice firmly outside the realm of rhetoric.[55]

The report presumes that inexperience with devising suitable communication strategies has resulted in the international community becoming witness to "how poorly planned (or unplanned) communications can set back the work of an IJI with both local populations and international public opinion."[56] The report's purpose, therefore, was to offer a "practical policy document" with "practical ideas and guidelines" so that IJIs can develop "effective strategic communications policies and tools."[57] As such, the report served as a primer on using rhetorical strategies to circulate knowledge and promote support of IJIs.

In addition to the ambiguous position IJIs occupy by virtue of their institutional constraints, they also encounter challenges due to the relatively low public acceptance of their purpose, role, and work. The lack of public acceptance is not based on well-thought-out and soundly argued cases against IJIs in general or the ICC in specific. Rather, lack of public acceptance is based on a lack of knowledge, partisan adherence, or perceived threats to concepts such as autonomy or sovereignty. This creates the need for rhetorical campaigns to present these ideas to U.S. audiences. We will see in chapter 6 that levels of support for the ICC grow exponentially once U.S. audiences become better informed about the court. Strikingly, the increase of support that comes alongside increased knowledge transcends right-left ideological lines. Generating support is not, however, as simple as offering people comprehensive information. If it was so easy, NGOs working on behalf of the court would have a simple task ahead of them. Instead, pro-ICC NGOs must rely on strategic communication to generate attention, frame the discussion, and then provide more comprehensive information.

" . . . AND JUSTICE FOR ALL: HOW TO TALK ABOUT THE ICC IN THE U.S."

Based on the particular challenges IJIs pose for generating public support, Citizens for Global Solutions has devised a "strategic communications plan" to promote the ICC, a report aptly entitled " . . . And Justice for All: How to Talk about the ICC in the U.S." The fifty-six-page document published by Citizens for Global Solutions in October 2005 serves as a communications guide with the purpose of providing "advice to supporters of the ICC on communicating with American audiences about the ICC and the U.S. relationship with the Court."[58] Citizens for Global Solutions encourages supporters of the ICC to utilize the strategies outlined in the report to learn how to communicate "with Americans about positive, constructive U.S. global engagement."[59] The strategies provided in the handbook respond to a felt need among advocates of the ICC for a "common strategy and approach to deal with the crippling polarization and lack of genuine debate on the issue."[60] The report characterizes the general U.S. sentiment toward the ICC as a "toxic" topic about which public statements "were rarely made by influential figures."[61] It thus came as no surprise that "the American debate about what role the U.S. should play regarding the Court had become both marginalized and one-sided."[62] Against the background of this attitude of skepticism toward the ICC in the United States, the communications guide was developed when a group of leading U.S. ICC advocates from Citizens for Global Solutions started to develop strategies for main audiences of ICC-related communications.[63] The handbook was drafted with the intent of building support for the court in the United States in advance of additional conferences where the court would continue to be shaped. The goal would be to drum up support for the court while the United States could still play a role in the ongoing conversations and modification of the court.

One of the key messages of the report is that the United States "should move toward constructive engagement with the International Criminal Court, assisting the Court's efforts to bring to justice the world's worst criminals while monitoring and guiding its development from 'inside the tent.'"[64] In this sense, the Citizens for Global Solutions' "communications guide" is a form of activism designed to "provide advice to supporters of the ICC on communicating with American audiences about the ICC and the U.S. relationship with the Court."[65] It accomplishes this by presenting itself like a handbook for rhetorical action, adopting, for a major part of the report, a tone that is reminiscent of a chapter in an introductory textbook on public speaking. Accordingly, much of the report appears to be based on "public speaking truisms."[66]

The handbook starts with a one-page "Quick Reference Guide" listing the primary audiences for the report and the desired outcomes and key messages to be promoted. The report identifies its "priority target audiences for International Criminal Court-related communications" as members of the military, Jewish organizations, and experts who form and influence foreign policies.[67] In addition, the handbook is designed to address the media and the general public. The handbook's explicitly stated goal is to help ICC supporters "understand how key American audiences perceive the ICC and how to best engage these audiences in a constructive dialogue about the court."[68] Based on interviews with focus groups, the handbook aims to "identify the messages that—if totally believed by our target audiences and the public—would lead them to agree with us that the U.S. should join the ICC."[69] Hence, the handbook's "desired policy outcome" was to "soften" the Bush administration's "anti-International Criminal Court stance and persuad[e] Congress that the U.S. should be a constructively engaged observer of the Court's proceedings."[70] The link to Jewish organizations, although not clearly outlined at this point in the report, is based on the report's findings that some Jewish American groups have been "skeptical of international organizations that are linked to the United Nations," as they see such institutions potentially taking actions against Israel because some member states might be negatively predisposed toward Israel's foreign policy.[71]

PUBLIC OPINION POLLING AND PRINCIPLES OF STRATEGIC COMMUNICATION

The handbook discusses the general misconceptions that guide public opinion about the ICC. Drawing on a series of polls, the handbook concludes that while administration officials reflect the larger U.S. population's opinion on the ICC and hence back the court, congressional staff "mis-reads" the public on the issue: "Because the debate about the International Criminal Court

(ICC) in the U.S. has been so one-sided, policymakers and the media tend to assume that the public does not support the ICC. However, public opinion polls consistently show strong American public support for U.S. ratification of the Rome Statute establishing the ICC."[72] Employing the phrase "misread," the report calls for better informing congresspeople rather than decrying or denouncing them for their anti-ICC stance. Here we see a strategic use of rhetoric as a way of being by inviting the targeted audiences into a program of communicative action rather than calling them out for the dogmatic criticism of the ICC.[73] This allows U.S. audiences to see policy makers as misunderstanding the level of support and to call for a more accurate representation of their views while at the same time allowing representatives to change their stance on the ICC without risking embarrassment or loss of votes.

Drawing from the poll results regarding public opinion on the ICC, the handbook operates from the general presumption that "American audiences" must be adequately informed and educated about the ICC in order to support it. Responding to this deficit in public knowledge about the court, the communications guide offers "advice to supporters of the ICC"[74] to engage audiences in effective and informative communication about the ICC. The authors claim to have come to a clearer understanding of the public's attitudes and "the ideas and values that motivate these beliefs" as the research brought to light "themes and patterns in how some key groups of people think about the ICC and what kinds of arguments they regard as credible and motivating."[75]

Highlighting "principles of strategic communication," the report introduces a set of key rules to consider in designing persuasive messages and links those principles to the specific demands of U.S. audiences in discussions about the ICC. Noting that "the conclusions we draw from any information" are shaped by "those deeply held beliefs and stories about the world that we already have in our heads,"[76] the handbook suggests advocates "use 'big ideas' or stories" that strike a familiar chord when entering discussions about the court. The communications guide instructs its readers to ask themselves a series of questions, including "What is U.S. participation in the International Criminal Court 'about' to you? Building a world with justice for the victims of atrocious crimes? The legacy of American leadership at Nuremberg? An interconnected world that requires teamwork to solve problems? Making smart choices in our foreign policy? The U.S. working in partnership with other countries? Putting bad guys in prison?"[77] The implicit assumption is that readers would draw conclusions about the positions their audiences are likely to hold based on their own views. The series of questions is significant in that it acknowledges the principles underlying the ICC's work—international cooperation and responsibility—while its focus is decidedly on U.S. values, concerns, and interests, and on establishing how the

United States can benefit from the ICC. Each question is designed to invoke American values to demonstrate that these are not at odds with the values enshrined in the ICC.

Although the authors argue that using "research-based messages"[78] is an important aspect of communicating about the ICC, a predominant theme that emerges in this text is that providing factual information is oftentimes not sufficient to convince opponents of the ICC of the necessity of the institution. In fact, the authors admit that in working with the ICC in the United States, "one of the most frustrating aspects . . . is the persistence of myths about what the Court is, how it works, and how it will affect Americans."[79] The handbook illustrates this point, referring to the commonly held view that the United States spends too much on foreign aid. This belief, the authors write, "is not something that is negotiable—no amount of education or advocacy will change it."[80] What we see here is that the rhetoric of Citizens for Global Solutions presupposes a persuasive discourse with a rational audience that makes informed and reasonable decisions based on the available evidence. What we see instead are entrenched positions that make the ICC not subject to rational rhetorical discourse. Recognizing that even the most factually accurate and historically faithful account would not be able to debunk certain positions, the authors suggest that if the arguments provided do not offer a mode of existence that is favorable to the audience, the audience will reject the idea as a whole.[81]

Given that in ICC-related public discourse research-based messages have not proven to be effective, the handbook borrows from the sociological concept of framing, "tell[ing] a story that incorporates people's values."[82] Framing provides a familiar context for the "facts that you are presenting and open[s] their minds to the conclusions you'd like them to reach."[83] The handbook emphasizes the need for establishing common ground by invoking stories and values audience members "already accept" to help them "accept your point of view."[84] The text recommends a list of six "useful frames" deemed particularly helpful to engage U.S. audiences that oppose the ICC in discussions about the court. These frames are offered as tools to "give meaning" to facts and figures about the ICC and are, once again, designed specifically for targeting the beliefs and concerns of U.S. audiences and U.S. political culture.[85]

The first frame the authors' focus group research identified as one that U.S. audiences respond favorably to is "pragmatics." To the tested audiences, pragmatics connoted results, effectiveness, and common sense. The second cluster of ideas that was identified as resonating with U.S. audiences is "farsightedness," suggesting prevention, investment, and stewardship for future generations. The third theme, clustered under the heading "comprehensiveness," invokes seeing the big picture, using all available tools, and a balanced approach. "Trustworthiness," the fourth theme, echoes traits such as keeping promises, practicing what we preach, and avoiding double standards, while "collaboration" is associated with teamwork, team leadership, and respecting and listening to others. Lastly, the "principled" category suggests putting the United States' strength to great purpose, fairness, justice, being ethical, common decency, living up to our values, the American way. These concepts are thought of as concepts "familiar to Americans."[86] As suggested by the communications guide, these values reflect a set of distinctly American values and offer modes of being that Americans can connect to their "own life experiences." As such, they function like "a connective tissue," or key elements of a "shared vision for how America should be in the world."[87]

So far, the handbook seems to suggest circumventing the central issue at hand—the ICC—by avoiding direct advocacy of the ICC. Instead, the objective appears to be to frame the discussion of the ICC in such a way that it does not directly assault the "deeply held beliefs" invoked in criticisms or dismissals of the court in specific and cosmopolitanism in general. Consequently, the handbook seems to suggest thwarting the discussion of cosmopolitanism by redirecting the attention to discussions about U.S. interests that U.S. audiences may better understand and more willingly accept.

FRAMING JUSTICE AND JOINING THE INTERNATIONAL COMMUNITY

To frame the work of the ICC, the handbook buttresses its strategies for challenging audiences' existing beliefs and values to identify a set of concepts to avoid while communicating about the ICC. Conversely, it discusses key arguments that invoke particularly resonant and thus persuasive values with the respective audiences primarily targeted with the handbook. For instance, the communications guide discourages the use of "language that implies a bureaucratic body," as this latches on to many Americans' beliefs that international institutions are "wasteful" and ineffective. Specifically, the authors advise against using phrasings such as "international body" or "institution," for these terms would reinforce the already existing skepticism of such entities for crucial audiences.[88] Alternatively, supporters of the ICC are encouraged to "speak of the Court as an improvement on *ad hoc* tribunals," for the public is generally inclined to see the benefits of these courts.[89] As a variation of the theme of invoking fear responses, the handbook advises against drawing on the principle of "the rule of law," because the concept is easily misconstrued and associated with an overly regulated society. Use of the term "rule of law," the handbook explains, could "play into the public's fears" over totalitarian structures; hence the handbook advises to use the phrase "sparingly and with some consideration for how [a] specific target audience will interpret it."[90] In each case, the rhetorical discourses are working to shape audiences' perceptions of the court.

Corresponding to the concepts and narratives familiar to "Americans" outlined above, the handbook emphasizes how appeals to *national* concerns are more persuasive than appeals to an international community. A prominent example of this emphasis can be found in the context of the text's discussion of the significance of the United States joining the international community. The reasons to join the international community are presented in a way that highlights the benefits for the United States with regard to its leadership role. While the handbook discusses community-oriented benefits that would result from the United States joining the court, it simultaneously draws heavily on appeals to the United States' self-interest in its recommendation of how to communicate about the court. The authors are hesitant to advise supporters of the ICC to make arguments invoking cosmopolitan ideals because large parts of the audience may not respond favorably. For instance, the argument to join the pro-ICC international community based on the grounds that "all other major democracies" are party to the statute while the United States is "isolated from its allies because of its opposition to the Court" might draw a favorable response from some audiences, including "certain sections of internationalist policymakers."[91] It could, however, also be interpreted as a "weakminded 'me too' policy" and could hence "backfire" with those audiences "who see the U.S. as a force for good (in its own right), and take pride in its ability to challenge the entire world as needed."[92] So, in short, the opponents of the court need only provide a rationale that reflects their narrow worldview. Proponents, armed with data indicating wide support, must take the idiosyncrasies of their audience into account lest they fall into an argumentative trap.

Similarly, the degree to which the "Americanness of the ICC" should be emphasized in ICC-related discussions remains ambiguous in the handbook. Again, the authors make it a point to mention that the resonance of this argument depends strongly on the particular audience. For instance, the message that the ICC "embodies fundamental American values of accountability, equality, and justice" is considered to strike a balance between two different perspectives on the ICC: those who view the ICC as an institution grounded primarily in American values and one that considers the ICC an institution based on universal principles.[93] On the one hand are those who consider the ICC an institution that "upholds universal human rights values." On the other hand, the ICC is viewed as primarily promoting "American" values because "America has . . . been at the vanguard of promoting these universal values."[94]

The authors recognize that audiences may differ in their responsiveness to such arguments. While the notion that the ICC upholds "American values that the rest of the world shares"[95] might resonate more strongly with audiences who are concerned about raising "other nations to our standards,"[96] other groups might be more responsive to the notion that the ICC upholds universal values. For instance, some audiences interviewed by the authors of the guidebook "cautioned that the Court is not simply American and should not be presented as such" and that "co-opting the Court as an American project undermines its larger purpose and appeal."[97] The text concludes that "these concerns do not preclude calling attention to the fact that the ICC stands for the same values that America holds dear,"[98] suggesting that emphasizing the court's "Americanness" is crucial to build support for the institution as the necessary first step toward developing cosmopolitan values.

The acknowledgment of the power of such Americentric argument comes as no surprise given that, from the outset, when treaty negotiations began in 1995, "conservatives in the United States have been concerned about its creation and its implications for American sovereignty and international actions."[99] Against this background of a climate of "fear and deep doubt about the reach, mandate and operation of the Court,"[100] the handbook offers a number of strategies for communication with U.S. conservatives, highlighting the integral role U.S. conservatives have played in the development of the court. Harkening back to one of the main themes or frames to which U.S. audiences would respond favorably, the communications guide warns that "the U.S. believes that human rights and justice for the victims of genocide are important—and that we should practice what we preach."[101] Thus, advocates are to affirm the belief that the United States has a noble and longstanding commitment to human rights, to acknowledge the role of conservatives in the creation of the court, and to then promote the conclusion that "American" conservatives ought to be pro–human rights and pro-ICC.

While much of the text avoids explicitly endorsing cosmopolitanism by focusing specifically on American values, concepts, and narratives, it does espouse cosmopolitanism more openly in its discussion of the concept of justice that is underlying the ICC. For instance, in the section entitled "Tough Questions (And How to Deal with Them)" that outlines thirteen questions and model responses advocating the ICC, the report openly challenges the widely held support of the death penalty by repudiating it and instead endorsing an alternative concept of justice. In the model response to the question "How can the Court say it delivers justice when it won't allow the death penalty for these horrible crimes?" the handbook suggests readers "reframe to focus on delivering justice."[102] The response leads into an explanation of the court's quest for accountability of the perpetrators and the benefits for the victims of such crimes under the ICC by claiming that "the very fact of hearing the truth in a court of law and putting the criminals in jail can be an important part of a healing process."[103] Referring to the "innovative Victims Trust Fund," designed to "rebuild lives and communities shattered by unimaginable violence," the handbook turns the discussion from a retributive to a restorative model of justice.[104] The goal is to shift a discussion of justice as the product of punishment to a notion of justice as a process of ending ills while aiding in the recovery or healing process of those who have survived. With this focus on a restorative model of justice, Citizens for Global Solutions more directly works to steer away from distinct American discourse to one that abstracts from this particularized conceptualization of justice. Although this approach, in itself, is not an endorsement of cosmopolitanism, it functions as an example of how other concerns regarding the ICC could be approached from a perspective that allows audiences to look beyond national borders.

In addition to advocating transcendence of national borders in the discussion of justice, Citizens for Global Solutions uses such arguments in discussing how to address foreign policy leaders regarding the ICC. Citizens for Global Solutions explicitly suggests an alternative framework to the instrumental view of international relations as a "power struggle" for nations to "maximize their economic and military advantage."[105] Its recommended alternative is the "global system frame" that offers a "larger perspective" by conceiving of the international community as an "interlinked and interdependent system" that is guided by the idea that "national borders seem less important than the global good."[106] Despite these examples that represent a more explicit endorsement of cosmopolitanism, the overriding impression of the handbook's recommendations for communicating about the ICC remains cast in discourses of U.S. exceptionalism and nationalism.

Citizens for Global Solutions, and specifically their materials on communication strategies, offer a perspective on educating about cosmopolitan ideals of global cooperation. These views are challenged by a range of conservative actors that view these ideals as threatening their conceptualizations of sovereignty. These documents demonstrate that Citizens for Global Solutions' appeals to the rhetorical framework of the nation-state outweigh references to the "global system" framework. Thus, while the overall objective is to create global support and cooperation through international justice institutions like the ICC and to produce cosmopolitan sensibilities, as a whole, appeals to the nation-state paradigm are favored over appeals to cosmopolitan values. Given the context of Citizens for Global Solutions' purpose and mission, the particular focus on U.S. concerns in the communications handbook is striking. Citizens for Global Solutions' objective to argue for an international criminal court and the cosmopolitan values it represents are heavily challenged by a memory of discourses, narratives, and values associated with the concept of the nation-state.

Rather than invoking cosmopolitan values, the handbook relies heavily on providing specific examples of narratives that an *American* audience can relate to and that invoke *American* frames of reference. As such, the handbook appeals to the audience as members of a nation-state and the shared set of values and beliefs of a bounded community. With this argument I do not mean to diminish Citizens for Global Solutions' efforts to publicize advice on how to approach the subject of the ICC with certain segments of the public. The organization's use of U.S. nationalist discourses reflects the origin, character, and degree of opposition with which U.S. audiences have encountered the ICC and, as such, the organization's discourse is designed to address the very real opposition of some of these audiences to the ICC. At the same time, the reliance on U.S. *national* concerns in the discourse promoting an *international* criminal court raises the question of whether an important opportunity to highlight ideals of international cooperation and responsibility was missed. That is, Citizens for Global Solutions recognized the need to speak to U.S. audiences in language that U.S. audiences understand. However, by so doing, might the NGO have sacrificed the production of a genuine cosmopolitan attitude for support of the court? As we will see in the next chapter, the challenges to the promotion of such cosmopolitan ideals were waged even at the level of UN conferences, which, by definition, are designed to promote cosmopolitanism.

NOTES

1. Benjamin N. Schiff, *Building the International Criminal Court* (New York: Cambridge University Press, 2008), 28–29.
2. For a more thorough discussion of this development, see Schiff, *Building the International Criminal Court*, 28–29.
3. Philippe Kirsch, "The International Criminal Court: Current Issues and Perspectives," *Law and Contemporary Problems* 64, no. 1 (Winter 2001): 3.
4. See, for instance, Margaret E. Keck and Kathryn Sikkink, *Activists Beyond Borders: Advocacy Networks in International Politics* (Ithaca, NY: Cornell University Press, 1998) for an overview of civil society in human rights legislation. See also Julie Mertus, *Bait and Switch: Human Rights and U.S. Foreign Policy* (New York: Routledge, 2004) for a discussion of several case studies in which civil society has been particularly influential. See Elizabeth Jay Friedman, "Gendering the Agenda: The Impact of the Transnational Women's Rights Movement at the UN Conferences of the 1990s," *Women's Studies International Forum* 26, no. 4 (2003) for a discussion of women's rights activists and their impact on UN conferences in the 1990s.
5. Marlies Glasius, "Expertise in the Cause of Justice: Global Civil Society Influence on the Statute for an International Criminal Court," in *Global Civil Society 2002*, edited by Marlies Glasius, Mary Kaldor, and Helmut Anheier (Oxford: Oxford University Press, 2002), 137. Glasius mentions a variety of global civil society actors and their strategies that have helped establish the International Criminal Court.
6. Coalition for the International Criminal Court (CICC) website "About the Coalition," http://www.coalitionfortheicc.org/about-coalition-0. The coalition started with twenty-five member organizations advocating for the ICC in 1995.
7. Coalition for the International Criminal Court (CICC), "Friends of the Coalition," CICC, https://web.archive.org/web/20050204074713/www.iccnow.org/gettinginvolved/friendsofthecoalition.html.
8. For a more detailed discussion of the campaign for an ICC in the 1950s, see Michael J. Struett, *The Politics of Constructing the International Criminal Court: NGOs, Discourse, and Agency* (New York: Palgrave Macmillan, 2008).

9. William Pace and Jennifer Schense, "The Role of Non-Governmental Organizations," in *The Rome Statute of the International Criminal Court: A Commentary*, edited by Antonio Cassese, Paola Gaeta, and John R. W. D. Jones (New York: Oxford University Press, 2002), 109.

10. Ibid., 110.

11. Glasius, "Expertise in the Cause of Justice: Global Civil Society Influence on the Statute for an International Criminal Court," 146.

12. The NGOs founding the coalition included Amnesty International, Fédération Internationale des Ligues des Droits de l'Homme, Human Rights Watch, the International Commission of Jurists, the Lawyers Committee for Human Rights, No Peace without Justice, Parliamentarians for Global Action, and the World Federalist Movement. See Pace and Schense, "The Role of Non-Governmental Organizations," 111.

13. Glasius, "Expertise in the Cause of Justice: Global Civil Society Influence on the Statute for an International Criminal Court," 146.

14. Pace and Schense, "The Role of Non-Governmental Organizations," 113–14. Pace and Schense note that over the course of that year, the group of like-minded governments grew from six or seven states to about twenty (p. 112).

15. Struett, *The Politics of Constructing the International Criminal Court: NGOs, Discourse, and Agency*, 105.

16. See William R. Pace and Mark Thieroff, "Participation of Non-Governmental Organizations," in *The International Criminal Court: The Making of the Rome Statute—Issues, Negotiations, Results*, edited by Roy S. Lee (The Hague; Boston: Kluwer Law International, 1999), 392. See also Marlies Glasius, "How Activists Shaped the Court," Crimes of War Project (December 2003), https://web.archive.org/web/20110209102851/http://www.crimesofwar.org/print/icc/icc-glasius-print.html.

17. Glasius, "How Activists Shaped the Court."

18. Ibid.

19. Glasius, "Expertise in the Cause of Justice: Global Civil Society Influence on the Statute for an International Criminal Court," 150.

20. Pace and Thieroff, "Participation of Non-Governmental Organizations," 392.

21. Struett, *The Politics of Constructing the International Criminal Court: NGOs, Discourse, and Agency*, 79.

22. Pace and Schense, "The Role of Non-Governmental Organizations," 125–26.

23. John Burroughs and Jacqueline Cabasso, "Confronting the Nuclear-Armed States in International Negotiating Forums: Lessons for NGOs," *International Negotiation* 4, no. 3 (1999): 473.

24. Ibid., 474.

25. William Pace, "Globalizing Justice," *Harvard International Review* 20, no. 2 (1998): 28.

26. Glasius, "Expertise in the Cause of Justice: Global Civil Society Influence on the Statute for an International Criminal Court," 147.

27. Pace and Thieroff, "Participation of Non-Governmental Organizations," 394.

28. Struett, *The Politics of Constructing the International Criminal Court: NGOs, Discourse, and Agency*, 109.

29. Ibid., 110.

30. Glasius, "Expertise in the Cause of Justice: Global Civil Society Influence on the Statute for an International Criminal Court," 151. Glasius notes the potentially problematic position these experts occupy, representing both state governments as well as their own positions. She notes that, overall, such efforts enhanced the participation of smaller and poorer countries in the Rome Conference. See Glasius, "How Activists Shaped the Court."

31. See Advocacy Project's website with links to its coverage of the ICC, https://web.archive.org/web/20120810062117/http://advocacynet.org/resource/308.

32. Glasius, "Expertise in the Cause of Justice: Global Civil Society Influence on the Statute for an International Criminal Court," 151.

33. Pace and Thieroff, "Participation of Non-Governmental Organizations," 392.

34. Glasius, "How Activists Shaped the Court."

35. Some scholars and commentators have criticized NGO involvement in the creation of the court for precisely that reason, arguing that NGOs are not democratically elected representatives and therefore should be limited in their influence on international law-making. For a more detailed discussion, see Glasius, "Expertise in the Cause of Justice: Global Civil Society Influence on the Statute for an International Criminal Court," 161. Similarly, Helen Durham discusses the complex question of NGO legitimacy in the context of geographical representation. Durham notes that the "fact that the ideology and origin of NGOs within the U.N. system is predominantly Western-oriented must not be forgotten." See Helen Durham, "Women and Civil Society: NGOs and International Criminal Law," in *Women and International Human Rights Law*, edited by Kelly D. Askin and Dorean M. Koenig (Ardsley, NY: Transnational, 1999), 3:825–26. For a critical discussion of some of the shortcomings of the NGO campaign in the drafting and negotiation process of the Rome Statute, see Glasius, "Expertise in the Cause of Justice: Global Civil Society Influence on the Statute for an International Criminal Court," 162–64.

36. Coalition for the International Criminal Court (CICC), "An Overview of the ICC and the CICC," CICC (2019), https://web.archive.org/web/20170401003936/http://www.iccnow.org/documents/CICCFS-ICC_Overview_current.pdf.

37. Citizens for Global Solutions, "Working Together, Finding Solutions," Citizens for Global Solutions, https://web.archive.org/web/20100715061347/http://globalsolutions.org/issues/Overview.

38. See World Federalist Movement website at https://web.archive.org/web/20090203224220/http://wfm.org:80/site/index.php/base/main.

39. Citizens for Global Solutions, "Vision and Mission," https://web.archive.org/web/20081007050159/http://oldsite.globalsolutions.org/who/vision_mission.html.

40. Citizens for Global Solutions, "International Law and Justice," Citizens for Global Solutions, https://web.archive.org/web/20081013054733/http://oldsite.globalsolutions.org/programs/law_justice/icc/icc_home.html.

41. Ibid.

42. Ibid.

43. Ibid.

44. Ibid.

45. Liu Institute for Global Issues at the University of British Columbia, *The Third Vancouver Dialogue: The Communications Gap*, Citizens for Global Solutions (December 2004), https://web.archive.org/web/20071027094612/http://oldsite.globalsolutions.org/programs/law_justice/vd3-finalreport-feb28.pdf (p. 2).

46. Ibid., 9.

47. See for instance Stephen H. Browne, "Remembering Crispus Attucks: Race, Rhetoric, and the Politics of Commemoration," *Quarterly Journal of Speech* 85, no. 2 (1999).

48. Liu Institute for Global Issues at the University of British Columbia, *The Third Vancouver Dialogue: The Communications Gap*, 2.

49. Ibid., 1.

50. Ibid., 6.

51. Ibid.

52. Ibid.

53. Ibid.

54. Ibid.

55. For a discussion of judicial institutions as rhetorical institutions in a U.S. context, specifically the U.S. Supreme Court, see Katie L. Gibson, "Judicial Rhetoric and Women's Place: The United States Supreme Court's Darwinian Defense of Separate Spheres," *Western Journal of Communication* 71, no. 2 (2007).

56. Liu Institute for Global Issues at the University of British Columbia, *The Third Vancouver Dialogue: The Communications Gap*, 4.

57. Ibid., 1.

58. Citizens for Global Solutions, " . . . And Justice for All: How to Talk about the ICC in the U.S.," Citizens for Global Solutions (Washington, DC, 2005), 6. The main author of the report is Heather B. Hamilton, vice president and chief of staff of Citizens for Global Solutions.

The report is available at https://web.archive.org/web/20071027094527/http://old-site.globalsolutions.org/programs/law_justice/icc/resources/FINAL_ICC_Comm_Guide.pdf.

59. Ibid., 8.
60. Ibid., 6.
61. Ibid.
62. Ibid.
63. Ibid., 7.
64. Ibid., 3.
65. Ibid., 6.
66. For instance, the authors surmise that "it is a truism in public speaking that your listeners will only remember three things from your speech" (13).
67. Citizens for Global Solutions, " . . . And Justice for All: How to Talk about the ICC in the U.S.", 3.
68. Ibid., 6.
69. Ibid., 13.
70. Ibid., 3.
71. Ibid., 27.
72. Ibid., 9. The handbook suggests that the referral of Darfur to the ICC "may have increased public support for cooperation with the ICC" (9).
73. See Thomas W. Benson, "Rhetoric as a Way of Being," in *American Rhetoric: Context and Criticism* (Carbondale: Southern Illinois University Press, 1989).
74. Citizens for Global Solutions, " . . . And Justice for All: How to Talk about the ICC in the U.S.," 6.
75. Ibid., 7.
76. Ibid., 11.
77. Ibid.
78. Ibid., 7. The authors argue that this is partly due to the fact that there often is "no effective feedback loop for many of our advocacy communications" (7).
79. Ibid., 12.
80. Ibid., 13.
81. For an elaboration on this concept of rhetoric as a way of being, see Benson, "Rhetoric as a Way of Being."
82. Ibid., 13.
83. Citizens for Global Solutions, " . . . And Justice for All: How to Talk about the ICC in the U.S.," 11.
84. Ibid., 12.
85. Ibid.
86. Ibid.
87. Ibid.
88. Ibid., 16.
89. Ibid.
90. Ibid., 30.
91. Ibid., 31.
92. Ibid.
93. Ibid., 20.
94. Ibid.
95. Ibid.
96. Ibid., 20–21.
97. Ibid., 30.
98. Ibid.
99. American Non-Governmental Organizations Coalition for the International Criminal Court, "The International Criminal Court: A Case for Conservatives" (August 30, 2005), https://web.archive.org/web/20100710035539/http://www.amicc.org/docs/Case%20for%20Conservatives.pdf.
100. Ibid., 2.

101. Citizens for Global Solutions, " . . . And Justice for All: How to Talk about the ICC in the U.S.," 15.
102. Ibid., 34.
103. Ibid.
104. Ibid.
105. Ibid., 26.
106. Ibid.

Chapter Five

Gender, Sexual Violence, and International Community

The Fight for and against Gender Justice at the ICC

As outlined previously, the atrocities committed during World War II set into motion a struggle to internationalize the enforcement of human rights with landmark developments in the post–World War II era. The international community's resolve was tested in the early 1990s when mass violence erupted in Rwanda and the former Yugoslavia. Against the background of the mass commission of atrocities in these conflict areas, the need to develop mechanisms for stronger enforcement of international law to safeguard human rights became clear once again and the movement for the establishment of a standing international criminal tribunal regained momentum. The envisioned permanent criminal court would have two main purposes: First, it would have the authority to prosecute and hold individuals accountable for committing some of the most serious crimes of international concern. Second, it would serve as a public memorial to the ongoing efforts of securing human rights internationally. The most promising step toward fulfilling these purposes came with the drafting of the international treaty to establish an international criminal court (ICC), the Rome Statute, in 1998.

Despite the broad consensus among advocates that a permanent ICC to prosecute individuals for genocide, war crimes, and crimes against humanity was desirable, the specific features of such a court were fiercely debated during the drafting process of the treaty. Advocates across the political spectrum saw the court as a potent force in influencing how human rights are spoken of, practiced, adjudicated, and remembered. As such, they recognized the court as a rhetorical institution. From this point of agreement emerged a contentious battle over the rhetoric of the court during which advocates struggled over the meaning and scope of the crimes the ICC could prosecute and, implicitly, how the court's protections of certain groups in times of war might lead to guaranteeing access to those protections in times of peace.

This chapter examines one of the most fiercely contested issues in the negotiations over the ICC—namely, the debates over how "gender sensitive" the court should be. Specifically, this chapter examines the rhetorical strategies social policy makers employed during the treaty negotiations with regard to the inclusion of a gender perspective in the Rome Statute of the ICC. The chapter focuses on the debates over the inclusion of a gender perspective during and in close proximity to the six-week Diplomatic Conference for an International Criminal Court held in Rome from June to July 1998. The UN conference constituted the final set of negotiations over a draft statute that had been submitted by the UN's International Law Commission and would usher in the adoption of the Rome Statute of the ICC on July 18, 1998.

Historically, gender and sexual violence had largely been ignored in international law prior to the establishment of the ICC. For instance, the 1907 Hague Conventions contain only one article that addresses gender violence, but it does so by only "vaguely and indirectly" prohibiting sexual violence as a violation of family honor.[1] The Geneva Conventions of 1949 and Additional Protocols to the Geneva Conventions of 1977 included some provisions prohibiting sexual violence but failed to categorize sexual violence as "grave breaches," or the most serious violations of international humanitarian law.[2] While the Geneva Conventions included rape and forced prostitution, they "erroneously link rape with crimes of honor or dignity instead of with crimes of violence."[3] Legal scholar Kelly Askin notes that "even in the twenty-first century, the documents regulating armed conflict either minimally incorporate, inappropriately characterize, or wholly fail to mention these crimes."[4] Similarly, legal scholar Kristen Boon argues that, on the whole, even when sexual violence was explicitly prohibited, it has historically been "dismissed as an inevitable by-product of war and rarely prosecuted."[5]

During the negotiations of the Rome Statute, the gender-related debates ignited over the inclusion of gender anywhere in the Rome Statute, over provisions that would explicitly criminalize certain forms of sexual or gender violence, and over a provision relating to gender parity in the institutional setup of the court. After intense debates over the inclusion of a gender perspective in the Rome Statute, the statute adopted at the end of the Rome Conference codified "rape, sexual slavery, enforced prostitution, forced pregnancy . . . enforced sterilization or any other form of sexual violence" as a "grave breach" of the Geneva Conventions,[6] making the Rome Statute the first international treaty to codify gender and sexual violence in line with the most serious violations of international law. Prior to the creation of the Rome Statute, international criminal law had only insufficiently sanctioned such crimes. The adoption of the Rome Statute was thus widely considered an enormous development in international criminal law in general (see chapter 3) and an achievement of feminist legal thought in particular.

The fundamental change in perspective compared to prior international treaties was wrought, in large part, by the advocacy campaigns of the Women's Caucus for Gender Justice, a coalition of several hundred organizations and individuals promoting the inclusion of gender provisions into international criminal law. The need for a more gender-sensitive court and specifically the inclusion of provisions on gender and sexual violence had become an acute concern in the aftermath of the conflicts in Rwanda and the former Yugoslavia in the early to mid-1990s. Specifically the experiences with the ad hoc tribunals that had been established in response to these conflicts had increased global awareness of the systematic use of gender and sexual violence as instruments of war.

Feminist advocates in the Women's Caucus for Gender Justice seized the historical opportunity in the months leading up to the Rome Conference to influence the proceedings. As the Women's Caucus for Gender Justice's goal of the integration of a gender perspective through gender-specific language began to be reflected in the negotiations and drafts of the statute at the Rome Conference, a loose coalition of conservative states and NGOs increased their advocacy in an attempt to counteract the inclusion of such language. This chapter focuses on the advocacy campaigns of these two main players, the Women's Caucus for Gender Justice promoting a more gender-sensitive court and a coalition of conservative states and civil society organizations that challenged the inclusion of a gender perspective in the Rome Statute. The debates over gender provisions held at the Rome Conference will serve as a representative example of the growing participation and influence of nonstate actors at transnational social policy-making fora such as UN-related conferences.

Despite the increasing involvement of NGOs, and conservative organizations in particular, in shaping discourses of international law, transnational treaty making has so far been understudied from a rhetorical perspective. The Rome Statute as a legal document and the debates over the treaty language are particularly productive sites for rhetorical investigation as the debates at this UN-hosted conference offer insight into the rhetoric of law from an international perspective. Rhetorical scholars have widely discussed the importance of analyzing legal texts as rhetorical documents and the role of law in shaping subjectivities in domestic contexts.[7] As rhetorical/feminist legal critic Carrie Crenshaw has pointed out, since the "law institutionalizes relations of power, it can authorize and order our conceptions of social justice."[8] More specifically, Katie Gibson has argued in the context of Supreme Court rulings on women's rights legislation that "representations of women and gender . . . become part of the Court's collective rhetorical framework for thinking and reasoning about the legal rights of women,"[9] creating "rhetorical 'communities'" that "prohibit, constrain, or allow future decisions."[10] Accordingly, as an international court, the ICC, through the legal document of the Rome Statute, will provide such a collective rhetorical framework operating at a transnational level.

Given the reach and implications of the laws and policies produced at international sites, it becomes imperative to examine the rhetorical advocacy of those involved in the development of such high-profile treaties like the Rome Statute. Since its legal framework is intended to be incorporated into nation-states' domestic law, the ICC and the trials it will conduct will function as important sites for constructing subjectivities, meaning, and a transnational memory of what constitutes gender and sexual violence and the protection of such rights. As a site for the codification of transnational gender justice via the human rights system, the advocates' discourses offer insight into how and to what effect advocates negotiated gender provisions in the ICC treaty and what the implications might be.

Furthermore, gaining a deeper understanding of the conservative actors' rhetorical discourses employed to influence the ICC treaty negotiations is crucial because international institutions like the UN produce discourses not only in a strict legal but also a more general sense. They provide, as suggested by Doris Buss, a vision of a particular political imaginary: "the UN conference appears to play an increasingly important role in not only generating international law and policy, but also in defining the scope and nature of 'community' at the international level."[11] Analyzing conservative actors' discourse on these international treaty stipulations will provide insight into these actors' larger understanding of the role and legitimacy of international institutions, the human rights framework, and concepts of international community and cosmopolitanism that could influence both domestic and foreign policy perspectives and decisions.

Lastly, an examination of conservative actors' advocacy campaign will shed light on how and to what extent conservative rhetors operating at the international level mirror conservative resistance rhetoric in domestic politics. In her study of movements that "block reform-oriented change" or what she calls conservative resistance movements, Barbara Warnick identified several characteristic features of these groups' rhetorical discourses.[12] First, conservative resistance rhetoric discourse argues for the status quo and will prevent changes to the current social order. Second, the conservative resistance genre draws heavily on reiteration of ideology and assumes a moralistic stance often grounded in religion.[13] Third, conservative resistance rhetorics express fear over the loss of "traditional" values.[14] Fourth, conservative resistance rhetorics tend to embrace a dualist worldview and rely on stark polarization of an issue while also resisting compromise.[15] Similar features have been identified by other rhetorical critics in their analyses of the women's rights movement in the United States, and they are also prominently featured in the transnational conservative actors' advocacy over gender provisions in the Rome Statute.[16]

Although the Rome Statute is celebrated for its inclusion of several gender-based provisions, the conservative coalition's influence is reflected in the ICC treaty. Examining newsletters, pamphlets, position papers, and online material from advocates involved in the drafting process over the Rome Statute published during the conference in the summer of 1998, this chapter illustrates how these advocates advanced or challenged gender provisions in the Rome Statute. Focusing on the rhetoric of the conservative coalition, the analysis will show that these actors worked primarily through rejecting key elements of the gender provisions in the Rome Statute of the ICC. I argue that their rhetorics of human rights are deeply at odds with the ideal of international cooperation on which international institutions like the ICC and the UN are founded. As a result, their advocacy campaign poses a significant challenge to how human rights in general and women's rights in particular can and will be remembered, practiced, and enforced and contributes to a more complex understanding of the modes of argumentation employed in the international realm by those concerned with national sovereignty and national interest.

The chapter begins with an overview of the rise of conservative organizations' influence at UN conferences. This is followed by a brief overview of the conceptualization of sexual violence in international law prior to the establishment of the ICC that served as the background for women's rights NGOs to advocate for the inclusion of sexual crimes in the Rome Statute. We then turn to a group of progressive members of the Coalition for the International Criminal Court—namely, the Women's Caucus for Gender Justice. The Women's Caucus, comprised of women's rights advocacy organizations and individuals, crafted a rhetorical campaign for the inclusion of a gender perspective in the legal foundations of the ICC. This is followed by an examination of the rhetorical strategies of a set of conservative NGOs involved in the negotiation process at the Rome Conference who attempted to challenge the court's inclusion of provisions criminalizing gender and sexual violence as war crimes and crimes against humanity. These actors specifically targeted the inclusion of the term "gender" anywhere in the Rome Statute and the inclusion of "forced pregnancy" as a crime subject to ICC jurisdiction.

This analysis draws on materials from the Women's Caucus for Gender Justice (representing the proponents of the inclusion of a gender justice perspective) and conservative organizations (representing opposition to such a perspective) that were published and distributed primarily during the time of the Rome Conference. These materials include newsletters, pamphlets, and online material published on the websites hosted by these various organizations. Many of these materials were specifically targeting policy makers involved in the treaty-making process, especially online materials were also addressing the groups' respective constituents. While these audiences may be considered insular in the sense that a particular group's website would be sought out primarily by the respective target audience, these texts and the discourses they produced warrant closer examination. Given the milestone development in international law the Rome Statute represented, the issues that the negotiations brought to the fore were relevant not only for those directly involved in the proceedings. They also received considerable attention in national and international media in the context of the coverage of the ICC treaty negotiations at the Rome Conference.

THE RISE OF CONSERVATIVE CIVIL SOCIETY ACTORS IN THE INTERNATIONAL ARENA

Scholarly attention to women's rights issues across disciplines has typically focused on the work of progressive reformers, which acknowledges the accomplishments of the progressive members of the transnational women's rights movement. In addition to the growing influence of women's rights advocates in these contexts, however, there is a growing number of conservative actors that have become involved in international policy-making fora, such as UN conferences, and whose influence needs further scrutiny. Religious conservative actors represent an emerging alliance of what legal scholars Doris Buss and Didi Herman call Christian Right organizations that include primarily North American Catholic, Protestant, and Mormon organizations and that have built powerful alliances with the Vatican and representatives of conservative religious governments in an attempt to influence social policy making at international political fora including UN conferences. Having emerged in the context of the 1995 Fourth World Conference of Women in Beijing, China, to counter what they perceived as an increasing and thus dangerous influence of women's rights organizations at UN-related venues during the 1990s, these religious conservative organizations campaign against women's rights, reproductive rights, abortion, and the extension of civil or human rights protections to members of the LGBTQ+ community. At the same time, they lobby for the restriction of children's rights and promote what they perceive to be "traditional" gender roles. By their own description, these groups consider themselves advancing "family values" or a "pro-family" perspective at an international level.

Despite their growing presence and influence at these sites, however, there is to date relatively scant scholarship in social movement studies, international relations, and communication studies on those actors opposing reform at a transnational level.[17] The prominent role of religious conservative/

Christian Right forces and their rhetorical strategies is only beginning to be analyzed, even though, as Buss and Herman have pointed out, the Christian Right "is intent on both internationalizing its domestic concerns and shaping its domestic activism in light of [Christian Right] global understandings."[18] Buss and Herman insist that a nuanced understanding of the Christian Right's "domestic agenda is not possible without understanding how that agenda is intimately locked into a global program of action."[19] The relative dearth of attention these conservative activists operating at the transnational level have garnered is even more surprising given that this well-organized conservative alliance opposes the "women's movement at every UN forum that has any relevance to sexual and reproductive issues."[20] Hence, with the deeply divisive discussions over the inclusion of gender provisions, the Rome Conference was not unlike other international UN conferences in which civil society actors were involved in drafting human rights–related legislation. Political scientist Louise Chappell has noted, for instance, that international UN conferences, such as the Rome Conference, have emerged as "key international sites where contentious politics around women's rights take place" because they provide a "structured venue" for governments and civil society actors to "meet, formulate, express and contest views on women's rights."[21] The documents created at these conferences serve as the "battleground over which the framing of women's rights is fought"[22] and as important sites of both international law and the production of transnational memory.

The lack of attention paid to these conservative actors and their rhetorical discourses may be due to the prevailing notion that transnational civil society or fora such as international UN conferences are the realms of like-minded actors promoting human rights and social justice that embrace so-called emancipatory values. As political scientist Marlies Glasius has previously argued, however, global civil society is "not the exclusive domain of progressive human rights, environmental, social justice and women's rights activists; it is a space co-inhabited by conservatives, anti-abortionists and religious fundamentalists."[23] An examination of the discourses of conservative advocacy groups contesting the inclusion of a gender perspective in the Rome Statute serves as a case in point to illustrate the growing role of actors challenging this emancipatory trajectory and addresses the "clear need for further research into the beliefs, tactics and leadership" of conservative organizations at the transnational level.[24]

THE PATH TO WOMEN'S RIGHTS GROUPS' INVOLVEMENT IN THE ROME STATUTE

Given that women's experiences during armed conflict had been largely overlooked, what led to the inclusion of gender and sexual violence in the statute of the ICC? The integration of a gender perspective in the ICC owes to a series of developments in human rights politics and international criminal law that set the stage for women's rights groups' advocacy during the ICC treaty negotiations. First, the ICC negotiations occurred at a "critical moment in the history of the international women's human rights movement," which included women's rights activists' involvement in a series of UN conferences prior to the Rome Conference.[25] While women's rights NGOs had been influential in the campaign for the League of Nations and the drafting of the Universal Declaration of Human Rights,[26] women's rights advocacy gained momentum particularly in the context of the second wave feminist movement in the 1970s that was itself a "global phenomenon" that linked up with a window of opportunity created by UN-hosted conferences in the 1970s and 1980s.[27] These fora, including the UN Decade for Women in Mexico City 1975, Copenhagen in 1980, and Nairobi in 1985 gave rise to transnational feminist organizing proliferating in the 1990s at the World Conference on Human Rights in Vienna in 1993, the 1994 Cairo Conference on Population and Development, and the Fourth World Conference on Women in Beijing in 1995. Political scientist Elisabeth Friedman concludes that the rise of this transnational feminist movement resulted from a confluence of factors, including the "interaction of the political opportunities of UN Conferences and international politics, the mobilizational structures stemming from national, as well as regional and transnational women's movement organizations, and increasingly shared frames on women's oppression."[28] Through its participation in these conferences, the transnational feminist movement had contributed to a heightened concern for gender mainstreaming, or the recognition and implementation of gender perspectives in policy making to achieve gender equality in the UN system, and, especially in the 1990s, focused its efforts on including gender-related issues in the final conference documents.[29]

The Vienna and Beijing Declarations and Platforms of Action were particularly important stepping stones for the inclusion of a gender perspective in the Rome Statute because they called for the integration of a gender perspective in armed conflict.[30] However, while the declarations were significant for their conceptual and promotional contributions, their primary rhetorical function was limited to shaping perceptions of international jurisprudence. Like the documents produced at most UN conferences, the declaration was a nonbinding plan of action rather than a binding treaty; it thus did not provide the legal basis for enforcement and compliance by states.

A second set of catalysts for women's rights groups' involvement in the ICC treaty negotiations were the experiences with the war crimes tribunals for Rwanda (ICTR) and the former Yugoslavia (ICTY). The work of these ad hoc war tribunals strengthened the concern for establishing a permanent institution like the ICC. Moreover, the nature of the crimes, specifically the crimes committed against women in Rwanda and the former Yugoslavia, created a heightened sense of awareness about the prevalence of crimes of gender and sexual violence. Specifically, it was the use of rape "as a component of ethnic cleansing in the former Yugoslavia [that] brought the lack of legal protection [of women] to international attention."[31] The larger outcome of the cases brought before these tribunals was that they provided insight into a more general problem inherent in the relationship between the codification of sexual and gender violence in international law and women's rights in general.[32]

In order to better understand the significance of the achievements made by women's rights activists in including a gender perspective in the ICC, an overview of the traditional construction of gender in international law is in order. First, international law is based on a universalist conception of human rights and the concomitant notion that gender difference would not have to be addressed in documents relating to international law. At the same time, this seeming universalist conception of human rights simultaneously belies a "gender bias" in international law that privileges male perspectives as the norm and a seemingly impartial construction of the law. As men historically tended to be those who wrote the law, international law in many ways reflected this gender bias. This asymmetry in the law-making process—along with more general societal notions of gender—resulted in the system of international law being suffused with patriarchal gender constructions that imply distinct gender roles for men and women.[33] Reviewing the construction of the legal subject in international law, legal scholar Vasuki Nesiah writes that the "iconic 'perpetrator' of political violence of bodily injury is the male political actor."[34] By contrast, the dominant understanding of females is that they are "innocent civilians but typically they are not seen to be targeted for their politics, for the views they hold; rather, their injuries are collateral damage."[35] More specifically, as several feminist legal scholars have noted, women were defined in international law not as autonomous individual beings but rather through their relationship with others, usually as mothers to their children or as spouses. Hilary Charlesworth and C. M. Chinkin argue that "women's presence on the international stage is generally focused on their reproductive and mothering roles that are accorded 'special' protection. The woman of international law is painted in heterosexual terms within a traditional family structure. . . . She is constructed as 'the other,' the shadow complement to the man of decision and action."[36] This implicit understanding of women as dependent rather than autonomous, rights-bear-ing subjects is manifest, for instance, in the Hague Conventions and the four 1949 Geneva Conventions. As Zakia Afrin and Amy Schwartz note, the Hague Conventions "provided for the protection of women in armed conflict only in terms of their relationship with others, for instance as pregnant women, mothers or valued property of men or family, but not as legal persons themselves."[37] As another concomitant result of these particular gender biases, those crimes that were more commonly experienced by women had been considered lesser crimes.

Third, international law was modeled after a classical distinction between the public and the private sphere. Women's rights in international law were based on "stereotypical concepts of femininity and the 'place' of women in the private sphere."[38] This framework provided jurisdiction of international law over public life, including the political and economic realm, while leaving "unregulated the private world of home, hearth and the family."[39] The consequence of this framework is that "many of the distinctive harms that women experience are relegated to the private or domestic sphere of States"; thus, these harms do not fall under the jurisdiction of international law.[40] Since crimes of sexual violence were considered to take place within the private sphere, they could not be adequately addressed in international law.

The lack of legal protection from gender and sexual violence under international law was in part due to the underlying focus on men as agents and women as dependents rather than autonomous subjects inscribed into the international law system. At the same time, it became increasingly clear that the very omission or lack of express gender provisions in international law was part of the problem. Alda Facio, then director of the Women's Caucus for Gender Justice, noted that it is "precisely because the vast majority of laws, legal instruments and institutions have been created without a gender perspective that the everyday violations of women's human rights are invisible to the law and the most atrocious violations have been rendered trivial."[41] The context of the strategic use of sexual violence (mass rape) in Rwanda and Yugoslavia in the early 1990s painfully demonstrated the pitfalls of a system of international law that does not *explicitly* address sexual violence or gender-specific crimes. The cases brought before the ad hoc tribunals demonstrated once again that due to "socially-constructed power imbalances and culturally-defined stereotypes," women are particularly vulnerable to certain crimes.[42] It was in part the experiences with the ICTY and ICTR, then, that raised greater awareness about the fact that certain crimes are perpetrated against women because of their gender and that an "ostensibly gender-neutral justice system would in fact fail to address gender-specific abuses."[43]

Assessing the history of the treatment of women in international law, Rhonda Copelon, legal scholar and one of the founding members of the Women's Caucus, notes, there is "an almost inevitable tendency for crimes that are seen simply or primarily as crimes against women to be treated as of secondary importance."[44] The categorization of rape or sexual assault under international law illustrates this point. The Hague Convention of 1907 and the Geneva Conventions categorized rape variously as an "attack against honor" or "humiliating and degrading treatment," rather than as acts of violence.[45] Rape was thus treated differently from other crimes of violence in international law.[46] The terminology of "honor," Copelon explains, is problematic because the fact that rape was conceived of as an offense against honor turned women into "the object of a shaming attack, the property of objects of others, needing protection perhaps, but not the subject of rights."[47] Implicitly, the language of "honor" invokes a proprietary relationship between a man and a woman and "obfuscates the fact that rape is fundamentally violence against women—violence against her body, autonomy, integrity, selfhood, security, and self-esteem as well as her standing in the community."[48] In the context of the crises in Yugoslavia and Rwanda in the early 1990s—that is, at the time when the work on proposals for an international criminal court had just resumed after decades of inaction—Copelon argued that rape, when used as a tool of war, should be considered a "crime of the gravest dimension,"[49] as a form of torture and thus as a "grave breach." Categorizing rape as a "grave breach" rather than a "lesser crime" would entail the possibility of universal jurisdiction of that crime—that is, jurisdiction over crimes regardless of the perpetrator's nationality or whether the crimes were committed within or outside the boundaries of the prosecuting state. The crimes could then be heard before an international tribunal and would not have to be relegated to the domestic jurisdiction.[50] It would take women's rights advocates serious work for a similar proposal to become reality.

The heightened awareness about such issues led to the inclusion of sexual violence in the statutes of the ICTY established in 1993 and the ICTR established in 1994. These statutes included the classification of rape as a crime against humanity, although it was not included in other categories of crimes.[51] The classification of rape as a crime against humanity has far-reaching consequences because the threshold for prosecution of a crime against humanity is higher than the threshold for prosecution of a war crime, the former requiring evidence that the crime was committed on a widespread or systematic basis.[52] Moreover, by not classifying rape as a grave breach of the Geneva Conventions, the ICTY and ICTR failed to acknowledge the seriousness of the crime.[53] Yet, while some advances had been made in the statutes of the ICTY and ICTR with regard to gender and sexual violence provisions and the interpretation of those provisions,[54] the specific definition of rape under these statutes and under previous treaties neglected the gendered dimension of how rape has been used as a violent act against women and was thus insufficient. As a whole, Bedont and Martinez argue, the discriminatory and "inferior treatment of gender crimes perpetuated their under-investigation" and limited the ability to prosecute such crimes.[55] The inclusion of rape as a crime against humanity in the ad hoc tribunals was a step in the right direction, though it was not enough to prosecute some of the most heinous atrocities committed.

The political developments in Rwanda and Yugoslavia during the 1990s had paved the way for a heightened concern about gender-specific crimes and gender representation in international law. Moreover, the jurisprudence of the ICTY and ICTR with the adjudication of sexual and gender violence created the background for women's rights advocacy in the ICC treaty negotiations. For instance, some of the advances that were made in regard to the integration of a gender perspective in international criminal law have been attributed to the work of specific judges and prosecutors who were committed to such causes.[56] Against this backdrop, women's rights advocates across the world "recognized the existence of the ICC negotiations as an opportunity to codify the integration of gender in international criminal law."[57]

In order for the ICC to divert from the male bias and gender blindness of international law and to contribute to an emerging jurisprudence that would take into account gender and sexual violence, human rights advocates recognized that the ICC statute needed to reflect a more gender-sensitive international criminal law. Still, despite a generally increased awareness about the need for the explicit inclusion of a gender perspective in international law, Chappell notes that during the Rome Statute negotiations, "the onus remained with gender justice advocates to demonstrate the importance and relevance of their objectives. They had to work hard to convince states, global governance representatives, and other NGOs that their concerns were, in the first instance, worth deliberating upon, and in the second, worth protecting."[58]

Since the initial engagement with the proposed court in the early 1990s focused on the court's basic structure, the original drafts of a statute for the court prepared by the International Law Commission in 1994 did not include the term "gender," nor did they include articles "that could be characterized as gender sensitive."[59] As suggested above, this reflected the "existing state of humanitarian law and international criminal law" prior to the Rome Statute, as codified in the Hague Conventions, the Geneva Conventions, and the more recently created war tribunals for Yugoslavia and Rwanda.[60] The document adopted at the end of the six-week conference included a series of express provisions on gender and sexual violence and thus constituted a significant "reconceptualization of women's experiences as requiring legal recognition."[61] With the inclusion of "rape, sexual slavery, enforced prostitution, forced pregnancy, enforced sterilization, or any other form of sexual violence of comparable gravity"[62] as war crimes and crimes against humanity in the Rome Statute, women's rights advocates' demands for the recognition of sexual violence "as part of and encompassed by, other recognized egregious forms of violence" were realized.[63] As the first international legal body to "independently enumerate and define a range of sexual and reproductive crimes relating specifically to women and gender,"[64] it laid the groundwork for a new approach toward the sanction of gender and sexual violence.[65] The inclusion of express listing of these gender-based crimes ensures that they need not be negotiated on a case-by-case basis.[66] Boon summarizes the significance of the Rome Statute as reconceptualizing sexual violence in international law. She notes that the Rome Statute "shifts the legal framework of sexual crimes in armed conflict from assuming that the central legal harm is the violation of honor, to considering the harms to the victim's bodily integrity and infringement of their agency. This structure signals a new paradigm for the international criminalization of sexual crimes—one based on broader principles of human dignity, autonomy, and consent."[67] As such, the establishment of the International Criminal Court is considered by many a milestone in the codification of international law and human rights.[68]

Feminist legal scholars contend that besides the integration of a gender perspective in international law that holds perpetrators of sexual violence accountable for their past actions, the ICC's gender perspective has the potential to strengthen women's rights more generally at both national and international levels. At the national level, the Rome Statute is thought to be significant because the domestic law of those states that have ratified the Rome Statute should reflect the law enshrined in the international treaty. Since states are "encouraged, though not required" to integrate the Rome Statute into domestic legislation,[69] this does not necessarily forge an immediate advancement for women's rights at the national level. Still, the inclusion of a gender perspective at the international level, working through domestic law, is conceived of as a means to address not only the effects of gender violence but also the causes that produce such violence in the first place.

At the international level, the inclusion of a gender perspective may contribute to a larger cultural understanding of gender violence and to challenging constructions of masculinity in general that create the climate in which such crimes can be committed. Facio argues that "since the vast majority of those who commit the crimes or are responsible for them are men, one of the probable causes of these crimes may well be the social construction of the masculine gender and therefore one of the solutions may well lie in creating mechanisms that will help construct less violent men."[70] The ICC could thus contribute to the emergence of new understandings of masculinity that can be reconfigured by new transnational institutions and the power relations that they engender.[71] By implication, the crimes of gender and sexual violence are manifestations of a culture in which gender violence has been normalized. International law, then, represents one of many mechanisms by which gender violence can be challenged, both legally and rhetorically.

THE WOMEN'S CAUCUS FOR GENDER JUSTICE

In December 1995, the UN General Assembly had established the first Preparatory Committee on the Establishment of an International Criminal Court to revise the draft statute and prepare a final version of the statute. In addition to delegates who attended the PrepComs, a large number of NGOs were involved, including the Coalition for an International Criminal Court (CICC), an alliance comprising several hundred nongovernmental organizations promoting various aspects of the statute, including human rights, women's rights, children's rights, peace, international law, humanitarian assistance, victims' rights, faith-based issues, and disarmament.[72] Convinced that women's concerns were not sufficiently engaged in the coalition, women's rights groups created the Women's Caucus for Gender Justice during the PrepCom meeting in February 1997.[73] The caucus grew from originally two hundred organizations to eventually comprising over three hundred organizations from around the world, many of which "came out of the movement to combat violence against women."[74] With its "high visibility" and a membership comprised of individuals and organizations with expertise in international law on the one hand and expertise in human rights–related issues on the other, the Women's Caucus developed into a powerful voice in the negotiation process at the Rome Conference.[75]

Against the background of international law not having used or defined the word "gender" in an international treaty before, the principal objective of the Women's Caucus was to ensure that gender and sexual violence would be explicitly included in the list of crimes under ICC jurisdiction.[76] The caucus advocated to include "what had developed in the customary law and jurisprudence of the [ad hoc] tribunals, that sexual violence must be seen as part of, and encompassed by, other recognized egregious forms of violence, such as torture, enslavement, genocide, and inhumane treatment."[77] The *ICC Monitor* summarized the core principles of the Women's Caucus as follows:

> For the International Criminal Court to effectively dispense and promote universal justice, . . . it must necessarily incorporate gender perspectives in all aspects of its jurisdiction, structure and operations. To achieve this, the Court must have the capacity to ensure that crimes against women are not ignored or treated as trivial or secondary. It must take account of the disproportionate or distinct impact of the core crimes on women. The Court should be equipped and enabled to eliminate common assumptions about and prejudices against women and their experiences.[78]

In its advocacy campaign, the Women's Caucus pursued three main goals:

1. Worldwide participation of women's human rights advocates in the negotiations of the ICC treaty to lobby for an effective and independent court

2. To educate governments delegations and mainstream Human Rights NGOs on their commitments to women and the need to integrate a gender perspective into the U.N.
3. To use this historical event as a means for popular education on women's human rights and raise public awareness of the horrific nature of crimes committed against women[79]

Finally, the Women's Caucus advocated for a balanced representation of female and male judges and staff, victim and witness protection procedures to ensure their safety and social or psychological support, and a victim reparations fund to help victims rebuild their lives.

The Women's Caucus's advocacy efforts to integrate a gender perspective into the Rome Statute included producing position papers and commentaries on legal provisions that "contributed greatly to the discussions and variety of options states had to eventually consider."[80] The Women's Caucus also lobbied delegates and governments by publicizing press releases and disseminating open letters and petitions to garner support for particular initiatives.[81] Building on its legal network and alliances with a range of organizations and state delegates who were particularly sympathetic to the Women's Caucus's agenda, the caucus assumed an influential role over the course of the Rome Conference in July 1998. Their advocacy campaign culminated in the final weeks of the Rome Conference. When negotiations deadlocked on crucial gender provisions in the final week of the negotiations, the Women's Caucus felt confident enough to threaten that "if these minimal criteria are not present in the final Statute, the Women's Caucus will not support the resulting weak court and will consider actively lobbying their governments against ratification."[82]

As a result of what many consider the outcome of the Women's Caucus for Gender Justice's advocacy campaign, the Rome Statute that was eventually adopted on July 17, 1998, differed substantially from the original drafts of the treaty. While the International Law Commission's draft statute that was the basis for negotiations in Rome did not include the term "gender" or any gender-sensitive language, the adopted Rome Statute included nine explicit references to gender.[83] Specifically, the inclusion of a gender perspective was accomplished in the following ways: Key changes included definitions of sexual and gender violence under provisions regarding the court's jurisdiction under the definitions of war crimes and crimes against humanity. Specifically, Article 7 (1) (g) codifies "rape, sexual slavery, enforced prostitution, forced pregnancy, enforced sterilization, or any other form of sexual violence of comparable gravity" as crimes against humanity; Article 7 (1) (h) lists persecution on the grounds of gender as crimes against humanity; and Article 8 includes sexual violence as constituting war crimes. Moreover, Article 21 prohibits gender-based discrimination in the application and interpretation of the law. Article 7 (3) explicitly defines gender. Gender is included in Articles 42 and 54 relating to the powers and duties of the prosecutor with respect to choosing personnel and conducting investigations. Other successful lobbying efforts included structural safeguards of the court, such as the provision regarding gender equity in the representation of judges in Article 46 (8) (a) (iii) and the provision that the court must include judges with "legal expertise" on issues involving violence against women and children as well as witness protection procedures in Article 68 (1).

Having made significant achievements during the negotiations over the adoption of the Rome Statute in 1998, the Women's Caucus continued its campaign during the subsequent Preparatory Commission meetings held from 1999 to 2000 during which supplementary materials to the Rome Statute were negotiated—namely, the Elements of Crimes and the Rules of Procedure and Evidence.[84]

CONSERVATIVE ORGANIZATIONS AT THE UN AND THE ROME CONFERENCE

As the negotiations over the draft statute moved into the final stages in the summer of 1998, a coalition of conservative organizations and states that had previously been relatively subtle in their criticism of the inclusion of gender provisions attempted to create "sustained public opposition" to gender provisions that had already been integrated into the draft statute.[85] Chappell notes that central "counter-actors" that advanced a conservative agenda on gender issues included the Holy See, Ireland, Guatemala, and several countries from the "Middle East and Africa, including Syria, the United Arab Emirates, Qatar, and Nigeria"[86] that argued that the inclusion of gender-specific rights "offended their religious standards."[87] These countries were joined by several North American–based conservative, self-declared "pro-life" or "pro-family" organizations. The latter represent a growing movement of conservative NGOs influencing international social policy in international fora. These advocates' primary target for intervention is the UN, including both UN agencies and conferences, where their primary objective is to block consensus on issues relating to women's rights, reproductive rights, gay and lesbian rights, and children's rights.[88]

Although clearly a minority in terms of numbers, these conservative organizations' influence on international social policy hinges in large part on their ability to build powerful alliances in the international political arena. Chappell notes that "although no single multi-denominational organization operated in ICC forums to voice shared traditional values, it was nevertheless clear that a network of religious actors advanced a consistent and complementary conservative position on gender issues."[89] Similarly, Buss and Herman argue that while the organizations active at the UN focus on promoting a Christian orthodox worldview and therefore should be considered a "particular subset of the U.S. Christian Right as a whole,"[90] the coalition of religious conservative organizations has built global interfaith alliances on some issues with conservative Muslim and Jewish activists and delegates and are on many issues supported by the Vatican.[91]

Prominent religious conservative organizations involved in the ICC negotiations (and other UN conferences) included groups such as REAL (Realistic, Equal, Active, for Life) Women of Canada, the International Human Life Committee, the JMJ (Jesus, Mary and Joseph) Children's Fund of Canada, and the Catholic Family and Human Rights Institute (C-FAM), some of whom have made UN activism their primary focus.[92] C-FAM for instance, has established a permanent office at the United Nations in New York in an attempt to "monitor and affect the social policy debate at the United Nations and other international institutions."[93] Other vocal participants were the World Family Policy Center—previously known under the name NGO Family Voice—whose mission is to "provide balanced, pro-family input and effectively educate the United Nations System on moral, religious and other value-based" international policy issues.[94] The World Family Policy Center is based at and sponsored by Brigham Young University Law School. The NGO's founder and director, BYU professor of law Richard Wilkins, has published widely and spoken frequently on the International Criminal Court.

In their effort to stifle progressive reform in the international realm, this loose coalition of conservative organizations has employed similar tactics as their progressive counterpart, including the lobbying of state delegates and publicizing materials via newsletters.[95] Moreover, just as their progressive counterpart, they recognized influencing language as central to their advocacy campaigns to shape documents produced at the international conferences. For instance, Austin Ruse, president of C-FAM, casts his organization's primary work as controlling the language used in international policy in a way that mirrors the work of women's rights advocates. In preparation for the Cairo +5 Conference (1999), Ruse argued that C-FAM "took the initiative from the other side on a new piece of language. Our side has generally been content with scanning the document which the other side writes and trying to improve their language. This still remains the most important part of our work. But we will not win until we begin writing language and getting governments to introduce it for us."[96] C-FAM thus sought to not only identify language to oppose and alter but also to introduce its own proposals. The conservative NGO Family Voice had previously accomplished such a task during the negotiations over the draft statute in Rome. There, NGO Family Voice had introduced a proposal that expressly limited the definition of "gender" as "male and female."[97] That this language was ultimately adopted in the Rome Statute illustrates that these organizations and their allies are influential enough to shape international legal instruments according to their worldviews. Moreover, the statement may demonstrate a shift in conservatives' advocacy campaigns. While their strategies in the 1990s were marked by "symbolic protests and blocking progressive agendas," by the mid-2000s, Butler notes, they were more strongly lobbying for their "own proactive agenda through the U.N. General Assembly."[98]

Conservative NGOs' efforts to draw from women's rights activists' strategies were not limited to the changing of the language in legal documents but extended to other mobilization and lobbying strategies. Drawing on the experiences with conservative NGOs' advocacy during the Beijing +5 Conference, Friedman concludes that by 2000, the conservative movement's "repertoire of actions drew from the highly successful models of women's rights advocates," which included holding their own preparatory meetings, employing communication technology to distribute their materials to supporters, and lobbying delegates with their positions.[99] In addition to these, some conservative organizations also used less reputable forms of influence, such as intimidation tactics and breaking UN rules of procedure.[100] Anick Druelle observed that at the Beijing +5 Conference held in 2000, conservative NGOs' strategies included the spreading of false information in leaflets and brochures, destroying other progressive NGOs' information, and displaying visible signs of religion, such as Bibles in hand or ashen crosses on their foreheads.[101]

A final characteristic feature of conservative organizations' advocacy campaigns influencing UN-related conferences is that they tend to focus on a set of narrowly defined issues that relate to social policy. Working toward preventing the adoption of specific gender-sensitive language in the final ICC treaty, their efforts concentrated on the following issues: blocking the inclusion of the term "gender" anywhere in the statute; preventing the inclusion of a provision defining gender and sexual violence as war crimes and crimes against humanity, specifically the inclusion of forced pregnancy; and impeding the inclusion of provisions regarding gender parity in the structural setup of the court. What follows is a discussion of the rhetorical advocacy over these issues and the underlying concerns and attitudes toward women's rights and the international community they reveal.

THE INCLUSION OF REFERENCES TO "GENDER" IN THE ROME STATUTE

As indicated above, the nonexistent or inadequate definition and treatment of gender in international treaties prior to the Rome Statute reflected a general "pattern of misrecognizing and ignoring gender injustices within the international relations system."[102] The inclusion of the term in an international treaty was known to mark a significant development in international criminal law with implications for the prosecution of gender or sex-based crimes and had developed into a core objective for women's rights activists operating in the transnational realm over the decade prior to the adoption of the Rome Statute. In fact, against the backdrop of the gendered history of international law outlined above and the growing awareness of its significance among feminist legal scholars and activists, Chappell notes, the "disagreement over how and whether gender should be defined was not new; it had been a longstanding area of dispute between progressive and conservative transnational actors at other recent UN conferences."[103] The significance of the inclusion of "gender" in the Rome Statute is explained by Valerie Oosterveld, a member of the Canadian delegation to the ICC's Preparatory Commission from 1999 until 2002 and the 1998 Rome Conference: "How the ICC interprets 'gender' will have a direct impact on the kinds of cases of persecution that the Court may be able to prosecute, as well as on the law applied, on how the Prosecutor undertakes his/her duties, and on the protection and participation of victims and witnesses. It could also profoundly affect the legal construction of 'gender' under international law."[104]

That the inclusion of a "gender" definition in the Rome Statute would have far-reaching implications was also recognized by a set of conservative NGOs and several state delegations, including, but not limited to, members of the Arab League.[105] Conservative states and NGOs most notably increased their lobbying efforts after the term "gender" had been included in the proposed treaty draft a few weeks into the Rome Conference.[106] While women's rights advocates, and specifically the Women's Caucus for Gender Justice, worked hard to include the term, conservative actors sought to object to gender references altogether or to define the term in ways that reflected an understanding of gender more in line with biological sex.[107] While the Women's Caucus strongly advocated for using the term "gender," signifying the social construction of gender roles, conservative NGOs countered their campaign by first objecting to any references to it and, when this avenue did not seem successful, by shifting their advocacy campaign to replacing the term "gender" with "sex" in an attempt to solidify the notion of differences between the sexes as innate and biologically determined. The concern over the gender versus sex terminology reveals conservative state actors' and NGOs' concerns that the new language might pose a threat to their understanding of gender identity and relations. The gender essentialism generally endorsed by these conservative actors is based on the notion of two biologically determined sexes that provides the basis for much of their politics.

Another line of argument advanced by conservative state actors in alliance with conservative NGOs was that the inclusion of "gender-based" crimes (rather than sex-based crimes) could be interpreted as creating protection on the grounds of homosexuality.[108] REAL Women of Canada objected to the inclusion on these grounds. Invoking feminist scholar Anne Fausto-Sterling's 1993 article "The Five Sexes: Why Male and Female Are Not Enough," the organization argued that gender—"sprinkled throughout" the draft statute—"does not always mean a male and female but can also be interpreted (especially by a feminist prosecutor) in a way which could provide protection for 'other genders' including homosexuals, lesbians, bisexuals, transgendered, etc."[109] REAL Women suggested that the inclusion of the term "gender" would ultimately require the recognition of homosexuality, which they considered incompatible with their self-proclaimed "traditional" view of gender relations. Similarly, C-FAM explained its opposition to including the term "gender," claiming that "gender" could be "interpreted as criminalizing any national laws or policies that favor heterosexual marriage over homosexual couplings, on the grounds that homosexuality is a recognized 'gender.'"[110] The articulation of gender to homosexuality illustrated above recurs as a common trope in the rhetoric produced by these conservative state actors and organizations in their ICC campaign. Conservatives built their arguments against the inclusion of "gender" on the premise that "gender" as such refers to homosexuality. Their rhetorical strategy had thus been to "equate use of the term 'gender' with endorsement of homosexuality."[111] Moreover, in conservatives' discourse relating to the Rome Statute, the concept of homosexuality is inextricably bound up with a moral determinism according to which homosexuality inevitably leads to the degeneration of social and moral values.[112] By doing so, they articulated an established anti-gay discourse to a discourse about stifling international human rights legislation.

The conservative discourse about gender was characterized by slippery slope arguments that suggested that if the concept of gender was introduced into the legal document of the ICC, the court would ultimately develop into an institution that could regulate other areas of social policy. A position paper of REAL Women of Canada projects the potential for large-scale manipulation of social behavior if "gender justice" were to be implemented:

> If "gender," as used in the ICC Draft Statute, in fact means something beyond "male" and "female," the ICC will drastically restructure societies throughout the world. The possibilities include everything from hiring quotas to sexual orientation to abortion—hardly an appropriate agenda for a "criminal" court. The ICC was never intended, nor should it be used, to redefine and regulate all "socially constructed roles" that exist throughout the globe. . . . One might ask what fuels the continual quest for "gender justice." No one opposes equal treatment of women and men before the law. If "gender justice" means more than this, the concept dramatically expands the role of the International Criminal Court, changing the Court from a Court aimed at the "most serious crimes" of "international concern," into a potent judicial engine for social engineering.[113]

As seen here, what looms large in conservatives' ICC discourse is that this social reorganization, as their logic implies, would happen if states were required to offer legal protections that would include women's and human rights that they deem immoral. Pragmatically, such legal protections and recognition would, as they clearly sense, marginalize their views of "tradition."

In the course of the ICC treaty negotiations, conservative organizations shifted their goal from eliminating the word "gender" from the statute to replacing the term "gender" with "men, women, and children" or with "sex."[114] The substitution was an effort to see a biologically deterministic language in the legal document. By contrast, the Women's Caucus for Gender Justice and delegates in support of retaining the term "gender" promoted a definition of gender based on the understanding that "differences between men and women are not essential or inevitable products of biological sex differences" but rather "socially constructed differences between men and women and the unequal power relationships that result."[115] In addition, women's rights advocates rejected the proposal to replace "gender" with "sex" by arguing that it contradicted the language used by the UN system, which has used the term "gender" rather than "sex."[116]

Due to the objections to the inclusion of the term "gender" that were raised by conservative advocates, finding agreement proved to be a difficult undertaking, with the result being a "delicate, hard-fought compromise among delegations."[117] After a long series of formal and informal negotiations over the definition, those who opted for the definition that emphasized the constructivist dimension of gender roles won.[118] The victory, however, came with concessions. Delegates eventually adopted a definition of gender as "the two sexes, male and female, within the context of society. The term 'gender' does not indicate any meaning different from the above."[119]

The phrase "within the context of society" is the outcome of a series of debates over language that would reflect the commitment to a definition of gender as socially constructed and that would be acceptable to those who opposed the inclusion of "gender." The phrase codifying that "the term 'gender' does not indicate any meaning different from the above," Oosterveld explains, "gave comfort to those opposed to 'gender' because they saw it as reaffirming the 'two sexes, male and female,' while those supportive [of the inclusion of the term 'gender'] felt that it was harmless because it reaffirmed the valuable sociological reference to 'context of society.'"[120] Even after contentious negotiations, this was "the only definition of 'gender' to which the Arab States and others were willing to agree"[121] and in that sense represents a concession to conservative advocates. Nonetheless, the definition expresses the drafters' concern for "constructive ambiguity," leaving the definition relatively open to future interpretation.[122]

This negotiation history reflects competing notions of gender and sex in the various strands of feminist thought. The arguments over gender during the Rome Conference reveal that advocates on both sides of the political spectrum subscribed to the binary distinction between sex as biologically determined and gender as the socially constructed meaning of sex roles. Moreover, the question that arose was whether or not "gender" was meant to include sexual orientation. While for some progressive activists, sexual orientation was part of the definition of "gender" in the sense that the concept highlights the social construction of identity within a society based on the norms and expectations of what constitute appropriate or inappropriate expressions of masculinity or femininity,[123] members of the Women's Caucus have maintained that there was no consensus over the connection between gender and sexuality among progressive activists.[124]

Conservative actors began their advocacy on "gender" by insisting on the biological basis for the determination of sex. When that goal seemed no longer attainable over the course of the negotiations, conservative actors shifted in their application of feminist thought. Conservative actors' discourse that charges women's rights activists with advocating for "gender" (rather than "sex") to introduce "sexual orientation" concurrently with "gender" seemingly invokes even more radical notions of social constructionism than the sex/gender approach that was favored by the Women's Caucus and women's rights advocates. According to theories that had become more prominent in the 1990s, both sex and gender are socially or discursively constructed. These theories posited that the construction of the natural binary sexed body leads to binary gender constructions that map onto binary constructions of sex, which in turn leads to the normalization of heterosexuality.[125] Due to their potential of reinscribing heterosexuality as natural and normative, the binary system of gender versus sex had come to be seen as problematic by some feminist theorists.[126] Some contemporary analyses of how the gender perspective of the Rome Statute has been interpreted by academics indeed suggest that this newer thinking of the gender/sex binary may not have been sufficiently reflected in the Rome Statute.[127] Counterintuitively, it is conservatives that seem to have incorporated some of these tenets of a more "radical" understanding of social constructionism (relating to both gender *and* sex) into their discourse.[128] As Diane Richardson notes, "A less essentialist reading of the sexual/social split assumes a sexual which is to a greater or lesser extent modified by the social, thus allowing for the possibility that if society changed then so might (hetero)sexualities."[129] The recurring references to the idea that societal changes—brought about by the inclusion of "gender" (in this case, the inclusion of "gender" in an international legal statute)—will lead to larger social transformations may be interpreted as reflecting tenets of some more radical notions of social construction in feminist theory. In this sense, some of the conservative actors' concerns over the definition of gender comprising homosexuality/sexual orientation is not entirely inaccurate as such but reveals that conservatives have co-opted more "radical" approaches in feminist theory in their advocacy than many self-declared feminist advocates.

Conservative actors tended to claim the agreed-upon definition as a victory of religious conservative advocacy efforts. Wilkins, William Perry, and Marcus Mumford of the NGO Family Voice argued that "while the ICC definition is not perfect, advocates can no longer assert (without further explanation) that 'gender' is a mere 'social construct' unrelated to 'immutable biological differences.'"[130] At the same time, NGO Family Voice was cognizant that the phrase "within the context of society" could potentially reopen the definitional issues in the future: "Although the precise meaning of this phrase is presently unknowable, it does provide room to argue that 'gender' is not limited exclusively to biology. Accordingly, over time, the ICC definition may once again become open-textured enough to accommodate Fausto-Sterling's 'five sexes.'"[131] Despite the concessions to conservative advocates, as a whole, the definition of gender in the Rome Statute is significant as it constitutes the first definition of gender in a legally binding international treaty.

FORCED PREGNANCY AS ANTI-ABORTION DISCOURSE

Besides attempting to hinder the inclusion of the term "gender"—an issue that seeped into other gender-related provisions in the Rome Statute—conservative organizations' efforts to influence the Rome Statute largely centered on questions concerning the crimes that should fall under the court's jurisdiction. More specifically, there was "no serious opposition" to the inclusion of rape, sexual slavery, enforced prostitution, and enforced sterilization as grave breaches of Article 3 of the Geneva Convention.[132] For most delegations, the inclusion of these crimes amounted to merely "codifying the current state of international law" and as such enjoyed the consensus of most state delegations.[133] Unlike the crimes listed above, however, the proposal for the inclusion of "forced pregnancy" as a sexual crime represented a highly controversial subject. While women's rights advocates strongly argued for including the provision as a continuation of their efforts to explicitly address gender and sexual violence in an international treaty, conservative actors strongly opposed its inclusion in the Rome Statute. Looking closely at their advocacy allows us to see how conservative actors relied on definitional arguments in their rhetorical campaigns to obstruct the inclusion of "enforced pregnancy" as a core crime under the Rome Statute. By relying on definitional arguments that created strong associations between "enforced pregnancy" and "abortion," conservatives attempted to dissociate "enforced pregnancy" from genocide out of a fear that such a legal articulation would undermine a key tenet of their moralistic stance.

As a result of the conference participants' "fundamentally different philosophical, legal, and cultural approaches,"[134] the forced pregnancy provision evolved into the "most contentious" and "most emotionally charged" issue of all gender provisions.[135] The *New York Times* reported one week prior to the end of the Rome Conference that the battle over the issue of "enforced pregnancy" had developed into "one of the most glaring and painful examples of just how contentious and intractable the process of negotiating a treaty on war crimes is."[136] Originally introduced as "enforced pregnancy" by the Women's Caucus for Gender Justice, after intense debates between women's rights and conservative actors, the lawmakers agreed to the following definition of "forced pregnancy" in the Rome Statute: "the unlawful confinement of a woman forcibly made pregnant, with the intent of affecting the ethnic composition of any population or carrying out other grave violations of international law. This definition shall not in any way be interpreted as affecting national laws relating to pregnancy."[137] The inclusion of this provision makes the Rome Statute the first international treaty to expressly list and define forced pregnancy as a crime.[138]

The international community became more acutely aware of this particular crime of forced pregnancy within the context of witness testimony given before the ad hoc tribunals for Rwanda and the former Yugoslavia in the 1990s that brought to light the prevalent use of sexual violence and forced pregnancy in particular as a tool of war being fought with the aim of genocide. The cases heard before the tribunals revealed the systematic attempts to forcibly impregnate women, confine them, and to subsequently deny them the opportunity to terminate their pregnancies for the purpose of having women give birth to children of a different ethnicity, thereby changing the ethnic composition of the population. During the ICC treaty negotiations, women's rights activists and feminist legal scholars drew heavily from this testimony in their demands for incorporating a subparagraph that explicitly names crimes of gender and sexual violence in the definition of crimes subject to ICC jurisdiction. Their insistence on the inclusion of an explicit enumeration reflects how the lack of express gender provisions in international law has hindered the prosecution of such crimes.

While women's rights advocates advocated for the inclusion of the forced pregnancy provision, conservative organizations, along with some state delegates of the Arab League countries and the Vatican, strongly opposed it on the grounds that it constituted an attempt to secure the expansion of reproductive rights. Their rhetorical efforts to obstruct the inclusion of forced pregnancy in the Rome Statute centered on arguments defining the enforced pregnancy provision as women's rights advocates' attempt to either create the basis for legalization of abortion or directly create the universal right to abortion. David Zarefsky's classification of different types of definitional arguments is useful for helping to understand conservatives' argumentative strategies. Zarefsky identified several types of definitional arguments, including argument about definition, in which advocates argue over what a particular definition should be; argument from definition, which refers to arguments about the parameters of a definition; and arguments by definition, which refers to persuasive arguments in which a new definition is merely advanced without making the argumentative and definitional moves explicit.[139]

Conservatives employed the strategy of argument from definition by casting the enforced pregnancy provision as a *denial of access* to abortion as a criminal act and framing the provision as subsequently creating global access to abortion. Wilkins and Kathryn Balmforth of NGO Family Voice argued,

> The thrust of the proposed "crime" of "enforced pregnancy" was clear: Any legal regime that forbade termination of unwanted pregnancies would be guilty of "enforced pregnancy." The pro-family coalition argued that, while rape or sexual violence properly should be condemned, the status of "pregnancy" should not be criminalized. While rape or other sexual misconduct that could result in pregnancy might properly be considered criminal, it is straining the bounds of logic to assert that pregnancy (in any circumstance) is itself a "crime."[140]

The passage demonstrates how conservative organizations drew on the strategy of using argument about definition by framing the forced pregnancy provision as women's rights advocates' attempt to criminalize the "denial of access to abortion."[141] Similarly, the Holy See had argued that the crime could be seen as consisting of the "denial to terminating pregnancy."[142] Conservative discourse defined the crime of "enforced pregnancy" as the *failure to provide* abortion in the case of pregnancy as a result of rape (in the context of war or genocidal campaign to alter the composition of the population) rather than the act of making a woman pregnant through rape and forcing her to bear children from that rape. In legal terms, this argument about definition regarding the crime of "enforced pregnancy" criminalized what is considered an omission under criminal law—the failure to act—rather than the commission of an act.[143]

Conservatives' portrayal of the forced pregnancy provision thus misrepresented the nature of the sexual crime being addressed—a woman forcibly made pregnant and confined to give birth as a tool of war or as part of a genocidal campaign. Conservatives' campaign against the issue of enforced pregnancy was thus not primarily about defining crimes of sexual violence to be sanctioned by the international community when domestic states are not able or willing to do so. Instead, the debate over the definition of enforced pregnancy redirected the debate to arguments about definitions about the proper scope of international law. Conservative actors argued that defining "enforced pregnancy" as a war crime would harm states who outlawed abortion domestically if they applied their law and disallowed the termination of pregnancies that resulted from war crimes and/or genocidal violence. The Holy See argued that "retention of 'forced' or 'enforced pregnancy' raises the ironic prospect of making the enforcement of legitimate State and conventional law a 'war crime.'"[144]

This line of argument was then applied to address the definition of the proper role of international law. The Holy See argued that "the international community can now address juridically the violence which gravely harms innocent victims, but it must do so within clearly understood and accepted principles of international criminal law rather than with dangerously ambiguous constructions."[145] Conservatives advanced an argument about definition by denying "enforced pregnancy"—as a yet to be codified international crime—the status of a crime under international criminal law. According to this argument, "enforced pregnancy" as defined and envisioned by women's rights advocates was outside the purview of international criminal law and instead "can and must be prosecuted within the framework of existing legal norms."[146] By placing the provision outside the purview of international law, the argument evidenced the Holy See's resistance to social reform the provision would create in international criminal law. Drawing on this strategy of resistance to reform, they employed one of the characteristics of resistance movements identified by Warnick in the context of domestic politics. Moreover, conservatives used argument by definition to establish the parameters of international law. Arguments by definition, rather than arguments from or about definition, are a form of persuasive definition that merely stipulates, rather than provides evidence for, their conclusion.[147] Conservatives posited that existing (international) legal norms of genocide and war crimes were sufficient tools to address crimes of gender and reproductive violence and implied that it is not the proper role for international law to guide or supersede domestic laws if it violated domestic abortion laws. The definitional work of conservative actors dissociated the "enforced pregnancy" provision from core elements of the crime that were intended—through its explicit reference in the statute—to more effectively and consistently address gender and sexual violence that have proved so often to be a constitutive element of crimes of international concern. By reading the provision as criminalizing domestic states' refusal to provide abortion, the discourse allowed for the strengthening of the association of "enforced pregnancy" to a discourse about abortion rather than the prosecution of perpetrators of grave human rights violations. Redirecting the discourse over the integration of provisions to protect against sexual violence in a way that placed limiting access to abortion in the foreground of the enforced pregnancy debates, conservatives co-opted the issue for a more familiar anti-abortion discourse around which many conservative organizations have rallied in domestic policy.

Conservative advocacy also drew heavily on articulating the "enforced pregnancy" negotiations to a discourse over national sovereignty that conservatives have raised on other issues relating to the International Criminal Court (see chapter 3). This association occurred through a number of different strategies. First, conservatives' advocacy against the "enforced pregnancy" provision emphasized that women's rights advocates employed the enforced pregnancy provision as an attempt to open "a back door to allow abortion" via international law.[148] These fears over the provision globally creating a more liberal stance toward abortion "through the back door"[149] emerged as a common trope in conservatives' advocacy. For instance, the Population Research Institute, founded as part of the conservative Human Life International organization, cast the ICC's forced pregnancy provision as tantamount to legalizing abortion globally and hence as creating the possibility for an international institution to "impose 'anti-natal views'" on states' domestic law.[150]

In addition to defending nation-states' anti-abortion legislation in general, a second strategy that conservatives drew from and that permeated conservatives' advocacy against the enforced pregnancy provision was to create a strong association between international population control policies as a matter of national sovereignty and individual autonomy. As a set of programs designed to limit population growth, this area of international social policy is intricately connected to issues such as women's rights and reproductive rights and has hence received considerable attention from religious conservative organizations targeting the UN.[151] To illustrate the co-optation of forced pregnancy for a discourse about population control policies, a closer look at the rhetoric of the Population Research Institute (PRI) is instructive.

PRI combines an agenda of being "against abortion, against euthanasia, in favor of traditional marriage, against artificial contraception, and in favor of family-friendly societies and economies, all of which are essential to maintaining healthy populations."[152] A central strand of its advocacy has focused on advancing anti-population control policies by "expos[ing] human rights abuses committed in population control programs." [153] In a variation to other conservative actors who defined "enforced pregnancy" as a denial of access to abortion, PRI's advocacy drew on argument by definition to posit that the provision is a form of "population control," or more evaluative, a "coercive" population control measure. Echoing fears over the international reach of the provision, PRI warned against the provision creating an avenue toward prosecution of those "who oppose coercive population-control policies."[154] As a logical conclusion, the International Criminal Court, as the vehicle for such policies, must be rejected. Scott Weinberg, formerly PRI's director of governmental affairs, urged that the "imposition of anti-natal views on the poorest of the poor by corrupt governments or through an international criminal court, and the prosecution of individuals who heroically oppose coercion, is something which must be opposed with the utmost vigilance."[155] Weinberg cast PRI as the defender of state sovereignty committed to aiding "poor" or developing countries in their struggle against repressive measures of family planning programs imposed by global institutions. With this, PRI exemplifies a common trope of conservative resistance rhetoric identified—namely, the perception of itself as protecting traditional and moral values.[156]

PRI positioned itself as assuming a leadership role and a moral force legitimated to oppose the repressive measures imposed by family planning programs and cast PRI as the mouthpiece for developing countries that are subject to such "coercion." The language PRI employs, including "poor countries," "family planning programs," and "global institutions," invokes a discourse of development and globalization. As a result, at a quick glance, PRI's critique of population control policies could be perceived as a plausible argument against some of the more troublesome aspects of global family planning programs, for instance those instituted by the World Bank that have been made by feminist scholars in the context of critiques of globalization. [157] Upon closer examination, however, PRI's argument is more complex and includes several interconnected argumentative moves. First, similar to other conservative actors' advocacy, "enforced pregnancy" gets defined as nation-states becoming subject to prosecution if they denied access to abortion or what PRI reclassifies as "population control policies." Then, employing a slippery slope argument, PRI casts international law that recognizes "enforced pregnancy" as a crime that will necessarily impose access to abortion on nation-states and attaches the attribute "coercive" (thereby masking PRI's own categorical anti-abortion stance that is arguably "coercive" in the same way). Lastly, PRI draws on metonymy to associate the institution of the ICC with "coercive" international law that is threatening and violating nation-state sovereignty. PRI invoked the ICC, at the macro level, as a dangerous intervention in nation-states' ability to determine their laws and, at the micro level, to shore up fears over the loss of women's and families' reproductive decisions. Reassuming a moralistic stance, Weinberg simultaneously claimed the potent idiom of agency, autonomy, and individual rights for the PRI: "We're concerned about violations of the sovereign rights of nations, and the inalienable rights of women and families to determine for themselves the timing and spacing of their pregnancies."[158]

As these passages illustrate, PRI assumed for itself the voice of the world's oppressed, drawing on a common rhetorical trope of conservative discourse targeting international social policy. Buss and Herman have noted the insidiousness of the "development-friendly" rhetoric conservatives focusing on population control policies have employed:

> By arguing that population policy is irredeemably racist and imperialist, and by characterizing feminism as western and single-focused, the CR UN [Christian Right working to influence the UN] has introduced a new question into the population debate: who speaks most authentically for the third world? Using the language of racism, inequality, and the needs of the poor, the CR UN has laid claim to a progressive stance that it says is more authentic, more compassionate, and more sensitive than that of feminists.[159]

Having positioned itself as defending developing countries against imperialist population control programs—that is, international law promoting abortion rights through the "back door"—conservative organizations are competing with feminists over an important rhetorical position at transnational sites such as the UN. Moreover, by articulating "enforced pregnancy" to the issue of overpopulation and by framing the issue in a language that invokes the provision as a struggle of individual autonomy against state-sanctioned coercion, PRI ushers the "enforced pregnancy" debate into a familiar discourse of conservative talking points and obfuscates the definition of "enforced pregnancy" as a war crime or crime against humanity with genocidal intent to further PRI's moral agenda.

The rhetorical efforts of conservative advocates to influence the lawmaking process had a significant impact on the definition of the crime of forced pregnancy in the Rome Statute. The disagreements between the supporters and opponents of a forced pregnancy provision were eventually resolved by a compromise to change the provision from the original wording of "enforced pregnancy" to "forced pregnancy" and to include a definition of the crime itself in the statute.[160] Moreover, the definition of the crime included a clause that protects states from having to make domestic law correspond with the Rome Statute's provision and thus protects domestic abortion law from the reach of the ICC.[161] This addition, stating that "this definition shall not in any way be interpreted as affecting national laws relating to pregnancy,"[162] was included as a compromise to the Holy See and several Arab League countries that feared that the definition of forced pregnancy would undermine domestic abortion law.[163] The very definition of forced pregnancy is thus contradictory. On the one hand, it recognizes forced pregnancy as a punishable crime; on the other hand, by recognizing the sovereignty of domestic anti-abortion legislations, it does not establish rights for women to terminate pregnancies resulting from rape used as a tool of war. Thus, those believed to have used rape and forced pregnancy as genocidal tools for altering ethnic composition or carrying out other grave violations of international law may be tried for such crimes; however, the victims are not offered any additional medical or legal recourse beyond that which their nation of origin provides.[164] Moreover, the strategy of defining the crime of enforced pregnancy as primarily an issue of abortion and its proper locus of jurisdiction as a matter of national sovereignty rather than international law, conservatives' rhetorical strategies laid the groundwork for an understanding of international law in a way that constrains it in addressing gender, sexual, and reproductive violence as war crimes or genocide.

THE ICC AND HUMAN RIGHTS: A THREAT TO NATIONAL SOVEREIGNTY

A third gender-related issue that conservatives prominently advocated against during the ICC negotiations was the question over gender parity in the ICC. In these discussions, conservative organizations created a discourse that framed gender parity as an expression of a "radical feminist" agenda carried out through the institution of the ICC, drew on restrictive definitions of human rights, and articulated gender parity to an issue of waning national sovereignty. Further examination of the rhetorical strategies that were employed in matters of gender parity illustrates how the trope of a global feminist movement was articulated to the institution of the ICC and human rights discourses. This analysis sheds light on conservatives' larger conceptualization of the proper role of international relations and the role the ICC plays in it.

Similarly to discussions over the definition of "gender" outlined previously, the debates over the proposed inclusion of a gender parity provision ensuring a "fair representation of female and male judges" in the structural setup of the court provided the context in which conservatives' concerns about the ICC contributing to a subversion of traditional gender relations came to the fore. In the gender parity discourse, the institution of the ICC figured prominently as a force employed by women's rights advocates to shape not only the ICC but also social relations at a global level. Conservative advocacy employed unspecified claims about the ICC's dangerous potential to "change the world,"[165] or, more specifically, portrayed the ICC as a means of the global feminist movement designed to advance a feminist agenda that would expand from the realm of international law into other areas of international social policy. For instance, REAL Women of Canada claimed that the institution of the ICC is being instrumentalized as a means to endorse the very concept of "radical feminism": "Sadly, any hope of achieving an impartial, objective Court to bring the tyrants of this world to justice dissolved in the wake of actions taken by a Canadian delegation determined to turn the ICC into a powerful vehicle to promote world-wide radical feminism, including abortion and homosexual rights."[166] Elsewhere, the ICC was described in militaristic language as a tool of the global feminist movement: "While an ICC could be a wonderful tool for building true justice and freedom everywhere, in the context in which the court has been established and will be used, we fear it will be an extremely powerful weapon in the hands of the international anti-life, anti-family movement."[167]

The label "feminist" is almost exclusively accompanied by the attribute "radical." Rather than describing a particular theoretical strand of feminism within the larger feminist movement, conservative organizations employed the label to invoke existing negative connotations of feminism circulating in the larger public discourse. These kinds of discourses are prominent and resonate as feminists and feminism have a long history of being both trivialized and demonized in media representations.[168]

Conservative organizations' strategy of associating feminists with radicalism echoes a common trope employed in coverage of the *transnational* women's movement. As Lauren Danner and Susan Walsh have shown, U.S. print news coverage of the global feminist movement at international conferences has contributed to an image of feminists as extreme women, as unfeminine "misfits," or as disorganized "bickering" women in conflict.[169] These frames emphasize extremism and suggest that feminists act outside the realm of the reasonable. Such representations of "radical feminists" contribute to reproducing an already pervasively negative image of feminism and invite audiences to further discredit objectives of the transnational feminist movement as out of touch and irrational.

Moreover, conservatives' discourse of rejecting the gender parity provisions in the ICC treaty portrayed the ICC as the workings of an intellectual minority. Conceived by extremist but influential women's rights advocates, conservative organizations argued, the progressive values enshrined in the ICC treaty have little relevance for the larger public. NGO Family Voice claimed that the crimes defined under the ICC "pose a chilling potential for misuse: rather than deterring horrendous atrocities and vindicating mankind's just vengeance on mass murderers, the ICC could well become an engine for eliminating all cultural, ethnic and religious values that dare to stray from the modern convictions of the ICC's judicial elite."[170] Crafting a narrative of a gender-sensitive ICC drafted by a radical minority of women's rights activists, conservative discourse reinforced an image of feminists and the ICC poised to transform traditional gender roles and, by extension, transform "traditional-minded societies."[171] Conservative organizations employed "feminism" as synonymous with "total autonomy, personal gratification and non-accountability for women,"[172] while depicting their own members as protecting convention. This line of argument is summarized succinctly in a statement from NGO Family Voice:

> Millions of women find support, opportunity for growth and protection within the structure of the traditional family. Millions of women find distinctions between gender roles to be a workable and satisfactory mechanism for division of labor and enhancement of productivity. The fact that these women are

> typically too busy with their own full and productive lives to become involved in international politics is no justification for subjecting them to the jurisdiction of judges selected for views and ideologies that are utterly foreign to the experience and the desires of these women.[173]

Framing the drafters and judges of the ICC as a privileged minority with illegitimate and unrepresentative social, political, cultural, and religious worldviews, and by dissociating itself from that identity, NGO Family Voice constituted itself as legitimate and as supported by a broad base while simultaneously constructing mutually exclusive identities for these two groups. With this construction of a Manichean worldview of "pro-family" advocates versus the "radically feminist Women's Caucus,"[174] conservative rhetors' strategies exemplify another common feature of the conservative resistance genre. Moreover, by drawing on fear appeals in the portrayal of the reach and impact of the ICC brought about by a "radical" or "extremist" group of feminist bureaucrats, conservative organizations reproduced a common "caricature of feminism as a movement of man-hating, power-mongering ideologues who do not really represent most women anyway."[175]

While targeting specific gender-based provisions during the ICC negotiations, conservative organizations reinforced broader but related discourses of anti-cosmopolitanism that they had employed at other UN-related events prior to the Rome Conference. Their charges against the inclusion of gender-based protections in the Rome Statute thus often worked in tandem with a more general critique of a system of global governance. At the core of this anti-internationalist stance is the concern over the nation-state's loss of sovereignty to the authority of global institutions. In short, conservative organizations targeted the ICC for shifting the locus of decision making from the domestic to the international level at the expense of domestic control over the definition of social policy.

For this line of argument focusing on a critique of global governance that emerged in the context of gender parity at the court, conservative actors' advocacy once again relied on argument from definition. Specifically, conservative organizations' rhetorical discourse employed strategies limiting the definition of human rights in the context of negotiations over gender parity provisions. Specifically, their strategies involved framing gender-specific rights as particularistic concerns of the feminist movement and using argument from definition to deny reproductive rights the status of human rights. In December 1997, months before the Rome Conference convened, C-FAM alarmed its like-minded community about the attendance of feminist activists at the conference, fueling concerns of its constituents over the impact women's rights advocates could have on solidifying reproductive rights in the international legal system: "Of grave concern to the pro-family activists is the strong presence of many feminist NGOs in the preparation for the upcoming ICC conference. Feminists look longingly at the equation of 'reproductive rights' with human rights. They may not suggest it yet, but the question is obvious; will these feminist NGOs, who will be allowed to make official presentations to the conference next summer, one day push to make pro-life crimes against humanity."[176] The excerpt illustrates that conservative advocates employed argument from definition to classify reproductive rights as outside the realm of human rights. While denying reproductive rights the status of human rights, conservative organizations draw on argument from definition to define political and religious rights as "true" human rights. Wilkins of the World Family Policy Center clarified the concept of "human rights" as it has been widely understood and used by conservative organizations in the context of the ICC negotiations and beyond: "Key among fundamental human rights are the rights to democratic self-governance and self-determination, the right to maintain diverse cultural and religious practices, and even the right, if people so choose, to 'vote their conscience' and to establish governments based on religious principles."[177] Like C-FAM, Wilkins strategically champions select human rights that emphasize national sovereignty and religious freedom.

The conservative rhetors' strategic definition of "human rights" that acknowledged political and religious rights but excluded reproductive rights to be included in that definition also involved framing gender-specific rights as particularistic concerns of the feminist movement. For instance, conservative rhetors cast the human rights system as a primary channel through which feminists work to achieve their policy agenda. In her speech "Hijacking Human Rights," delivered before the World Congress of Families II, Balmforth claimed "the anti-family faction has targeted the human rights system because it is a direct path to power. The power they seek is the power to curtail the freedom of most of humanity and to do it, ironically, in the name of 'human rights.'"[178] Balmforth framed the inclusion of a certain set of rights—arguably women's rights or rights for previously underprivileged communities—as the product of an exclusive feminist discourse, alienated from the experiences and needs of the majority of society:

> The hijacking of the human rights system by the anti-family movement must be rejected by nations and people who value their families and their sovereignty. It is undemocratic when judges—who are part of a sovereign government with jurisdiction over its people—invent new rights and impose them on the majority. However, it is far, far worse and, I believe, completely illegitimate when committees of "experts"—whatever that word means—invents new rights, and attempt to force them on sovereign nations who have not and would not consent to them.[179]

The statement illustrates how religious conservative discourse over the ICC articulates the issue of what crimes should be codified into an issue of sovereignty. Rather than attending to women's rights as codifications of internationally recognized norms of conduct in conflict situations, Balmforth's discourse of human rights focuses on women in need of protection from feminist judges' ideologies. Balmforth reiterates the trope of the feminist bureaucrat that is too removed from ordinary women's lives and concerns encountered previously. Balmforth indicts the human rights system as victimizing both governments and women. Her claim illustrates how religious conservative NGOs have crafted for themselves an identity of being victimized by feminist lawmakers who have supposedly created the possibility for the ICC to criminalize what conservatives perceive as marginalized pro-life views. In doing so, questions over crimes of gender and sexual violence as the subject of internationally recognized norms of conduct in conflict situations retreat into the background while a critique of stripping rights to autonomy and sovereignty from individuals and states becomes the overriding issue. Consequently, this discourse emphasizes matters of power, force, and imposition that turn the debate over human rights primarily into a matter of self-determination both at the micro level of the family and the macro level of the nation-state.

As is evident in these materials, much of the conservative organizations' discourse related to the negotiations over a more gender-sensitive International Criminal Court expressed a broader rejection of global governance and cosmopolitanism. In this discourse, the ICC, though central to conservative organizations' discourse, served primarily as a projection surface for concerns including global feminism and its attendant notions of "anti-family" politics, specifically the recognition of homosexuality and the decline of traditional gender roles. That is, their rejection of the ICC serves as a touchstone for conservative social policy arguments that restrict the rights of women, children, and the LGBTQ+ community. Rather than posing any unique and specific concerns, international institutions like the ICC are thought of as having a dangerous power to influence social policy, a realm that conservatives perceive to be the prerogative of domestic legislation. Wilkins's plea for domestic social policy making is revealing in its allusions to where international institutions are thought to interfere. He argues that "these human rights and individual freedoms are best served if countries preserve their sovereignty and the right to govern their own domestic affairs. An autonomous international court will not be responsive to the culturally diverse peoples of the world. Moreover, governance by judges is inherently undemocratic. The power to determine the contours of domestic policies must be kept close to home—close to the people being governed."[180] Wilkins constructs the nation-state as the only viable locus for human rights legislation. According to this discourse, a social policy agenda set by international institutions like the ICC would lead to a universalization of social values that would override national or cultural differences—that is, social policy would not be subject to local religious influence, guidance, or control. What we see in this discourse is an attack on international institutions and legal frameworks waged in the name of national sovereignty, the nation-state, and "traditional" notions of the social order.

CONCLUDING REMARKS

As a whole, the outcome of the advocacy efforts to influence the Rome Statute with regard to the inclusion of a gender perspective is ambiguous. In many respects, the treaty functions as a landmark development for the recognition of gender in international law. The United Nations special rapporteur on violence against women, Radhika Coomaraswamy, noted optimistically that "the Rome Statute's gender provisions are an encouraging example of how the development of the international women's rights movement is positively impacting international human rights and humanitarian law despite the strong influence of conservative political forces. . . . While much remains to be done, the progress made since 1994 is extraordinary."[181] At the same time, conservative NGOs participating in the ICC treaty negotiations, with the backing of several state delegations, have left their imprint on a long-fought-over international treaty like the Rome Statute. While their advocacy was not successful on all fronts, their efforts attest to the growing influence of a movement comprised of relatively few actors. This is no small feat. The Rome Statute is quite unlike many other UN conference documents that function primarily as manifestations of international values and aspiration. Instead, an international treaty like the Rome Statute serves as the basic legal foundation for the International Criminal Court, which will play a profound role in the ways in which we remember human rights, war crimes, and the responsibility for such crimes, and it will consequently have a significant impact on the community that emerges from that memory. In this sense, conservative organizations have influenced and will continue to alter the way in which human rights, women's rights, and crimes of sexual and gender violence will be adjudicated and remembered at a global scale.

Whereas the Women's Caucus saw the creation of the ICC as an opportunity to shape an international criminal court and international criminal law according to universal human rights, including women's rights, conservative organizations' discourses promoted parochial understandings of rights in which the nation-state is summoned as a safeguard against the intrusion of universal rights. At the core of conservative organizations' rhetoric of social maintenance lies the attempt to preserve a traditionalist view of the social order. In the context of the ICC negotiations, their discourse focused on a rather narrowly defined realm of issues: the potential expansive interpretation of the term "gender," the right to abortion under the stipulation of forced pregnancy, and ideological bias of the court and its staff. With their focus on those issues, conservatives have employed a rhetorical discourse that obfuscated questions over how to establish safeguards to protect women from war crimes and crimes against humanity that had not been sufficiently accounted for in existing international law. Moreover, given that the ICC is designed to bring to trial and hold accountable perpetrators who have committed some of the most heinous crimes on a mass scale, conservative discourse that emphasized the illegitimacy of expanding rights for marginalized communities is disproportionate to the *benefits* that a system of legal protection from gender and sexual violence would provide for many. By rejecting, obstructing the inclusion, and defining core categories of crimes as outside the human rights system, the discourse of conservative state and nonstate actors involved in negotiations over gender provisions in the Rome Statute suggests that women and marginalized communities do not deserve legal protection from such crimes if it comes at the cost of challenging national sovereignty, regardless of the nature of the crimes committed. As such, their discourse implicitly discounts the experience of thousands of victims who are specifically targeted for their gender in times of conflict.

Having succeeded in eliminating crucial provisions relating to sexual and gender violence and potentially limiting the scope of the definition of the term "gender," conservative NGOs' transnational advocacy successes demonstrate that their rhetorical prowess is not to be denied. Their campaign demonstrated that they pose a significant challenge to the future of cosmopolitan rights and memory, even in political arenas that are generally thought of as the territory of advocates embracing progressive visions of the future. Since international legal institutions, such as the ICC, form the basis for a set of shared values and norms that function as a type of transnational memory for (gender) justice, the discursive strategies of conservative organizations demand our collective attention and reflection. For, when the ICC sets out to do its work, the possibility of achieving some form of justice, gender or otherwise, where inhumanity has reigned hangs in the balance.

NOTES

1. Kelly D. Askin, "Prosecuting Wartime Rape and Other Gender-Related Crimes under International Law: Extraordinary Advances, Enduring Obstacles," *Berkeley Journal of International Law* 21, no. 2 (2003): 295. Askin's article offers a historical account of the recognition of sexual violence in international law.
2. Cate Steains, "Gender Issues," in *The International Criminal Court: The Making of the Rome Statute—Issues, Negotiations, Results*, edited by Roy S. Lee (The Hague, Netherlands: Kluwer Law International, 1999), 361–62.
3. Askin, "Prosecuting Wartime Rape," 304.
4. Ibid., 295.
5. Kristen Boon, "Rape and Forced Pregnancy under the ICC Statute: Human Dignity, Autonomy, and Consent," *Columbia Human Rights Law Review* 32, Rev. 625 (2001): 628.

6. United Nations Diplomatic Conference of Plenipotentiaries on the Establishment of an International Criminal Court, *Rome Statute of the International Criminal Court* (July 15–17, 1998), UN document A/CONF. 183/9, https://www.icc-cpi.int/nr/rdonlyres/ea9aeff7-5752-4f84-be94-0a655eb30e16/0/rome_statute_english.pdf. Article 8(2)(b)(xxii). The four Geneva Conventions of 1949 and Protocol 1 of 1977 include definitions of what constitutes a grave breach. While the various conventions provide varying specific details, what the definitions of these texts share is the definition of "grave breaches" as involving "willful killing, torture or inhuman treatment, including biological experiments, willfully causing great suffering or serious injury to body or health, and extensive destruction and appropriation of property, not justified by military necessity and carried out unlawfully and wantonly." See *Geneva Convention (I) for the Amelioration of the Condition of the Wounded and Sick in Armed Forces in the Field*, adopted August 12, 1949, Article 50; *Convention (II) for the Amelioration of the Condition of Wounded, Sick and Shipwrecked Members of Armed Forces at Sea*, adopted August 12, 1949, Article 51. See also *Convention (III) Relative to the Treatment of Prisoners of War*, adopted August 12, 1949, Article 130 as well as *Geneva Convention (IV) Relative to the Protection of Civilian Persons in Time of War*, adopted August 12, 1949, Article 147. The texts of the Geneva Conventions are available at the website of the International Committee of the Red Cross (ICRC) at http://www.icrc.org/ihl.nsf/CONVPRES?OpenView.

7. See for instance Carrie Crenshaw, "The 'Protection' of 'Woman': A History of Legal Attitudes towards Women's Workplace Freedoms," *Quarterly Journal of Speech* 81, no. 1 (February 1995): 63–82; Katie L. Gibson, "Judicial Rhetoric and Women's 'Place': The United States Supreme Court's Darwinian Defense of Separate Spheres," *Western Journal of Communication* 71, no. 2 (April 2007): 159–75; Angela G. Ray and Cindy Koenig Richards, "Inventing Citizens, Imagining Gender Justice: The Suffrage Rhetoric of Virginia and Francis Minor," *Quarterly Journal of Speech* 93, no. 4 (November 2007): 357–402.

8. Carrie Crenshaw, "The Normality of Man and Female Otherness: (Re)Producing Patriarchal Lines of Argument in the Law and the News," *Argumentation and Advocacy* 32, no. 4 (1996): 183.

9. Katie L. Gibson, "United States v. Virginia: A Rhetorical Battle between Progress and Preservation," *Women's Studies in Communication* 29, no. 2 (2006): 136.

10. Ibid., 135.

11. Doris Buss, "Robes, Relics, and Rights: The Vatican and the Beijing Conference on Women," *Social and Legal Studies* 7, no. 3 (1998): 342.

12. Barbara Warnick, "The Rhetoric of Conservative Resistance," *The Southern Speech Communication Journal* 42, no. 3 (Spring 1977): 273. See also Barbara Warnick, "Conservative Resistance Revisited—A Reply to Medhurst," *Western Journal of Speech Communication* 46, no. 4 (1982): 376–78.

13. Barbara Warnick, "Conservative Resistance," 273.

14. Ibid., 268–70.

15. Ibid., 272.

16. For similar discussions of conservative advocacy in the context of women's rights, see Martha Solomon, "The 'Positive Woman's' Journey: A Mythic Analysis of the Rhetoric of STOP ERA," *Quarterly Journal of Speech* 65, no. 3 (1979): 262–74; Martha Solomon, "The Rhetoric of STOP ERA: Fatalistic Reaffirmation," *Southern Speech Communication Journal*, 44 (1978): 42–59; and Sonja K. Foss, "Equal Rights Amendment Controversy: Two Worlds in Conflict," *Quarterly Journal of Speech* 65, no. 3 (October 1979): 275–88.

17. The rise of the influence of conservative forces in the context of women's rights, especially in the context of the Beijing Conference in 1995 and its successor conference Beijing +5 in 2000 has been noted over the last two decades, but sustained analyses of their advocacy is still sparse. Recent scholarship in this area includes Elizabeth Jay Friedman, "Gendering the Agenda: The Impact of the Transnational Women's Rights Movement at the UN Conferences of the 1990s," *Women's Studies International Forum* 26, no. 4 (2003); Buss, "Robes, Relics, and Rights: The Vatican and the Beijing Conference on Women"; Didi Herman, "Globalism's 'Siren Song': The United Nations and International Law in Christian Right Thought and Prophecy," *The Sociological Review* 49, no. 1 (2001); Jennifer S. Butler, *Born Again: The Christian Right Globalized* (Ann Arbor, MI: Pluto, 2006).

18. Doris Buss and Didi Herman, *Globalizing Family Values: The Christian Right in International Politics* (Minneapolis: University of Minnesota Press, 2003), xv.
19. Ibid.
20. Marlies Glasius, *The International Criminal Court: A Global Civil Society Achievement* (Routledge Advances in International Relations and Global Politics) (New York: Routledge, 2005), 78. See also Margaret E. Keck and Kathryn Sikkink, *Activists Beyond Borders: Advocacy Networks in International Politics* (Ithaca, NY: Cornell University Press, 1998), 189.
21. Louise Chappell, "Contesting Women's Rights: Charting the Emergence of a Transnational Conservative Patriarchal Network," *Global Society* 20, no. 4 (2006): 495.
22. Ibid., 496. Similarly, children's rights have emerged as an area in which conservative forces have been particularly active.
23. Glasius, *The International Criminal Court: A Global Civil Society Achievement*, 78.
24. Ibid., 78.
25. Pam Spees, "Women's Advocacy in the Creation of the International Criminal Court: Changing the Landscape of Justice and Power," *Signs: Journal of Women in Culture and Society* 28, no. 4 (2003): 1237.
26. Helen Durham, "Women and Civil Society: NGOs and International Criminal Law," in *Women and International Human Rights Law*, edited by Kelly D. Askin and Dorean M. Koenig (Ardsley, NY: Transnational, 1999), 824. See also Lois West, "The United Nations Women's Conferences and Feminist Politics," in *Gender Politics in Global Governance*, edited by Mary K. Meyer and Elisabeth Prügl (Lanham, MD: Rowman and Littlefield, 1999), 178.
27. Friedman, "Gendering the Agenda: The Impact of the Transnational Women's Rights Movement at the UN Conferences of the 1990s," 317.
28. Ibid.
29. West, "The United Nations Women's Conferences and Feminist Politics," 184.
30. Steains, "Gender Issues," 360.
31. Glasius, *The International Criminal Court: A Global Civil Society Achievement*, 79.
32. In addition to these larger outcomes, the ICTR ruled in the landmark Akayesu judgment that rape is a form of genocide. The ICTY ruled in two cases that rape can be a form of torture.
33. Louise Chappell, *The Politics of Gender Justice at the International Criminal Court: Legacies and Legitimacy* (New York: Oxford University Press, 2016), 37–38.
34. Vasuki Nesiah, "Missionary Zeal for a Secular Mission: Bringing Gender to Transitional Justice and Redemption Feminism," in *Feminist Perspectives on Contemporary International Law: Between Resistance and Compliance?*, edited by Sari Kouvo and Zoe Pearson (Portland, OR: Hart, 2011), 142.
35. Ibid.
36. Hilary Charlesworth and C. M. Chinkin, *The Boundaries of International Law: A Feminist Analysis, Melland Schill Studies in International Law* (Manchester: Manchester University Press, 2000), 308.
37. Afrin Zakia and Amy Schwartz, "A Human Rights Instrument That Works for Women: The ICC as a Tool for Gender Justice," in *Defending Our Dreams: Global Feminist Voices for a New Generation*, edited by Shamillah Wilson et al. (New York: Zed Books, 2005), 151.
38. Ibid., 153.
39. Judith Gardam, "Women and the Law of Armed Conflict: Why the Silence?," *The International and Comparative Law Quarterly* 46, no. 1 (1997): 65.
40. Ibid., 66.
41. Alda Facio, "A Word (or Two) about Gender," *ICC Monitor*, no. 6 (November 1997): 10.
42. Marsha A. Freeman, "International Institutions and Gendered Justice," *Journal of International Affairs* 52, no. 2 (1999): 529.
43. Glasius, *The International Criminal Court: A Global Civil Society Achievement*, 79.
44. Rhonda Copelon, "Gender Crimes as War Crimes: Integrating Crimes against Women into International Criminal Law," *McGill Law Journal* 46, no. 1 (2000): 234.
45. Ibid., 221. Article 27 of *Geneva Convention (IV)* reads: "Women shall be especially protected against any attack on their honour, in particular against rape, enforced prostitution, or any form of indecent assault."

46. Rhonda Copelon, "Surfacing Gender: Re-Engraving Crimes against Women in Humanitarian Law," *Hastings Women's Law Journal* 5, no. 2 (1994): 248–49. See also Louise Chappell, "Women, Gender and International Institutions: Exploring New Opportunities at the International Criminal Court," *Policy and Society* 22, no. 1 (2006): 7.
47. Copelon, "Gender Crimes as War Crimes," 221.
48. Copelon, "Surfacing Gender," 249.
49. Ibid.
50. Ibid., 250–53.
51. Steains, "Gender Issues," 362.
52. Ibid., 361–62.
53. Barbara Bedont and Katherine Hall Martinez, "Ending Impunity for Gender Crimes under the International Criminal Law," *The Brown Journal of World Affairs* 6, no. 1 (1999): 71.
54. For a discussion of the crime of rape under the ICTY and ICTR, see Mark Ellis, "Breaking the Silence: Rape as an International Crime," *Case Western Reserve Journal of International Law* 38, no. 2–3 (2006–2007).
55. Bedont and Martinez, "Ending Impunity," 71.
56. See Copelon, "Gender Crimes as War Crimes." See also Chappell, "Women, Gender and International Institutions," 10. Steains notes that the Office of the Prosecutor in the ICTY was able to overcome certain obstacles with regard to the rape provisions laid out in the statute "through creative interpretation of the Statute in a manner reflecting development of the law." Steains, "Gender Issues," 362–63.
57. Copelon, "Gender Crimes as War Crimes," 233.
58. Chappell, *The Politics of Gender Justice*, 41.
59. Glasius, *The International Criminal Court,* 89–90.
60. Ibid., 85.
61. Afrin and Schwartz, "A Human Rights Instrument," 154.
62. United Nations Diplomatic Conference of Plenipotentiaries on the Establishment of an International Criminal Court, *Rome Statute of the International Criminal Court.* See Articles 7(1)(g) referring to crimes against humanity; 8(2)(b)(xxii) referring to war crimes in international armed conflict; (8)(2)(e)(vi) referring to war crimes in noninternational armed conflict.
63. Copelon, "Gender Crimes as War Crimes," 234.
64. Boon, "Rape and Forced Pregnancy," 630.
65. Copelon, "Gender Crimes as War Crimes," 234.
66. Freeman, "International Institutions and Gendered Justice," 529.
67. Boon, "Rape and Forced Pregnancy," 630–31.
68. It should be noted here that while the gender provisions included in the Rome Statute have generally been considered a positive development, some feminist legal scholars have argued that these provisions do not go far enough. For instance, Charlesworth and Chinkin have pointed to the continuing challenges women's rights face in international law. They argue that despite the fact that advancements were made in several ICC provisions, the construction of women still emphasizes their reproductive identities. See Charlesworth and Chinkin, *The Boundaries of International Law: A Feminist Analysis*, 334.
69. Copelon, "Gender Crimes as War Crimes," 239.
70. Facio, "A Word (or Two) about Gender," 10.
71. See for instance R. W. Connell, "Masculinities and Globalization," *Men and Masculinities* 1, no. 1 (July 1998): 3–23.
72. The CICC started with 25 members in 1995 and has grown to include more than 2,500 legal and civil society organizations. Coalition for the International Criminal Court, "An Overview of the ICC and the CICC," CICC, 2019, http://www.iccnow.org/documents/CICCFS-ICC_Overview_current.pdf.
73. Glasius, *The International Criminal Court*, 80. Glasius notes that although the Women's Caucus initially evolved out of the coalition, the coalition strongly supported the Women's Caucus's campaign and made it a member of the coalition's steering committee.
74. Ibid., 86.
75. Ibid., 80–81.

76. Valerie Oosterveld, "The Definition of 'Gender' in the Rome Statute of the International Criminal Court: A Step Forward or Back for International Criminal Justice?," *Harvard Human Rights Journal* 18 (2005): 55.
77. Copelon, "Gender Crimes as War Crimes," 234.
78. *ICC Monitor*, "Core Principles of the Women's Caucus," *ICC Monitor*, no. 8 (June 1998): 13.
79. Women's Caucus for Gender Justice, "About the Caucus," Women's Caucus for Gender Justice, https://web.archive.org/web/20090108203343/http://www.iccwomen.addr.com/caucus/about.htm.
80. Durham, "Women and Civil Society," 829.
81. Chappell, "Women, Gender and International Institutions," 14.
82. Women's Caucus for Gender Justice, "No More Compromises: Bring the Issues of Justice to a Vote," The Advocacy Project (July 13, 1998), https://web.archive.org/web/20081119150159/http://www.advocacynet.org/resource/375. Advocacy Project (AP) provided detailed coverage of the negotiations and texts distributed. "AP was established in June 1998 at the request of the NGO Coalition for an International Criminal Court (CICC). The Coalition asked for help in covering the Rome conference to draft an ICC statute and AP produced an online newsletter (On the Record) from the conference which was sent out to CICC members worldwide. AP continued on a project-by-project basis until July 2001, when the project acquired 501c3 (nonprofit) status, registered in Washington, DC." See Advocacy Project, "Frequently Asked Questions," Advocacy Project, https://web.archive.org/web/20130629014544/http://advocacynet.org/page/questions.
83. Laura McLeod, Rachel Johnson, Sheila Meintjes, Alice Brown, and Valerie Oosterveld, "Gendering Processes of Institutional Design: Activists at the Negotiating Table," *International Feminist Journal of Politics* 16, no. 2 (2014): 359.
84. The Women's Caucus for Gender Justice dissolved in March 2003 after the drafting of ICC-related documents were completed. Since 2004, the women's rights organization Women's Initiatives for Gender Justice has been monitoring and advocating gender justice in the work of the ICC. See http://www.iccwomen.org/.
85. McLeod et al., "Gendering Processes," 358.
86. Chappell, *The Politics of Gender Justice*, 43.
87. Afrin and Schwartz, "A Human Rights Instrument," 152.
88. Jennifer Butler, "For Faith and Family: Christian Right Advocacy at the United Nations," *Public Eye* 14, no. 2–3 (2000): 10.
89. Louise Chappell, "Women's Rights and Opposition: The Politics of Gender at the International Criminal Court," in *Gendering the Nation-State: Canadian and Comparative Perspectives*, edited by Yasmeen Abu-Laban (Vancouver: University of British Columbia Press, 2008), 147.
90. Buss and Herman, *Globalizing Family Values: The Christian Right in International Politics*, xxi. Buss and Herman prefer the label Christian Right (or CR)—even though the movement does comprise non-Christian advocates and delegations—because the movement remains spearheaded by the Christian Right and is largely based on the worldviews of the Christian Right. See Buss and Herman, *Globalizing Family Values: The Christian Right in International Politics*, xiv.
91. The Vatican, or Holy See, is the only state that is not a member of the United Nations and therefore does not have the power to vote in UN decisions. It does, however, have permanent observer status at the UN. This analysis mainly focuses on the rhetoric employed by conservative NGOs. These NGOs did, however, find a relatively powerful ally in the Vatican that converged with many of their positions. For a more detailed discussion of the rhetorical discourse the Vatican employed at the UN Beijing Conference in 1995, see Buss, "Robes, Relics, and Rights: The Vatican and the Beijing Conference on Women." For a discussion of the rhetorical discourses employed by the Vatican on issues of sexual reproduction and sexuality during the UN-sponsored International Conference on Population and Development in Cairo in 1994, see Palena R. Neale, "The Bodies of Christ as International Bodies: The Holy See, Wom(b)an and the Cairo Conference," *Review of International Studies* 24, no. 1 (1998): 101–18.

92. Copelon, "Gender Crimes as War Crimes: Integrating Crimes against Women into International Criminal Law," 233. See also Glasius, *The International Criminal Court: A Global Civil Society Achievement*, 82–83.

93. C-FAM, "About C-FAM," https://c-fam.org/about-us/. C-FAM's mission is to "publish" and "[promote] scholarship related to the proposition that the UN and other international institutions harm a true understanding of international law and in the process undermine the family and other institutions man requires for a just, free and happy life." C-FAM was established in response to the organization Human Life International having been denied accreditation for consultative status with the UN Economic and Social Council in the 1990s. See Butler, "For Faith and Family," 4.

94. World Family Policy Center, "About the World Family Policy Center," World Family Policy Center, https://web.archive.org/web/20160820050512/http://www.law2.byu.edu/wfpc/about.htm.

95. Jennifer Butler, "300 Religious Right Participants Attend Beijing Prepcom: The Religious Right at the Beijing+5 Prepcom," Global Policy Forum Policy Paper, no. 16 (June 2000), Global Policy Forum, http://www.globalpolicy.org/ngos/ngo-un/access/2000/beij5-2.htm.

96. Austin Ruse, "Toward a Permanent United Nations Pro-Family Bloc. Remarks to the World Congress of Families II," World Congress of Families (1999), https://web.archive.org/web/20160128001948/http://worldcongress.org/wcf2_spkrs/wcf2_ruse.htm. Another tactic Ruse cited as particularly successful was the publication and distribution of a daily newspaper (rather than fliers) during the conference.

97. Richard Wilkins, William Perry, and Marcus Mumford, "The United Nations Diplomatic Conference of Plenipotentiaries on the Establishment of an International Criminal Court," World Family Policy Center (1998), http://web.archive.org/web/20040628194703/http://www.worldfamilypolicycenter.org/wfpc/About_the_WFPC/papers/ICC_Report.html#N_5_. See also "'The Two Sexes' in the Various Versions of the Draft Statute: The Need for Conformity," position paper prepared by the David M. Kennedy Center for International Studies. Position paper in Wilkins, Perry, and Mumford, "The United Nations Diplomatic Conference of Plenipotentiaries on the Establishment of an International Criminal Court," Appendix F.

98. Butler, *Born Again*, 51.

99. Friedman, "Gendering the Agenda: The Impact of the Transnational Women's Rights Movement at the UN Conferences of the 1990s," 326.

100. Butler, "300 Religious Right Participants." Butler describes additional tactics employed by the conservative NGOs used at the Beijing +5 PrepCom Conference in 2000, including the specific targeting of youth and health caucuses; intimidation tactics, such as wearing large red buttons with the words "motherhood" or "family" written on them; and refusing to make their own materials openly available.

101. Anick Druelle, "Right-Wing Anti-Feminist Groups at the United Nations," Institut de recherches et d'études féministes, Université du Québec à Montréal, Centre de documentation sur l'éducation des adultes et la condition féminine (CDÉACF) (May 2000), p. 10–16,https://web.archive.org/web/20100509022101/http://netfemmes.cdeacf.ca/documents/Anti-Feminist%20Groups-USLetter.pdf.

102. Chappell, *The Politics of Gender Justice*, 41

103. Ibid., 44.

104. Oosterveld, "The Definition of 'Gender,'" 57.

105. Governments that opposed the inclusion of the term "gender" included "Qatar, Libya, Egypt, Venezuela, Guatemala (but flexible), United Arab Emirates, Saudi Arabia, Kuwait, Syria, Turkey, Sudan, Bahrain, Iran, Yemen, Brunei, and Oman." See Bedont and Martinez, "Ending Impunity," 81.

106. McLeod et al, "Gendering Processes," 358. Oosterveld, "Constructive Ambiguity," 565.

107. Oosterveld, "Constructive Ambiguity," 567.

108. Chappell, *The Politics of Gender Justice*, 45.

109. REAL Women of Canada, "Canada Courts Disaster with World Court," Newsletter XVI, no. 10 (July–August 1998), REAL Women of Canada, http://web.archive.org/web/20020822011010/http://www.realwomenca.com/html/newsletter/1998_July_Aug/Article_1.html.

110. Austin Ruse, "Feminists Refuse to Define Their 'Gender Agenda' for the International Criminal Court," C-FAM (June 26, 1998), https://c-fam.org/feminists-refuse-to-define-their-gender-agenda-for-the-international-criminal-court/.

111. Glasius, *The International Criminal Court: A Global Civil Society Achievement*, 90.

112. See for instance a paper delivered by Farooq Hassan at the World Congress in 2004 in which he employs a language invoking deviance and evil when referring to "certain lifestyles that violate all accepted canons of decent living." Specifically, Hassan voiced concerns over ICC provisions posing a threat to "traditionalists of Family values" in the context of gender persecution. With the ICC having jurisdiction over persecution looming large, he painted apocalyptic scenarios in which "teaching or forceful dissemination of the moral and realistic evils about the actions of the sexual deviant community of a group may be sufficient for having infringed the law relating to 'prosecution.'" See Farooq Hassan, "International Criminal Court: Family Related Issues." Synopsis of Paper Presented at the World Congress of Families III Mexico City, Family and the UN Mexico, World Congress of Families (March 30, 2004) http://web.archive.org/web/20150925164331/http://worldcongress.org/wcf3_spkrs/wcf3_hassan.htm

113. REAL Women of Canada, "What's the Argument for 'Gender Justice?'" Position paper prepared by the David M. Kennedy Center for International Studies. Position paper in Wilkins, Perry, and Mumford, "The United Nations Diplomatic Conference of Plenipotentiaries on the Establishment of an International Criminal Court," Appendix G.

114. Steains, "Gender Issues," 372–73.

115. Women's Caucus for Gender Justice, "Clarification of Term 'Gender,'" Women's Caucus for Gender Justice, http://web.archive.org/web/20150409235023/http://www.iccwomen.org/wigjdraft1/Archives/oldWCGJ/resources/gender.htm.

116. Steains, "Gender Issues," 373. For a comparison to the use of "gender" in other UN documents, see Oosterveld, "The Definition of 'Gender' in the Rome Statute of the International Criminal Court: A Step Forward or Back for International Criminal Justice?," 66–71.

117. Steains, "Gender Issues," 371.

118. There is some debate among scholars about whether the definition adopted in the Rome Statute emphasizes social construction rather than biological essentialism.

119. United Nations Diplomatic Conference of Plenipotentiaries on the Establishment of an International Criminal Court, *Rome Statute of the International Criminal Court*, Article 7(3).

120. Oosterveld, "The Definition of 'Gender' in the Rome Statute of the International Criminal Court: A Step Forward or Back for International Criminal Justice?," 65.

121. Steains, "Gender Issues," 374–75.

122. Oosterveld, "The Definition of 'Gender' in the Rome Statute of the International Criminal Court: A Step Forward or Back for International Criminal Justice?," 57. Oosterveld has provided an account of how gender has been interpreted and applied in the ICC context more recently. See Oosterveld, "Constructive Ambiguity," 568–74.

123. For a more detailed discussion of more or less probable interpretations of the term "gender" in the Rome Statute and the term's implications for the recognition of sexual orientation and transgendered individuals, particularly in the context of gender-based persecution, see Oosterveld, "The Definition of 'Gender' in the Rome Statute of the International Criminal Court: A Step Forward or Back for International Criminal Justice?," 78.

124. Oosterveld, "Constructive Ambiguity," 570. Oosterveld cites a personal conversation with Steains, a participant of the negotiations, on that issue.

125. Doris Buss, "Finding the Homosexual in Women's Rights: The Christian Right in International Politics," *International Feminist Journal of Politics* 6, no. 2 (2004): 271. Oosterveld, "Constructive Ambiguity," 569.

126. Representative works include Judith Butler, *Gender Trouble: Feminism and the Subversion of Identity* (New York: Routledge, 1990), 1–46.

127. Oosterveld, "Constructive Ambiguity," 568–71.

128. Buss, "Finding the Homosexual," 271.

129. Diane Richardson, *Rethinking Sexuality* (London: Sage, 2000), 31. Cited in Buss, "Finding the Homosexual," 271.

130. Wilkins, Perry, and Mumford, "The United Nations Diplomatic Conference of Plenipotentiaries on the Establishment of an International Criminal Court."

131. Ibid.
132. Steains, "Gender Issues," 365.
133. Ibid.
134. Boon, "Rape and Forced Pregnancy," 637.
135. Steains, "Gender Issues," 365–69.
136. Alessandra Stanley, "Semantics Stalls Pact Labeling Rape a War Crime," *New York Times*, July 9, 1998, p. A3.
137. United Nations Diplomatic Conference of Plenipotentiaries on the Establishment of an International Criminal Court, *Rome Statute of the International Criminal Court*, Article 7(2)(f).
138. Boon, "Rape and Forced Pregnancy," 656.
139. David Zarefsky, "Definitions," in *Argument in a Time of Change: Definitions, Frameworks, and Critiques*, edited by J. F. Klumpp (Annandale, VA: National Communication Association, 1998), 1–11. For recent discussions of definitional arguments in international policy-making, see Carol Winkler, "Encroachments on State Sovereignty: The Argumentation Strategies of the George W. Bush Administration," *Argumentation* 22, no. 4 (2008): 473–88.
140. Richard G. Wilkins and Kathryn O. Balmforth, "The International Criminal Court, Human Rights and the Family," in *Fifty Years after the Declaration: The United Nations' Record on Human Rights*, edited by Teresa Wagner and Leslie Carbone (Lanham, MD: University Press of America, 2001), 101–02.
141. Patrick Goodenough, "Pro-Family Groups Worry about Effects of International Court," Cybercast News Service (July 7, 2008), https://www.cnsnews.com/news/article/pro-family-groups-worry-about-effects-international-court. The article was published on cns.news.com (Cybercast News Service), a conservative news site that is a subsidiary of the conservative Media Research Center. See also the response to Goodenough's article by Anne Heindel, deputy convener, American Non-Governmental Organizations Coalition for the ICC, http://web.archive.org/web/20170116084510/http://www.amicc.org/docs/Feb11_02.pdf.
142. Holy See, "Intervention of the Holy See Diplomatic Conference of Plenipotentiaries on the Establishment of an International Criminal Court." Working Group on War Crimes, 1998. https://www.catholicculture.org/culture/library/view.cfm?recnum=459.
143. See Bedont and Martinez, "Ending Impunity," 74.
144. Holy See, "Intervention."
145. Ibid.
146. Ibid.
147. Zarefsky, "Definitions," 5.
148. *Terraviva*, "Africa Pushing Gender Concerns," Inter Press Service News Agency (June 30, 1998), https://www.legal-tools.org/doc/b051dd/pdf/.
149. Goodenough, "Pro-Family Groups Worry about Effects of International Court."
150. Ibid.
151. This issue has become a principal issue for religious conservatives as the issue is able to subsume a number of related causes, including women's rights, abortion, and questions regarding the waning sovereignty of the nation-state. For a more detailed discussion of how population control figures in conservative organizations' rhetoric at the international level, see Buss and Herman, *Globalizing Family Values: The Christian Right in International Politics*, chapter 4.
152. Population Research Institute, "PRI FAQ's (Frequently Asked Questions)."
153. The Population Research Institute, https://www.pop.org/simple/who-we-are/.
154. Goodenough, "Pro-Family Groups Worry about Effects of International Court."
155. Ibid.
156. Warnick, "Conservative Resistance," 268–70.
157. These family planning programs have been criticized for the implicitly operating assumptions about women's reproductive roles, for the focus on medical interventions rather than larger structural changes, and for the potential instrumentalization of such programs for political purposes. For an insightful discussion of the assumptions operating in transnational family planning programs and women's resistance to such policies in the case of World Bank-funded programs in Indonesia, see Leslie K. Dwyer, "Spectacular Sexuality: Nationalism, Develop-

ment and the Politics of Family Planning in Indonesia," in *Gender Ironies of Nationalism: Sexing the Nation*, edited by Tamar Mayer (London: Routledge, 2000).

158. Goodenough, "Pro-Family Groups Worry about Effects of International Court."

159. Buss and Herman, *Globalizing Family Values: The Christian Right in International Politics*, 77.

160. Originally introduced as "enforced pregnancy" by the Women's Caucus for Gender Justice, the Holy See made an alternative proposal during the PrepCom prior to the Rome Conference in April 1998 in which it labeled the issue as a provision on "forcible impregnation." Supporters of the "enforced pregnancy" provision, however, dismissed the Holy See's proposal as unacceptable because the phrasing was too narrow in that it referred only to the act of making a woman pregnant rather than the act of confining a woman—who had forcibly been made pregnant—during pregnancy in an attempt to make her carry the baby to full term (Steains, "Gender Issues," 366). Steains further notes that some countries argued that the inclusion of the "forced pregnancy" provision was altogether unnecessary because it would be covered in the Rome Statute under the crimes of rape and unlawful detention. See Steains, "Gender Issues," 367.

161. Boon, "Rape and Forced Pregnancy," 665–66.

162. United Nations Diplomatic Conference of Plenipotentiaries on the Establishment of an International Criminal Court, *Rome Statute of the International Criminal Court*, Article 7 (2)(f).

163. Boon notes that the clause is "meant to ensure that forced pregnancy will not be used to supplant anti-abortion laws or endanger Catholic hospitals that refuse to provide abortions to women who become pregnant through rape." See Boon, "Rape and Forced Pregnancy," 659.

164. Despite this clause that limits the reach of the ICC provision on forced pregnancy, the clause may be less restrictive than it may seem. Boon notes that even in countries with strict abortion laws on the books, these laws are not always categorically applied. See Boon, "Rape and Forced Pregnancy," 666.

165. "International Criminal Court Approved," *LifeSiteNews* (July 19, 1998), https://www.lifesitenews.com/news/international-criminal-court-approved-despite-major-victories-grave-concern.

166. REAL Women of Canada, "Canada Courts Disaster with World Court."

167. *Interim*, "ICC: Promise of Justice or Threat of Tyranny?" (August 1998), http://www.theinterim.com/politics/icc-promise-of-justice-or-threat-of-tyranny/.

168. See Rebecca Ann Lind and Colleen Salo, "The Framing of Feminists and Feminism in News and Public Affairs Programs in U.S. Electronic Media," *Journal of Communication* 52, no. 1 (2002). See also Solomon "The 'Positive Woman's' Journey," 270, for a similar analysis in the context of the Equal Rights Amendment.

169. See Lauren Danner and Susan Walsh, "'Radical' Feminists and 'Bickering' Women: Backlash in U.S. Media Coverage of the United Nations Fourth World Conference on Women," *Critical Studies in Mass Communication* 16, no. 1 (1999).

170. NGO Family Voice, "The ICC's 'New International Crimes': A Call for Caution." Position paper in Richard Wilkins, William Perry, and Marcus Mumford, "The United Nations Diplomatic Conference of Plenipotentiaries on the Establishment of an International Criminal Court," Appendix D.

171. Austin Ruse, "International Criminal Court Debate Begins in Rome: Feminists Face First Setback," C-FAM, June 19, 1998.

172. NGO Family Voice, "Judges and Prosecutors Must Be Professionally Qualified and Ideologically Neutral." Position paper in Richard Wilkins, William Perry, and Marcus Mumford, "The United Nations Diplomatic Conference of Plenipotentiaries on the Establishment of an International Criminal Court," Appendix D. World Family Policy Center, 1998.

173. Ibid.

174. Austin Ruse, "Protection for Families Dropped from New International Criminal Court," C-FAM (December 17, 1999), https://c-fam.org/friday_fax/protection-for-families-dropped-from-new-international-criminal-court/.

175. Sara Diamond, *Not by Politics Alone: The Enduring Influence of the Christian Right* (New York: Guilford, 1998), 127.

176. Austin Ruse, "International Criminal Court Takes a Giant Step in UN General Assembly," C-FAM (December 19, 1997), https://c-fam.org/friday_fax/international-criminal-court-takes-a-giant-step-in-un-general-assembly-john-paul-ii-accepts-diplomatic-credentials-from-new-american-ambassador-2/.

177. Richard Wilkins, "Doing the Right Thing: The International Criminal Court and Social Engineering," Address to the Second Annual World Family Policy Forum, Provo, Utah, (July 11, 2000), in *Proceedings of the World Family Policy Forum 2000*, http://web.archive.org/web/20051102032734/http://www.worldfamilypolicy.org/New%20Page/Forum/2000/WFPF2000.pdf.

178. Kathryn O. Balmforth, "Hijacking Human Rights. Remarks to the World Congress of Families II," World Congress of Families (November 17, 1999), https://web.archive.org/web/20160213211454/http://www.worldcongress.org/wcf2_spkrs/wcf2_balmforth.htm.

179. Ibid.

180. Wilkins, "Doing the Right Thing: The International Criminal Court and Social Engineering," 93.

181. United Nations Special Rapporteur on Violence against Women, *Integration of the Human Rights of Women and the Gender Perspective: Violence against Women*, Report E/CN.4/2003/75/Add.1, UN Economic and Social Council (February 27, 2003), https://documents-dds-ny.un.org/doc/UNDOC/GEN/G03/113/04/PDF/G0311304.pdf?OpenElement (p. 10). Cited in Amnesty International, "The International Criminal Court Fact Sheet 7: Ensuring Justice for Women," Amnesty International (April 12, 2005), http://web.archive.org/web/20081117121403/http://amnesty.org/en/library/asset/IOR40/006/2005/en/dom-IOR400062005en.pdf.

Chapter Six

Sovereignty/Cosmopolitanism Revisited

The U.S. Military and the International Criminal Court

The International Criminal Court (ICC)—as an international legal institution that emerged out of the international human rights system and that was designed to bring to justice perpetrators of war crimes, crimes against humanity, and genocide—figures as a key site for rhetorical inquiry into the study of transnational memory discourses. Specifically, the study examined the kinds of political subjectivities and rhetorical communities produced by discourses about the signing/unsigning of the court's treaty (chapter 3), advocacy promoting ratification and public support of the ICC (chapter 4), and advocacy over the court's design with specific emphasis on gender provisions (chapter 5). My analysis of these discourses provides insight into the rhetoric of advocacy campaigns that seek to produce more cosmopolitanism and those that attempt to resist it.

The analysis is informed by Levy and Sznaider's claim about the emergence of cosmopolitan memory against which I juxtaposed four moments in the development of the ICC that document not only the emergence or existence but also the resistance to such transnational memory discourses at various levels. With this approach I do not intend to discount their position. Rather, I intend to add to Levy and Sznaider's analysis by illustrating that, while the formation of transnational memories is very real at certain sites and locations, we are simultaneously witnessing a stronghold of forces counteracting the formation of transnational or cosmopolitan subjectivities.

The primary means through which the development of transnational subjectivities and transnational memory is being contested is by domesticating discourses of international justice. The political subjectivities produced by the discourses around the ICC include the citizen of the globe and the citizen of the nation-state. To varying degrees, advocates supporting and critiquing the ICC invite us to see ourselves as subjects primarily associated with the nation-state rather than as "global" or cosmopolitan citizens. Thus, rather than merely producing a transnational memory culture, the discourses discussed here serve as representative examples of how the formation of transnational memory is being hindered by social advocates both for and against cosmopolitan values.

Chapter 3 analyzed U.S. policy discourse over the creation of and opposition to the ICC with a focus on the rhetorical dimension of "unsigning" the Rome Statute of the International Criminal Court. The formation of transnational memory, embodied by an international juridical institution that would hold accountable some of the worst perpetrators of crimes against humanity, was impeded by a discourse that frames such concerns primarily as an issue of nation-state sovereignty. What emerged in this discourse over the ICC was an idiosyncratic "American internationalism" manifest in the unprecedented act of unsigning an international treaty. Here, resistance to the formation of a "genuine" international community was hindered by a rhetoric of strengthening national identification and claims to national sovereignty in dealing with international crime. The act of unsigning the Rome Statute, I argued, has both domestic and international consequences for the character and possibility of cosmopolitanism or internationalism as well as consequences for how U.S. citizens are invited to think of their role with respect to the international community, global responsibility, and justice.

Chapter 4 illustrated similarly how the memory work of transnational NGOs laboring to produce more cosmopolitan communities only marginally relies on the rhetoric of transnational memory and instead explicitly appeals to audiences of the nation-state. While organizations like Citizens for Global Solutions embrace and support cosmopolitan values, their persuasive strategies draw mostly on a rhetoric that invokes national interests that would be met with an institution like the ICC. As such, an important opportunity to educate and inform about cosmopolitan values was missed in these discourses. The opportunities are missed when advocates of cosmopolitanism forgo deeper and more genuine communication of their goals for pragmatic communication and tangible accomplishments.

Finally, chapter 5 analyzed advocates' intervention in the development of the Rome Statute that provides the legal foundation for the court. The chapter examined both the successes of the Women's Caucus for Gender Justice that culminated in the unprecedented inclusion of a series of gender provisions in an international treaty and the conservative backlash that their success sparked. This analysis of the rhetoric of conservative state actors and NGOs operating at the UN level illustrated how advocates rendered the legal institution into a public memorial that will influence how women's rights, and gender and sexual violence in particular, can and will be remembered. Moreover, the chapter illustrated how the strengthening of a cosmopolitan community is resisted by conservative anti–women's rights advocates in the codification process of international justice. By focusing on the ICC as a framework for legal and nonlegal memory production, we see how the ICC serves an important role in codifying which human rights and violations thereof will be remembered and which will be overlooked. Conversely, social conservative NGO rhetoric influences decisions about how women the world over are invited to remember themselves as bodies that matter. In this instance, the creation of an international community driven by cosmopolitan principles was obstructed by conservative forces that employ a rhetoric of social maintenance with a particularistic notion of human rights in an attempt to protect national sovereignty. In such discourses, international justice is being "domesticated" by rejecting a commitment to the ICC. Taken together, the book illustrates that there is a conspicuous absence of explicit attempts to create an international community in discourses shaping the ICC, and the formation of an international community is resisted primarily through a rhetoric of domestication.

THE PATH FROM KNOWLEDGE TO UNDERSTANDING AND SUPPORT: A MILITARY POSTSCRIPT

Throughout this manuscript we have borne witness to several advocacy attempts to produce or restrict cosmopolitanism through managing the resources of the rhetoric of public memory on national and international scales. Many of the advocates were quite effective. On the one hand were the progressive advocates. The Women's Caucus for Gender Justice helped codify women's rights into international law for the first time. Citizens for Global Solutions developed a rhetorical program for disseminating a positive view of the ICC to U.S. audiences. On the other hand were the conservative anticosmopolitan activists. The Bush administration made the unprecedented move of *unsigning* an international treaty, indicating a systematic effort to frame national sovereignty as a "new American internationalism" while turning away from the extant international community. A group of affiliated religious-conservative anti–women's rights organizations successfully coalesced to undermine the efficacy of the inclusion of gender provisions in the Rome Statute. These cases show how cosmopolitan advocacy is not conducted in a vacuum.

The news is not, however, that there are advocates sitting on both sides of an issue with some negotiation needed in order to move forward as a genuine international community. As seen in this project, those opposing the type of cosmopolitanism that the ICC represents do not appear to desire some form of open political dialogue. By weighing the court down with their own devil issues of abortion and homosexuality, women's rights and status, and threats to national sovereignty and identity, such advocates play on fear and promote ignorance to the faithful. They evoke an illusion of knowledge to protect their ability to maintain control over populations at the level of the nation-state.

It doesn't have to be this way. The Stimson Center published a report in 2006 that provides documentary evidence that a little knowledge can go a long way to changing the attitudinal tides toward cosmopolitanism and the ICC. Entitled *On Trial: The US Military and the International Criminal Court*, the report suggests that the military has recently shown a larger degree of acceptance regarding the ICC. Traditionally, the military—concerned with issues of national security and thus potentially more directly affected by the ICC—strongly opposed the idea of an international criminal court. The premise of the ninety-two-page report is the context of U.S. forces in Iraq and Afghanistan and the fact that, once the ICC would take on its first cases, "an improved understanding of the military concerns" regarding the ICC is "increasingly urgent."[1] Accordingly, the study conducted by Future of Peace Operations Program codirectors Victoria K. Holt and Elisabeth Dallas sought to identify U.S. military views regarding the ICC. Based on interviews with U.S. military personnel, politicians, and policy makers and a workshop on the ICC held by the center in January 2006, the study suggested that the military's long-established staunch opposition to the ICC has been waning.

The rationale for the project stemmed from a realization that, while there has been a "vigorous" debate over the ICC "among policymakers and non-governmental organizations, academics and legal scholars" in the United States,[2] the views of military personnel have been "largely absent from this public discussion." As a result, the views of military personnel "are not well-known or well-understood" even though they "are directly relevant and important to US policy considerations."[3] In the context of the ICC having begun its hearings and U.S. armed forces active "in places such as Afghanistan and Iraq where insurgents do not heed international humanitarian law or the laws of war,"[4] the authors conclude that there are "important reasons for a fresh assessment of US interests as it relates to the Court, today, as a non-state party."[5] The larger goal of the study was then to "move beyond the debate over whether or not to join the International Criminal Court" and "to identify current thinking within military circles and common interests—if not agreements—among experts and non-experts, critics and advocates of the Court."[6] The message that emerged from the year-long project was the imperative for the United States "to move from studied distancing to constructive engagement with the Court."[7]

Holt and Dallas point to a number of important findings in their study. Most of the military interviewees reported that their knowledge of the ICC was largely based on public sources as opposed to specific courses or professional briefings on the court. Most interviewees had little more than "rudimentary knowledge" about the court, and their views of the ICC were mostly "based on a minimal understanding of how it was designed to operate." Moreover, the study showed a direct correlation between knowledge, understanding, and support of the court as it demonstrated that "those most familiar with the Court were generally the least fearful of its implications for the US military and its operations."[8] These findings suggest that an informed citizenry, including citizen-soldiers, might be all that is necessary to develop a more cosmopolitan attitude among U.S. Americans. This conclusion is further supported by the finding that few of those who were interviewed "argued against the need for criminal accountability for those who commit systematic and grave violations of international humanitarian law."[9] The implication is that if the knowledge gap were closed, U.S. audiences would more or less automatically become more open-minded about the ICC, given that, on the whole, "deterring and punishing" crimes such as genocide and crimes against humanity were "seen as laudatory."[10] Given this generally favorable disposition of military personnel to the larger aims of the ICC once they are better informed, it is imperative that we develop an understanding of the rhetoric of conservative actors who continue to shape public and expert opinion by providing easily digestible factually incorrect information.

The Stimson Report identifies several main recommendations for a stronger support of the ICC among military personnel, including that military anxiety about the court must be reduced, which is likely to be accomplished by developing "educational tools" for military leaders. Furthermore, the report urged the United States to participate in the preparatory meetings prior to the 2009 Review Conference for the ICC. A trope repeatedly invoked is the notion that there is a necessity to move forward from the current state of immobility by establishing a new kind of attitude toward the ICC. For instance, the report talks about offering "a way ahead"[11] and of opening up "ways forward for the United States in developing a relationship with the Court." Similarly, the report attests to the existence of a "a genuine interest within military circles to develop a way forward to protect US interests and to relate to the Court better," suggesting that the current U.S. view is considered an impasse and a situation in need of rectification.[12]

The suggested step for the United States to propel itself out of this state of anti-ICC inertia is to gain "a better understanding of what concerns are central to US military personnel."[13] As we have seen in the context of Marc Grossman's speech and Bolton's call for an "American internationalism," as well as in the promotional material offered by Citizens for Global Solutions, these issues are approached in terms of how the ICC relates to U.S. interests.

The justification to change U.S. attitudes toward the ICC is offered via a recourse to national interests. Here we find again, perhaps not surprisingly, that for this particular audience, the creation of a stronger international community plays an insignificant role. The report concludes that the United States should engage in further defining the court by acting according to its own interests by "leaving aside the polarized domestic and international political debates about the US joining the Court, the United States should consider what is in its best interests today, and what role it should play in forming the Court."[14] Thus, the consensus among both supporters and critics of the ICC that "American interests would be best served by participating in discussions about the Court's development"[15] could be read as primarily motivated by "develop[ing] a way forward to protect US interests."[16]

The type of attitudinal shift detailed by the Stimson Report might seem bittersweet. Once again we see support for international law predicated on the support of national interests. Nonetheless, I am concluding with this report as indicative of good news. There are two key elements of this case that make it so. First, the specific audience addressed by this report was U.S. military personnel, a group with a mission of protecting U.S. national interest through the show or implementation of force. That this group of people who one might reasonably expect to be most resistant showed significant attitudinal change after becoming slightly better informed is good news for progressive advocates who wish to shape a more cosmopolitan world. Second, even though the attitudinal shift was expressed in conjunction with the desire to protect U.S. interests, the new position required a more genuine expression of internationalism. While not necessarily coded in a desire for cosmopolitanism, the position expressed by the military personnel acknowledged the interdependency of commitments to state interests and the international community. Rather than a retreat to the paradigm of the nation-state, this position advertises the necessity for cosmopolitan ideas and practices.

The topical focus of this book centers largely on the NGO advocacy work done in the context of the Bush administration's staunch opposition to the ICC. While the attitude of the Obama administration toward the ICC was guided by a somewhat more cooperative stance, with the rise of a new populist conservative nationalism and the Trump administration the clock has been turned back as evidenced by Bolton's and President Trump's remarks on the ICC in September 2018. These demonstrated a continuation of the United States' stance uttered two decades ago—that is, to actively resist the institution.[17] With regard to gender, the outcome has also been ambiguous. While the rhetorical discourses around the ICC and gender are no longer making headlines, the effects of conservative actors' influence are real. Oosterveld notes that the Holy See continues to use a narrow interpretation that it had advocated for.[18] On the other hand, a 2014 policy paper issued by the Office of the Prosecutor suggests that the prosecutor has applied and encourages a more inclusive interpretation of gender at the level of policy in its practice. Still, Oosterveld warns, it is unclear whether judges follow that interpretation.[19] The ambiguity in the definition of the Rome Statute allows for diverging interpretations and thus rests with those enacting it to fill it with meaning. With regard to forced pregnancy, some scholars have been skeptical about its ability to be prosecuted due to its particular definition that requires prosecutors to prove how harm done to individuals was part of a widespread or systematic attack.[20]

Since the start of its operation in 2002, the court has investigated eleven situations and has indicted forty-four individuals.[21] In July 2018, the international community celebrated its twenty-year anniversary of the signing of the Rome Statute. As an instrument of international justice, the ICC offers, in the words of William Pace, convener of the Coalition for the International Criminal Court, "'root-cause' relief across the entire peace and security spectrum—prevention, deterrence, cessation of conflict, peace-building and reconciliation."[22] There is some evidence to suggest that the existence of the ICC has affected how state leaders act.

OBSTACLES TO A COSMOPOLITAN POLITICAL IMAGINARY

While the Stimson Report suggests that basic knowledge is the key to attitudinal shifts promoting at least a rudimentary set of cosmopolitan values and commitments, advocates for transnational cooperation and transnational women's rights advocates are challenged by conservative groups who are devoting significant amounts of time and energy to derailing such reforms. Specifically, this has shown how several conservative organizations have claimed an influential position in framing political subjectivities at the international level. These groups have created their own idiosyncratic understanding of internationalism that is fundamentally at odds with cosmopolitan values. The stated purpose of this conservative rhetoric is to undermine the possibility of a more solidarist, cosmopolitan community. Since it was the rhetorical discourse of a relatively small group of actors that left its mark on important international treaties like the Rome Statute of the International Criminal Court with consequences beyond borders, the significance of their rhetoric that strictly upholds the nation-state paradigm should not be underestimated.

This focus on national interests and nation-state sovereignty in the conservative rhetoric detailed in this project is deeply troubling. This is not only because of the immediate material consequences their advocacy campaigns have for advances made in international law over the last sixty years. Their rhetorical discourses undermine the very goals of an institution like the ICC—that is, to punish and hold accountable those who violate standards of humanity. Moreover, as we saw in the discourse about the inclusion of gender and sexual violence in the Rome Statute, given that international law ought to be integrated into national law, conservative rhetoric at the UN level serves the status quo and sets a precedent by limiting the recognition of the relationship between gender and violence in domestic and international contexts.

But the focus on the nation-state paradigm is also profoundly disconcerting because it evidences a lack or failure of imagination. What is emerging in many of the discourses discussed in this study is a resistance to cosmopolitan ideals. Even those groups seeking to promote cosmopolitanism resign to a belief that direct appeals to cosmopolitanism would not have much clout. But the problem seems to lie deeper—that is, at the very level of the imagination. Cosmopolitanism as an ethic or an ideal to aspire to is given neither the recognition it deserves nor the status of a principle needed to create a more just world order. The tendency to resort to the nation-state as an easily harnessed rhetorical trope rather than fostering cosmopolitan values in public discourse figures as the most significant obstacle standing in the way of imagining ourselves as part of an emerging cosmopolitan community. As such, the failure to *discourse about* cosmopolitanism and a cosmopolitan community represents a failure to *imagine* it as both a real and desirable community. In sum, what each of these discourses offers is a memory of what it means to be a citizen at the trans/national level. This analysis of the rhetoric of advocates for and against cosmopolitan reforms in the development of the ICC shows how each attempt to influence an attitude toward the ICC and invites audiences to remember themselves in different ways. Both the target and consequence of such advocacy is public memory both in and beyond borders.

NOTES

1. Henry L. Stimson Center, "Project on International Humanitarian Law and the US Armed Services: Understanding US Military Concerns Regarding the International Criminal Court," Henry L. Stimson Center (2006), https://web.archive.org/web/20081127185224/ http://www.stimson.org/fopo/pdf/Descript_FOPO_ICC_Project.pdf.
2. Ibid.
3. Ibid.
4. Victoria K. Holt and Elisabeth W. Dallas, "On Trial: The US Military and the International Criminal Court," Henry L. Stimson Center (March 2006), https://www.stimson.org/sites/default/files/file-attachments/US_Military_and_the_ICC_FINAL_website_1.pdf.
5. Ibid.
6. Ibid.
7. Ibid.
8. Holt and Dallas, "On Trial: The US Military and the International Criminal Court," 32.
9. Ibid.
10. Ibid.
11. Ibid., 69.

12. Ibid.
13. Ibid., 13.
14. Ibid., 60.
15. Ibid., 8.
16. Ibid.
17. John Bolton, "Protecting American Constitutionalism and Sovereignty from International Threats," Speech presented to the Federalist Society in September 2018. Video and searchable transcript are available at https://www.c-span.org/video/?451213-1/national-security-adviser-john-bolton-addresses-federalist-society.
18. Valerie Oosterveld, "Constructive Ambiguity and the Meaning of 'Gender' for the International Criminal Court," *International Feminist Journal of Politics* 16, no. 4 (2014): 572.
19. Oosterveld, "Constructive Ambiguity," 575.
20. Milan Markovic, "Vessels of Reproduction: Forced Pregnancy and the ICC," *Michigan State Journal of International Law* 16 (2007): 456–58. For a discussion of the implications of the gender-related provisions in the ICC during its first decade in existence, see Fatou Bensouda, "Gender Justice and the ICC: Progress and Reflections," *International Feminist Journal of Politics* 16, no. 4 (2014): 540–41.
21. International Criminal Court (ICC), "Situations under Investigation," https://www.icc-cpi.int/pages/situations.aspx.
22. William Pace, "The Rome Statute System: Future Perspectives and Challenges," Statement on the occasion of the 10 Years' Celebration of the Adoption of the Rome Statute for the Coalition for the International Criminal Court, The Hague, CICC (July 3, 2008), https://asp.icc-cpi.int/iccdocs/asp_docs/ASP7/10th/ICC-ASP-10thAnni-Pace-ENG.pdf

Bibliography

Aceves, William J. "The President's Roman Holiday." *San Diego Union-Tribune*, September 5, 2002.

Advocacy Project. "The Advocacy Project: Supporting Advocates for Peace." Accessed May 20, 2019. http://www.advocacynet.org.

Advocacy Project. "Frequently Asked Questions." Accessed May 20, 2019. https://web.archive.org/web/20130629014544/http://advocacynet.org/page/questions.

Afrin, Zakia, and Amy Schwartz. "A Human Rights Instrument That Works for Women: The ICC as a Tool for Gender Justice." In *Defending Our Dreams: Global Feminist Voices for a New Generation*, edited by Shamillah Wilson, Anasuya Sengupta, Kristy Evans, and Association for Women's Rights in Development, 150–66. New York: Zed Books, 2005.

Alexander, Jeffrey C. "On the Social Construction of Moral Universals: The 'Holocaust' from War Crime to Trauma Drama." *European Journal of Social Theory* 5, no. 1 (2002): 5–85.

American Non-Governmental Organizations Coalition for the International Criminal Court (AMICC). "American NGO for the International Criminal Court: Advocating US Participation in the ICC." Accessed May 20, 2019. http://www.amicc.org/.

American Non-Governmental Organizations Coalition for the International Criminal Court (AMICC). "The International Criminal Court: A Case for Conservatives." AMICC, August 30, 2005. https://web.archive.org/web/20100710035539/http://www.amicc.org/docs/Case%20for%20Conservatives.pdf.

Amnesty International. "The International Criminal Court Fact Sheet 7: Ensuring Justice for Women." Amnesty International, April 12, 2005. http://web.archive.org/web/20081117121403/http://amnesty.org/en/library/asset/IOR40/006/2005/en/dom-IOR400062005en.pdf.

Anderson, Benedict. *Imagined Communities: Reflections on the Origin and Spread of Nationalism*, revised and extended edition. London: Verso, 1991.

Appadurai, Arjun. "Disjuncture and Difference in the Global Cultural Economy." *Theory, Culture and Society* 7 (1990): 295–310.

Askin, Kelly D. "Prosecuting Wartime Rape and Other Gender-Related Crimes under International Law: Extraordinary Advances, Enduring Obstacles." *Berkeley Journal of International Law* 21, no. 2 (2003): 288–349.

Balibar, Etienne. "Propositions on Citizenship." *Ethics* 98, no. 4 (July 1988): 723–30.

Balmforth, Kathryn O. "Hijacking Human Rights." Remarks to the World Congress of Families II. World Congress of Families, November 17, 1999. https://web.archive.org/web/20160213211454/http://www.worldcongress.org/wcf2_spkrs/wcf2_balmforth.htm.

Bass, Gary Jonathan. *Stay the Hand of Vengeance: Politics of War Crimes Tribunals*. Princeton, NJ: Princeton University Press, 2000.

Bassiouni, M. Cherif. "Policy Perspective Favoring the Establishment of the International Criminal Court." *Journal of International Affairs* 52, no. 2 (Spring 1999): 795–810.

Beck, Ulrich. "Wie Versöhnung möglich werden kann." *Die Zeit*, July 16, 2003.

Bedont, Barbara, and Katherine Hall Martinez. "Ending Impunity for Gender Crimes under the International Criminal Law." *The Brown Journal of World Affairs* 6, no. 1 (1999): 65–85.

Benedetti, Fanny, and John L. Washburn. "Drafting the International Criminal Court Treaty: Two Years to Rome and an Afterword on the Rome Diplomatic Conference." *Global Governance* 5, no. 1 (1999): 1–37.

Benson, Thomas W. "Rhetoric as a Way of Being." In *American Rhetoric: Context and Criticism*, 293–322. Carbondale: Southern Illinois University Press, 1989.

Bensouda, Fatou. "Gender Justice and the ICC: Progress and Reflections." *International Feminist Journal of Politics* 16, no. 4 (2014): 538–42.

Black, Edwin. "The Second Persona." *Quarterly Journal of Speech* 56, no. 2 (1970): 109–19.

Blair, Carole, Marsha S. Jeppeson, and Enrico Pucci Jr. "Public Memorializing in Postmodernity: The Vietnam Veterans Memorial as Prototype." *Quarterly Journal of Speech* 77, no. 3 (1991): 263–88.

Bloomfield, Lincoln. "Bloomfield Defends U.S. Course on International Criminal Court: Lincoln Bloomfield Remarks in New York to Parliamentarians for Global Action." Bureau of International Information Programs, U.S. Department of State, September 17, 2003.https://web.archive.org/web/20061001231803/http://usinfo.state.gov/xarchives/display.html?p=washfile-english&y=2003&m=September&x=20030917172946samohtj0.8693201.

Bloxham, Donald. "Genocide on Trial: Law and Collective Memory." In *The Nuremberg Trials: International Criminal Law since 1945*, edited by Herbert R. Reginbogin and Christoph J. M. Safferling, 74–84. Munich: K. G. Saur Verlag, 2006.

Bodnar, John E. *Remaking America: Public Memory, Commemoration, and Patriotism in the Twentieth Century*. Princeton, NJ: Princeton University Press, 1991.

Bolton, John R. "International Criminal Court: Letter to UN Secretary General Kofi Annan." U.S. Department of State, May 6, 2002. https://web.archive.org/web/20040630100111/https://www.state.gov/r/pa/prs/ps/2002/9968.htm.

Bolton, John R. "Protecting American Constitutionalism and Sovereignty from International Threats." Speech presented to the Federalist Society, New York, September 2018. Video and searchable transcript are available at https://www.c-span.org/video/?451213-1/national-security-adviser-john-bolton-addresses-federalist-society.

Bolton, John R. "The Risks and Weaknesses of the International Criminal Court from America's Perspective." *Law and Contemporary Problems* 64, no. 1 (2001): 167–80.

Bolton, John R. "Unsign That Treaty." *Washington Post*, January 4, 2001, p. A21.

Boon, Kristen. "Rape and Forced Pregnancy under the ICC Statute: Human Dignity, Autonomy, and Consent." *Columbia Human Rights Law Review* 32, Rev. 625 (2001): 624–75.

Broomhall, Bruce. *International Justice and the International Criminal Court: Between Sovereignty and the Rule of Law, Oxford Monographs in International Law*. New York: Oxford University Press, 2003.

Browne, Stephen H. "Reading Public Memory in Daniel Webster's Plymouth Rock Oration." *Western Journal of Communication* 57, no. 4 (1993): 464–77.

Browne, Stephen H. "Reading, Rhetoric, and the Texture of Public Memory." *Quarterly Journal of Speech* 81, no. 2 (1995): 237–50.

Browne, Stephen H. "Remembering Crispus Attucks: Race, Rhetoric, and the Politics of Commemoration." *Quarterly Journal of Speech* 85, no. 2 (1999): 169–87.

Burroughs, John, and Jacqueline Cabasso. "Confronting the Nuclear-Armed States in International Negotiating Forums: Lessons for NGOs." *International Negotiation* 4, no. 3 (1999).

Bush, George W. "A Distinctly American Internationalism." Speech delivered at the Ronald Reagan Presidential Library, Simi Valley, California, November 19, 1999.

Buss, Doris. "Finding the Homosexual in Women's Rights: The Christian Right in International Politics." *International Feminist Journal of Politics* 6, no. 2 (2004): 257–84.

Buss, Doris. "Robes, Relics, and Rights: The Vatican and the Beijing Conference on Women." *Social and Legal Studies* 7, no. 3 (1998): 339–63.

Buss, Doris, and Didi Herman. *Globalizing Family Values: The Christian Right in International Politics*. Minneapolis: University of Minnesota Press, 2003.

Butler, Jennifer. "300 Religious Right Participants Attend Beijing Prepcom: The Religious Right at the Beijing+5 Prepcom." Global Policy Forum Policy Paper no. 16, June 2000. http://www.globalpolicy.org/ngos/ngo-un/access/2000/beij5-2.htm.

Butler, Jennifer S. *Born Again: The Christian Right Globalized* (Ann Arbor, MI: Pluto, 2006).

Butler, Jennifer. "For Faith and Family: Christian Right Advocacy at the United Nations." *Public Eye* 14, no. 2–3 (2000): 1–17.

Butler, Judith. *Gender Trouble: Feminism and the Subversion of Identity*. New York: Routledge, 1990.

Calhoun, Craig. "Imagining Solidarity: Cosmopolitanism, Constitutional Patriotism, and the Public Sphere." *Public Culture* 14, no. 1 (2002): 147–71.

Casey, Edward S. *Remembering: A Phenomenological Study*. Bloomington: Indiana University Press, 1987.

Catholic Family and Human Rights Institute (C-FAM). "Center for Family and Human Rights." Accessed May 21, 2019. http://www.c-fam.org.

Catholic Family and Human Rights Institute (C-FAM). "About C-FAM." Accessed May 21, 2019. https://c-fam.org/about-us/.

Chandler, David. *Constructing Global Civil Society: Morality and Power in International Relations*. New York: Palgrave Macmillan, 2004.

Chappell, Louise. "Contesting Women's Rights: Charting the Emergence of a Transnational Conservative Patriarchal Network." *Global Society* 20, no. 4 (2006): 491–519.

Chappell, Louise. *The Politics of Gender Justice at the International Criminal Court: Legacies and Legitimacy*. New York: Oxford University Press, 2016.

Chappell, Louise. "Women, Gender and International Institutions: Exploring New Opportunities at the International Criminal Court." *Policy and Society* 22, no. 1 (2006): 1–25.

Chappell, Louise. "Women's Rights and Opposition: The Politics of Gender at the International Criminal Court." In *Gendering the Nation-State: Canadian and Comparative Perspectives*, edited by Yasmeen Abu-Laban, 139–64. Vancouver: University of British Columbia Press, 2008.

Charland, Maurice. "Constitutive Rhetoric: The Case of the Peuple Québécois." *Quarterly Journal of Speech* 73, no. 2 (1987): 133–50.

Charlesworth, Hilary, and C. M. Chinkin. *The Boundaries of International Law: A Feminist Analysis, Melland Schill Studies in International Law*. Manchester: Manchester University Press, 2000.

Cheah, Pheng. "Cosmopolitanism." *Theory, Culture and Society* 23, no. 2–3 (2006): 486–96.

Citizens for Global Solutions. " . . . And Justice for All: How to Talk about the International Criminal Court in the U.S." Citizens for Global Solutions, Washington, DC, 2005. https://web.archive.org/web/20071027094527/http://oldsite.globalsolutions.org/programs/law_justice/icc/resources/FINAL_ICC_Comm_Guide.pdf.

Citizens for Global Solutions. "International Law and Justice." Citizens for Global Solutions, October 13, 2008. https://web.archive.org/web/20081013054733/http://oldsite.globalsolutions.org/programs/law_justice/icc/icc_home.html.

Citizens for Global Solutions. "Vision and Mission." Citizens for Global Solutions, October 7, 2008. https://web.archive.org/web/20081007050159/http://oldsite.globalsolutions.org/who/vision_mission.html.

Citizens for Global Solutions. "Working Together, Finding Solutions." Citizens for Global Solutions, July 15, 2010. https://web.archive.org/web/20100715061347/http://globalsolutions.org/issues/Overview

Coalition for the International Criminal Court (CICC). "Global Justice for Atrocities." Accessed May 21, 2019. http://www.iccnow.org/.

Coalition for the International Criminal Court (CICC). "ICC Update." CICC, Special Edition, July 17, 2002. http://www.iccnow.org/documents/17July2002Update.pdf.

Coalition for the International Criminal Court (CICC). "Core Principles of the Women's Caucus." *ICC Monitor*, no. 8 (June 1998): 13.

Coalition for the International Criminal Court (CICC). "An Overview of the ICC and the CICC." CICC, 2019. http://www.iccnow.org/documents/CICCFS-ICC_Overview_current.pdf.

Coalition for the International Criminal Court (CICC). "Overview of the United States' Opposition to the International Criminal Court." CICC, December 2006. http://www.iccnow.org/documents/CICCFS_US_Opposition_to_ICC_11Dec06_final.pdf.

Connell, R. W. "Masculinities and Globalization." *Men and Masculinities* 1, no. 1 (July 1998): 3–23.

Conway, Brian. "Local Conditions, Global Environment and Transnational Discourses in Memory Work: The Case of Bloody Sunday (1972)." *Memory Studies* 1, no. 2 (2008): 187–209.

Copelon, Rhonda. "Gender Crimes as War Crimes: Integrating Crimes against Women into International Criminal Law." *McGill Law Journal* 46, no. 1 (2000): 217–40.

Copelon, Rhonda. "Surfacing Gender: Re-Engraving Crimes against Women in Humanitarian Law." *Hastings Women's Law Journal* 5, no. 2 (1994): 243–66.

Copple, Gideon, and Amitis Khojasteh. "The Normality of Man and Female Otherness: (Re)Producing Patriarchal Lines of Argument in the Law and the News." *Argumentation and Advocacy* 32, no. 4 (1996): 170–84.

Crenshaw, Carrie. "The Normality of Man and Female Otherness: (Re)Producing Patriarchal Lines of Argument in the Law and the News." *Argumentation and Advocacy* 32, no. 4 (1996): 183.

Crenshaw, Carrie. "The 'Protection' of 'Woman': A History of Legal Attitudes toward Women's Workplace Freedom." *Quarterly Journal of Speech* 81, no. 1 (February 1995): 63–82.

Cubilié, Anne. *Women Witnessing Terror: Testimony and the Cultural Politics of Human Rights*. New York: Fordham University Press, 2005.

Danner, Lauren, and Susan Walsh. "'Radical' Feminists and 'Bickering' Women: Backlash in U.S. Media Coverage of the United Nations Fourth World Conference on Women." *Critical Studies in Mass Communication* 16, no. 1 (1999): 63–84.

David M. Kennedy Center for International Studies. "'The Two Sexes' in the Various Versions of the Draft Statute: The Need for Conformity." Position paper in Richard Wilkins, William Perry, and Marcus Mumford, "The United Nations Diplomatic Conference of Plenipotentiaries on the Establishment of an International Criminal Court," Appendix F. World Family Policy Center, 1998. http://web.archive.org/web/20040628194703/http:/www.worldfamilypolicycenter.org/wfpc/About_the_WFPC/papers/ICC_Report.html#AppendixF.

Davenport, David. "The New Diplomacy." *Policy Review*, no. 116 (December 2002–January 2003): 17–30.

DeChaine, D. Robert. *Global Humanitarianism: NGOs and the Crafting of Community*. Lanham, MD: Lexington Books, 2005.

Derrida, Jacques. "Declarations of Independence." *New Political Science* 7, no. 1 (1986): 7–15.

Diamond, Sara. *Not by Politics Alone: The Enduring Influence of the Christian Right*. New York: Guilford, 1998.

Douglas, Lawrence. "History and Memory in the Courtroom: Reflections on Perpetrator Trials." In *The Nuremberg Trials: International Criminal Law since 1945*, edited by Herbert R. Reginbogin and Christoph J. M. Safferling, 95–105. Munich: K. G. Saur Verlag, 2006.

Douglas, Lawrence. *The Memory of Judgment: Making Law and History in the Trials of the Holocaust*. New Haven, CT: Yale University Press, 2001.

Druelle, Anick. "Right-Wing Anti-Feminist Groups at the United Nations." Institut de recherches et d'études féministes, Université du Québec à Montréal. Centre de documentation sur l'éducation des adultes et la condition féminine (CDÉACF), May 2000. https://web.archive.org/web/20100509022101/http://netfemmes.cdeacf.ca/documents/Anti-Feminist%20Groups-USLetter.pdf.

Durham, Helen. "Women and Civil Society: NGOs and International Criminal Law." In *Women and International Human Rights Law*, edited by Kelly D. Askin and Dorean M. Koenig, 819–43. Ardsley, NY: Transnational, 1999.

Dwyer, Leslie K. "Spectacular Sexuality: Nationalism, Development and the Politics of Family Planning in Indonesia." In *Gender Ironies of Nationalism: Sexing the Nation*, edited by Tamar Mayer, 25–62. London: Routledge, 2000.

Ellis, Mark. "Breaking the Silence: Rape as an International Crime." *Case Western Reserve Journal of International Law* 38, no. 2–3 (2006–2007): 225–47.

Engel, Matthew. "Rift with US: Distaste for 'International Entanglements' Runs Deep." *Guardian*, July 2, 2002, p. 4.

Facio, Alda. "A Word (or Two) about Gender." *ICC Monitor*, no. 6 (November 1997): 5, 10.

Farrell, Brian. "An Isolationist View of the International Criminal Court." *America* 187, no. 17 (2002): 19–20.

Fine, Robert. *Cosmopolitanism*. New York: Routledge, 2007.

Forsythe, David P. "The United States and International Criminal Justice." *Human Rights Quarterly* 24, no. 4 (2002): 974–91.

Foss, Sonja K. "Equal Rights Amendment Controversy: Two Worlds in Conflict." *Quarterly Journal of Speech* 65, no. 3 (October 1979): 275–88.

Fraser, Nancy. "Transnationalizing the Public Sphere: On the Legitimacy and Efficacy of Public Opinion in a Post-Westphalian World." *Theory, Culture and Society* 24, no. 4–30 (2007): 7.

Freeman, Marsha A. "International Institutions and Gendered Justice." *Journal of International Affairs* 52, no. 2 (1999): 529.

Friedman, Elizabeth Jay. "Gendering the Agenda: The Impact of the Transnational Women's Rights Movement at the UN Conferences of the 1990s." *Women's Studies International Forum* 26, no. 4 (2003): 313–31.

Gallant, Mary J., and Harry M. Rhea. "Collective Memory, International Law, and Restorative Social Processes after Conflagration: The Holocaust." *International Criminal Justice Review* 20, no. 3 (2010): 265–79.

Gardam, Judith. "Women and the Law of Armed Conflict: Why the Silence?" *The International and Comparative Law Quarterly* 46, no. 1 (1997): 55–80.

Gibson, Katie L. "Judicial Rhetoric and Women's 'Place': The United States Supreme Court's Darwinian Defense of Separate Spheres." *Western Journal of Communication* 71, no. 2 (2007): 159–75.

Gibson, Katie L. "United States v. Virginia: A Rhetorical Battle between Progress and Preservation." *Women's Studies in Communication* 29, no. 2 (2006): 133–64.

Glasius, Marlies. "Expertise in the Cause of Justice: Global Civil Society Influence on the Statute for an International Criminal Court." In *Global Civil Society 2002*, edited by Marlies Glasius, Mary Kaldor, and Helmut Anheier, 137–68. Oxford: Oxford University Press, 2002.

Glasius, Marlies. "How Activists Shaped the Court." Crimes of War Project, December 2003. https://web.archive.org/web/20110209102851/http://www.crimesofwar.org/print/icc/icc-glasius-print.html.

Glasius, Marlies. *The International Criminal Court: A Global Civil Society Achievement* (Routledge Advances in International Relations and Global Politics). New York: Routledge, 2005.

Glasius, Marlies, Mary Kaldor, and Helmut Anheier, eds. *Global Civil Society 2002*. Oxford: Oxford University Press, 2002.

Goodenough, Patrick. "Pro-Family Groups Worry about Effects of International Court." Cybercast News Service, July 7, 2008. https://www.cnsnews.com/news/article/pro-family-groups-worry-about-effects-international-court.

Grossman, Marc. "American Foreign Policy and the International Criminal Court." Remarks to the Center for Strategic and International Studies, Washington, DC, U.S. Department of State, May 6, 2002. https://2001-2009.state.gov/p/us/rm/9949.htm.

Habermas, Jürgen. *Die Postnationale Konstellation: Politische Essays*. Frankfurt: Suhrkamp Verlag, 1998.

Halbwachs, Maurice. *On Collective Memory*. Translated by Lewis A. Coser. Chicago: University of Chicago Press, 1992.

Hall, Christopher Keith. "The First Proposal for a Permanent International Criminal Court." *International Review of the Red Cross* 38, no. 322 (March 31, 1998): 57–74. https://www.icrc.org/en/doc/resources/documents/article/other/57jp4m.htm.

Hariman, Robert, and John Louis Lucaites. "Performing Civic Identity: The Iconic Photograph of the Flag Raising on Iwo Jima." *Quarterly Journal of Speech* 88, no. 4 (2002): 363–93.

Harvey, David. *The Condition of Postmodernity: An Enquiry into the Origins of Cultural Change*. Malden, MA: Wiley-Blackwell, 1989.

Hassan, Farooq. "International Criminal Court: Family Related Issues." Synopsis of paper presented at the World Congress of Families III, Mexico City, Family and the UN Mexico, World Congress of Families, March 30, 2004. http://web.archive.org/web/20150925164331/http://worldcongress.org/wcf3_spkrs/wcf3_hassan.htm.

Hayden, Patrick. *Cosmopolitan Global Politics , Ethics and Global Politics*. Farnham, UK: Ashgate, 2005.

Heater, Derek Benjamin. *What Is Citizenship?* Malden, MA: Polity, 1999.

Heindel, Anne. "Response from AMICC's Deputy Convener to Goodenough's 'Pro-Family Groups Worry about Effects of International Court.'" AMICC, 2002. http://web.archive.org/web/20170116084510/http://www.amicc.org/docs/Feb11_02.pdf.

Held, David. "Regulating Globalization." In *The Global Transformations Reader: An Introduction to the Globalization Debate*, edited by David Held and Anthony McGrew, 420–30. Malden, MA: Polity, 2000.

Held, David, and Anthony McGrew. "The Great Globalization Debate: An Introduction." In *The Global Transformations Reader: An Introduction to the Globalization Debate*, edited by David Held and Anthony G. McGrew, 1–50. Malden, MA: Polity, 2000.

Helms, Jesse. "We Must Slay This Monster." *Financial Times*, July 31, 1998, p. 18.

Henry L. Stimson Center. "Project on International Humanitarian Law and the US Armed Services: Understanding US Military Concerns Regarding the International Criminal Court." Henry L. Stimson Center, 2006. https://web.archive.org/web/20081127185224/http://www.stimson.org/fopo/pdf/Descript_FOPO_ICC_Project.pdf.

Herman, Didi. "Globalism's 'Siren Song': The United Nations and International Law in Christian Right Thought and Prophecy." *The Sociological Review* 49, no. 1 (2001): 56–77.

Higgins, Rosalyn. *Problems and Process, International Law and How We Use It*. New York: Oxford University Press, 1995.

Hirsh, David. *Law against Genocide: Cosmopolitan Trials*. London: GlassHouse, 2003.

Hirsch, Moshe. "Collective Memory and International Law." *ESIL Reflections* 3, no. 7 (September 2014): 1–4.

Hirsch, Moshe. "Collective Memory and International Law." In *Invitation to the Sociology of International Law*, 46–88. New York: Oxford University Press, 2016.

Holt, Victoria K., and Elisabeth W. Dallas. "On Trial: The US Military and the International Criminal Court." Henry L. Stimson Center, March 2006. https://www.stimson.org/sites/default/files/file-attachments/US_Military_and_the_ICC_FINAL_website_1.pdf.

Holy See, "Intervention of the Holy See Diplomatic Conference of Plenipotentiaries on the Establishment of an International Criminal Court." Working Group on War Crimes, 1998. https://www.catholicculture.org/culture/library/view.cfm?recnum=459.

Huyssen, Andreas. *Present Pasts: Urban Palimpsests and the Politics of Memory*. Stanford, CA: Stanford University Press, 2003.

"ICC: Promise of Justice or Threat of Tyranny?" *Interim*, August 12, 1998. http:// www.theinterim.com/politics/icc-promise-of-justice-or-threat-of-tyranny/.

Ignatieff, Michael. "Human Rights: The Midlife Crisis." *New York Review of Books*, May 20, 1999.

International Committee of the Red Cross (ICRC). *Geneva Convention for the Amelioration of the Condition of the Wounded and Sick in Armed Forces in the Field (First Geneva Convention)*, August 12, 1949, 75 UNTS 31. https://ihl-databases.icrc.org/applic/ihl/ihl.nsf/Treaty.xsp?documentId=4825657B0C7E6BF0C12563CD002D6B0B&action=openDocument.

International Committee of the Red Cross (ICRC). *Geneva Convention for the Amelioration of the Condition of Wounded, Sick and Shipwrecked Members of Armed Forces at Sea (Second Geneva Convention)*, August 12, 1949, 75 UNTS 85. https://ihl-databases.icrc.org/applic/

ihl/ihl.nsf/Treaty.xsp?documentId=2F5AA9B07AB61934C12563CD002D6B25&action=openDocument.

International Committee of the Red Cross (ICRC). *Geneva Convention Relative to the Protection of Civilian Persons in Time of War (Fourth Geneva Convention)*, August 12, 1949, 75 UNTS 287. https://ihl-databases.icrc.org/applic/ihl/ihl.nsf/Treaty.xsp?documentId=AE2D398352C5B028C12563CD002D6B5C&action=openDocument.

International Committee of the Red Cross (ICRC). *Geneva Convention Relative to the Treatment of Prisoners of War (Third Geneva Convention)*, August 12, 1949, 75 UNTS 135. https://ihl-databases.icrc.org/applic/ihl/ihl.nsf/Treaty.xsp?documentId=77CB9983BE01D004C12563CD002D6B3E&action=openDocument

"International Criminal Court Approved." *LifeSiteNews*, July 19, 1998. https://www.lifesitenews.com/news/international-criminal-court-approved-despite-major-victories-grave-concern.

International Criminal Court (ICC). "Situations under Investigation." Accessed May 22, 2019. https://www.icc-cpi.int/pages/situations.aspx.

Iriye, Akira. *Global Community: The Role of International Organizations in the Making of the Contemporary World*. Berkeley: University of California Press, 2002.

Jelin, Elizabeth. "The Politics of Memory: The Human Rights Movement and the Construction of Democracy in Argentina." *Latin American Perspectives* 21, no. 2 (Spring 1994): 38–58.

Kahn, Paul. "The International Criminal Court (ICC)—The End of Impunity: Why the United States Is So Opposed." *Crimes of War Magazine*, December 2003. https://web.archive.org/web/20110509102940/http://www.crimesofwar.org/print/icc/icc-kahn-print.html.

Keane, John. *Global Civil Society?* Cambridge: Cambridge University Press, 2003.

Keck, Margaret E., and Kathryn Sikkink. *Activists Beyond Borders: Advocacy Networks in International Politics*. Ithaca, NY: Cornell University Press, 1998.

Kelly, Michael. "Ignoring Criminal Treaty Harms U.S. Legacy." *USA Today*, April 16, 2002, p. 12A.

Kirsch, Philippe. "The International Criminal Court: Current Issues and Perspectives." *Law and Contemporary Problems* 64, no. 1 (Winter 2001): 3–11.

Korey, William. *NGOs and the Universal Declaration of Human Rights: A Curious Grapevine*. New York: St. Martin's, 1998.

Kritzman, Lawrence D. Foreword to *Realms of Memory: Rethinking the French Past Vol. 1—Conflicts and Divisions*, English language edition. New York: Columbia University Press, 1996.

Lemkin, Raphael. *Axis Rule in Occupied Europe: Laws of Occupation, Analysis of Government, Proposals for Redress*. Washington, DC: Carnegie Endowment for International Peace, Division of International Law, 1944.

Levy, Daniel, and Natan Sznaider. "The Institutionalization of Cosmopolitan Morality: The Holocaust and Human Rights." *Journal of Human Rights* 3, no. 2 (2004): 143–57.

Levy, Daniel, and Natan Sznaider. "Memory Unbound: The Holocaust and the Formation of Cosmopolitan Memory." *European Journal of Social Theory* 5, no. 1 (2002): 87–106.

Levy, Daniel, and Natan Sznaider. "Sovereignty Transformed: A Sociology of Human Rights." *The British Journal of Sociology* 57, no. 4 (2006): 657–76.

Lewis, Neil A. "U.S. to Renounce International Crime Tribunal." *Pittsburgh Post-Gazette*, May 5, 2002, p. A19.

Lewis, Neil A. "U.S. Will 'Unsign' Global Court Treaty: White House Fears Capricious Charges." *Chicago Tribune*, May 5, 2002, p. 4.

Lind, Rebecca Ann, and Colleen Salo. "The Framing of Feminists and Feminism in News and Public Affairs Programs in U.S. Electronic Media." *Journal of Communication* 52, no. 1 (2002): 211–28.

Liu Institute for Global Issues at the University of British Columbia. *The Third Vancouver Dialogue: The Communications Gap*. Citizens for Global Solutions, December 2004. https://web.archive.org/web/20071027094612/http://oldsite.globalsolutions.org/programs/law_justice/vd3-finalreport-feb28.pdf.

Lucaites, John Louis. "The Irony of 'Equality' in Black Abolitionist Discourse: The Case of Frederick Douglass's 'What to the Slave Is the Fourth of July?'" In *Rhetoric and Political*

Culture in Nineteenth-Century America, edited by Thomas W. Benson, 47–70. East Lansing: Michigan State University, 1997.

Lucaites, John Louis, and Celeste Michelle Condit. "Reconstructing [Equality]: Culturetypal and Counter-Cultural Rhetorics in the Martyred Black Vision." *Communication Monographs* 57, no. 1 (1990): 5–24.

Lyon, Janet. *Manifestoes: Provocations of the Modern*. Ithaca, NY: Cornell University Press, 1999.

Mandela, Nelson. "Opening Address." Speech presented at the Second Conference of African National Institutions for the Promotion and Protection of Human Rights, Durban, South Africa, July 1, 1998. http://www.mandela.gov.za/mandela_speeches/1998/980701_humanrights.htm.

Mansell, Wade, and Emily Haslam. "John Bolton and the United States' Retreat from International Law." *Social and Legal Studies* 14, no. 4 (2005): 459–85.

Markovic, Milan. "Vessels of Reproduction: Forced Pregnancy and the ICC." *Michigan State Journal of International Law* 16, (2007): 439–58.

Mayerfeld, Jamie. "Who Shall Be the Judge?: The United States, the International Criminal Court, and the Global Enforcement of Human Rights." *Human Rights Quarterly* 25, no. 1 (2003): 93–129.

McCarthy, Thomas. "Vergangenheitsbewältigung in the USA: On the Politics of the Memory of Slavery." *Political Theory* 30, no. 5 (2002): 623–48.

McGee, Michael Calvin. "The 'Ideograph': A Link between Rhetoric and Ideology." *Quarterly Journal of Speech* 66, no. 1 (1980): 1–16.

McGee, Michael Calvin. "In Search of 'the People': A Rhetorical Alternative." *Quarterly Journal of Speech* 61, no. 3 (1975): 235–49.

McLaurin, Luke A. "Can the President 'Unsign' a Treaty? A Constitutional Inquiry." *Washington University Law Review* 84, no. 7 (2006): 1941–82.

McLeod, Laura, Rachel Johnson, Sheila Meintjes, Alice Brown, and Valerie Oosterveld. "Gendering Processes of Institutional Design: Activists at the Negotiating Table." *International Feminist Journal of Politics* 16, no. 2 (2014): 354–69.

Mertus, Julie. *Bait and Switch: Human Rights and U.S. Foreign Policy*. New York: Routledge, 2004.

Miller, Alice M. "Realizing Women's Human Rights: Nongovernmental Organizations and the United Nations Treaty Bodies." In *Gender Politics in Global Governance*, edited by Mary K. Meyer and Elisabeth Prügl, 161–76. Lanham, MD: Rowman and Littlefield, 1999.

Minow, Martha. *Between Vengeance and Forgiveness: Facing History after Genocide and Mass Violence*. Boston, MA: Beacon, 1998.

Morris III, Charles E. "My Old Kentucky Homo: Lincoln and the Politics of Queer Public Memory." In *Framing Public Memory*, edited by Kendall R. Phillips, 89–114. Tuscaloosa: University of Alabama Press, 2004.

Mufson, Steven, and Alan Sipress. "U.N. Funds in Crossfire over Court: Exemption Sought for U.S. Troops." *Washington Post*, August 16, 2001, p. A01.

Murphy, John M. "The Language of the Liberal Consensus: John F. Kennedy, Technical Reason, and the 'New Economics' at Yale University." *Quarterly Journal of Speech* 90, no. 2 (2004): 133–62.

Murphy, Sean D. "U.S. Notification of Intent Not to Become a Party to the Rome Statute." *The American Journal of International Law* 96, no. 3 (2002): 724.

Myers, Steven Lee. "U.S. Signs Treaty for World Court to Try Atrocities." *New York Times*, January 1, 2001, p. A1.

Neale, Palena R. "The Bodies of Christ as International Bodies: The Holy See, Wom(b)an and the Cairo Conference." *Review of International Studies* 24, no. 1 (1998): 101–18.

Nesiah, Vasuki. "Missionary Zeal for a Secular Mission: Bringing Gender to Transitional Justice and Redemption Feminism." In *Feminist Perspectives on Contemporary International Law: Between Resistance and Compliance?*, edited by Sari Kouvo and Zoe Pearson, 137–59. Portland, OR: Hart, 2011.

Neuffer, Elizabeth. "US Pushes to Keep Its Troops Exempt from World Court." *Boston Globe*, May 23, 2002, p. A1.

Neuffer, Elizabeth. "US to Back out of World Court Plan Envoy: Bush Team May 'Unsign' Treaty." *Boston Globe*, March 29, 2002, p. A22.

New York Times. "Clinton's Words: 'The Right Action.'" January 1, 2001, p. A6.

New York Times. "The Coming War Trials." October 9, 1945, p. 20.

NGO Family Voice. "Judges and Prosecutors Must Be Professionally Qualified and Ideologically Neutral." Position paper in Richard Wilkins, William Perry, and Marcus Mumford, "The United Nations Diplomatic Conference of Plenipotentiaries on the Establishment of an International Criminal Court," Appendix D. World Family Policy Center, 1998. http://web.archive.org/web/20040628194703/http://www.worldfamilypolicycenter.org/wfpc/About_the_WFPC/papers/ICC_Report.html#AppendixD.

NGO Family Voice. "The ICC's 'New International Crimes:' A Call for Caution." Position paper in Richard Wilkins, William Perry, and Marcus Mumford, "The United Nations Diplomatic Conference of Plenipotentiaries on the Establishment of an International Criminal Court," Appendix D. World Family Policy Center, 1998. http://web.archive.org/web/20040628194703/http://www.worldfamilypolicycenter.org/wfpc/About_the_WFPC/papers/ICC_Report.html#AppendixD.

Nichols, Bill. "Clinton Backs a World Criminal Court Treaty Faces Opposition from Many Republicans in Senate." *USA Today*, January 2, 2001, p. 9A.

Nora, Pierre. "Between Memory and History: Les Lieux de Memoire." *Representations* 26 (Spring 1989): 7–25.

Oosterveld, Valerie. "Constructive Ambiguity and the Meaning of 'Gender' for the International Criminal Court." *International Feminist Journal of Politics* 16, no. 4 (2014): 563–80.

Oosterveld, Valerie. "The Definition of 'Gender' in the Rome Statute of the International Criminal Court: A Step Forward or Back for International Criminal Justice?" *Harvard Human Rights Journal* 18 (2005): 55–84.

Pace, William. "Globalizing Justice." *Harvard International Review* 20, no. 2 (1998).

Pace, William. "The Rome Statute System: Future Perspectives and Challenges." Statement on the Occasion of the 10 Years' Celebration of the Adoption of the Rome Statute, The Hague. CICC, July 3, 2008. https://asp.icc-cpi.int/iccdocs/asp_docs/ASP7/10th/ICC-ASP-10thAnni-Pace-ENG.pdf

Pace, William, and Jennifer Schense. "The Role of Non-Governmental Organizations." In *The Rome Statute of the International Criminal Court: A Commentary*, edited by Antonio Cassese, Paola Gaeta, and John R. W. D. Jones, 105–43. New York: Oxford University Press, 2002.

Pace, William, and Mark Thieroff. "Participation of Non-Governmental Organizations." In *The International Criminal Court: The Making of the Rome Statute—Issues, Negotiations, Results*, edited by Roy S. Lee, 391–98. The Hague, Netherlands: Kluwer Law International, 1999.

Phillips, Kendall R., and G. Mitchell Reyes. Introduction to *Global Memoryscapes: Contesting Remembrance in a Transnational Age*, 1–26. Tuscaloosa: University of Alabama Press, 2011.

Population Research Institute (PRI). "PRI FAQ's (Frequently Asked Questions)." Accessed May 22, 2019. http://www.pop.org/0000000094/pri-faqs-frequently-asked-questions.

Population Research Institute (PRI). "Who We Are." Accessed May 22, 2019. https://www.pop.org/simple/who-we-are/.

Ralph, Jason. "Between Cosmopolitan and American Democracy: Understanding US Opposition to the International Criminal Court." *International Relations* 17, no. 2 (2003): 195–211.

Ray, Angela G., and Cindy Koenig Richards. "Inventing Citizens, Imagining Gender Justice: The Suffrage Rhetoric of Virginia and Francis Minor." *Quarterly Journal of Speech* 93, no. 4 (November 2007): 357–402.

REAL Women of Canada. "Canada Courts Disaster with World Court." Newsletter XVI, no. 10, July–August 1998. http://web.archive.org/web/20020822011010/http://www.realwomenca.com/html/newsletter/1998_July_Aug/Article_1.html.

REAL Women of Canada. "What's the Argument for 'Gender Justice?'" Position paper prepared by the David M. Kennedy Center for International Studies. Position paper in Richard Wilkins, William Perry, and Marcus Mumford, "The United Nations Diplomatic Conference of Plenipotentiaries on the Establishment of an International Criminal Court," Appendix G. World Family Policy Center, 1998. http://web.archive.org/web/20040628194703/http://www.worldfamilypolicycenter.org/wfpc/About_the_WFPC/papers/ICC_Report.html#AppendixG.

Reilly, Niamh. "Cosmopolitan Feminism and Human Rights." *Hypatia* 22, no. 4 (2007): 180–98.

Richardson, Diane. *Rethinking Sexuality*. London: Sage, 2000.

Ricks, Thomas E. "U.S. Signs Treaty on War Crimes Tribunal: Pentagon, Republicans Object to Clinton Move." *Washington Post*, January 1, 2001, p. A1.

Roach, Steven C. *Politicizing the International Criminal Court: The Convergence of Politics, Ethics, and Law*. Lanham, MD: Rowman and Littlefield, 2006.

Roberts, Adam. "Analysis: Just the Beginning: This Week the Long-Awaited International Criminal Court Is Born." *Guardian*, April 8, 2002, p. 15.

Rumsfeld, Donald. "Secretary Rumsfeld Statement on the ICC Treaty." U.S. Department of Defense, News Release, May 6, 2002. https://web.archive.org/web/20061229224351/http://www.defenselink.mil/releases/release.aspx?releaseid=3337 .

Ruse, Austin. "Feminists Refuse to Define Their 'Gender Agenda' for the International Criminal Court." C-FAM, June 26, 1998. https://c-fam.org/feminists-refuse-to-define-their-gender-agenda-for-the-international-criminal-court/.

Ruse, Austin. "International Criminal Court Debate Begins in Rome: Feminists Face First Setback." C-FAM, June 19, 1998. https://c-fam.org/international-criminal-court-debate-begins-in-rome-feminists-face-first-setback/.

Ruse, Austin. "International Criminal Court Takes a Giant Step in UN General Assembly: John Paul II Accepts Diplomatic Credentials from New American Ambassador." C-FAM, December 19, 1997. https://c-fam.org/friday_fax/international-criminal-court-takes-a-giant-step-in-un-general-assembly-john-paul-ii-accepts-diplomatic-credentials-from-new-american-ambassador-2/.

Ruse, Austin. "Protection for Families Dropped from New International Criminal Court." C-FAM, December 17, 1999. https://c-fam.org/friday_fax/protection-for-families-dropped-from-new-international-criminal-court/.

Ruse, Austin. "Toward a Permanent United Nations Pro-Family Bloc." Remarks to the World Congress of Families II. World Congress of Families, 1999. https://web.archive.org/web/20160128001948/http://worldcongress.org/wcf2_spkrs/wcf2_ruse.htm.

San Francisco Chronicle. "No Way to Lead the World." April 23, 2002, p. A16.

Scharf, Michael P. "Results of the Rome Conference for an International Criminal Court." *ASIL Insights* 3, no. 10 (August 1998). https://web.archive.org/web/20120716203934/http://www.asil.org/insigh23.cfm.

Scheffer, David. "A Treaty Bush Shouldn't 'Unsign.'" *New York Times*, April 6, 2002, p. A15.

Scheffer, David, Richard Cooper, and Juliette Voinov Kohler. "The End of Exceptionalism in War Crimes: The International Criminal Court and America's Credibility in the World." *Harvard International Review*, November 21, 2007. https://web.archive.org/web/20090306061211/http://www.harvardir.org:80/articles/1647/.

Schiff, Benjamin N. *Building the International Criminal Court*. New York: Cambridge University Press, 2008.

Schwartz, Barry, and Horst-Alfred Heinrich. "Shadings of Regret: America and Germany." In *Framing Public Memory*, edited by Kendall R. Phillips, 115–44. Tuscaloosa: University of Alabama Press, 2004.

Schwenkel, Christina. "Recombinant History: Transnational Practices of Memory and Knowledge Production in Contemporary Vietnam." *Cultural Anthropology* 21, no. 1 (2006): 3–30.

Solomon, Martha. "The 'Positive Woman's' Journey: A Mythic Analysis of the Rhetoric of STOP ERA." *Quarterly Journal of Speech* 65, no. 3 (1979): 262–74.

Solomon, Martha. "The Rhetoric of STOP ERA: Fatalistic Reaffirmation." *Southern Speech Communication Journal* 44, no. 1 (1978): 42–59.

Soysal, Yasemin Nuhoğlu. *Limits of Citizenship: Migrants and Postnational Membership in Europe*. Chicago: University of Chicago Press, 1994.

Spees, Pam. "Women's Advocacy in the Creation of the International Criminal Court: Changing the Landscape of Justice and Power." *Signs: Journal of Women in Culture and Society* 28, no. 4 (2003): 1233–54.

Stacy, Helen. "Relational Sovereignty." *Stanford Law Review* 55 (May 2003): 2029–59.

Stanley, Alessandra. "Semantics Stalls Pact Labeling Rape a War Crime." *New York Times*, July 9, 1998, p. A3.

Steains, Cate. "Gender Issues." In *The International Criminal Court: The Making of the Rome Statute—Issues, Negotiations, Results*, edited by Roy S. Lee, 357–90. The Hague, Netherlands: Kluwer Law International, 1999.

Struett, Michael J. *The Politics of Constructing the International Criminal Court: NGOs, Discourse, and Agency*. New York: Palgrave Macmillan, 2008.

Stuckey, Mary E., and Joshua R. Ritter. "George Bush, [Human Rights], and American Democracy." *Presidential Studies Quarterly* 37, no. 4 (2007): 646–66.

Swaine, Edward T. "Unsigning." *Stanford Law Review* 55, no. 5 (May 2003): 2061–89.

Tan, Kok-Chor. *Justice without Borders: Cosmopolitanism, Nationalism, and Patriotism, Contemporary Political Theory*. New York: Cambridge University Press, 2004.

Teitel, Ruti G. "Humanity's Law: Rule of Law for the New Global Politics." *Cornell International Law Journal* 35 (2002): 355–87.

Terraviva. "Africa Pushing Gender Concerns." Inter Press Service News Agency, June 30, 1998. https://www.legal-tools.org/doc/b051dd/pdf/.

United Nations. "Security Council Requests International Criminal Court Not to Bring Cases against Peacekeeping Personnel from States Not Party to Statute." United Nations Press Release, Security Council Press Release SC/7450, July 12, 2002. http://www.un.org/press/en/2002/sc7450.doc.htm.

United Nations. "Vienna Convention on the Law of Treaties." United Nations Treaty Series Volume 1155, May 23, 1969. https://treaties.un.org/doc/publication/unts/volume%201155/volume-1155-i-18232-english.pdf.

United Nations Diplomatic Conference of Plenipotentiaries on the Establishment of an International Criminal Court. *Rome Statute of the International Criminal Court*. UN document A/CONF. 183/9, July 15–17, 1998. https://www.icc-cpi.int/nr/rdonlyres/ea9aeff7-5752-4f84-be94-0a655eb30e16/0/rome_statute_english.pdf.

United Nations General Assembly. *Convention on the Prevention and Punishment of the Crime of Genocide*. United Nations document A/RES/260, December 9, 1948. https://treaties.un.org/doc/publication/unts/volume%2078/volume-78-i-1021-english.pdf.

United Nations Special Rapporteur on Violence against Women. *Integration of the Human Rights of Women and the Gender Perspective: Violence against Women*. Report E/CN.4/2003/75/Add.1. UN Economic and Social Council, February 27, 2003. https://documents-dds-ny.un.org/doc/UNDOC/GEN/G03/113/04/PDF/G0311304.pdf?OpenElement.

U.S. Department of State. American Service-Members' Protection Act of 2003. Washington, DC, 2003. https://web.archive.org/web/20130310112048/http://www.state.gov/t/pm/rls/othr/misc/23425.htm.

United States House of Representatives Committee on International Relations. *The International Criminal Court*. 106th Congress, second session, July 25–26, 2000. No. 106–76. Washington, DC: US Government Printing Office, 2000.

United States Senate Subcommittee on International Operations of the Committee on Foreign Relations. *Is a U.N. International Criminal Court in the National Interest?* 105th Congress, second session, July 23, 1998. Senate hearing, 105–724. Washington, DC: US Government Printing Office, 1998.

Wall Street Journal. "A Global Special Prosecutor?" May 7, 2002, p. A26.

Wander, Philip. "The Ideological Turn in Modern Criticism." In *Readings in Rhetorical Criticism*, edited by Carl R. Burgchardt, 107–25. State College, PA: Strata, 2000.

Wander, Philip. "The Rhetoric of American Foreign Policy." *Quarterly Journal of Speech* 70, no. 4 (1984): 339–61.

Warnick, Barbara. "Conservative Resistance Revisited—A Reply to Medhurst." *Western Journal of Speech Communication* 46, no. 4 (1982): 373–78.

Warnick, Barbara. "The Rhetoric of Conservative Resistance." *The Southern Speech Communication Journal* 42, no. 3 (Spring 1977): 256–73.

Washburn, John. "The International Criminal Court Arrives: Establishing an Ethic of Peace and Justice." Speech delivered at the Ethical Society of New York. American NGO Coalition for the International Criminal Court, June 30, 2002. https://web.archive.org/web/20160814003230/http://www.amicc.org/docs/John_EthicalSoc.pdf.

Weller, Marc. "Undoing the Global Constitution: UN Security Council Action on the International Criminal Court." *International Affairs* 78, no. 4 (2002): 693–712.

West, Lois. "The United Nations Women's Conferences and Feminist Politics." In *Gender Politics in Global Governance*, edited by Mary K. Meyer and Elisabeth Prügl, 177–91. Lanham, MD: Rowman and Littlefield, 1999.

White, Geoffrey M. "Remembering Guadalcanal: National Identity and Transnational Memory-Making." *Public Culture* 7, no. 3 (1995): 529–55.

Whitehead, Anne. *Memory*. New York: Routledge, 2009.

Wilkins, Richard. "Doing the Right Thing: The International Criminal Court and Social Engineering." Address to the Second Annual World Family Policy Forum, Provo, Utah, July 11, 2000. In *Proceedings of the World Family Policy Forum 2000*, pp. 88–95. http://web.archive.org/web/20051102032734/http://www.worldfamilypolicy.org/New%20Page/Forum/2000/WFPF2000.pdf

Wilkins, Richard, William Perry, and Marcus Mumford. "The United Nations Diplomatic Conference of Plenipotentiaries on the Establishment of an International Criminal Court." World Family Policy Center, 1998. http://web.archive.org/web/20040628194703/http:/www.worldfamilypolicycenter.org/wfpc/About_the_WFPC/papers/ICC_Report.html#N_5_

Wilkins, Richard G., and Kathryn O. Balmforth. "The International Criminal Court, Human Rights and the Family." In *Fifty Years after the Declaration: The United Nations' Record on Human Rights*, edited by Teresa Wagner and Leslie Carbone, 99–108. Lanham, MD: University Press of America, 2001.

Wind, Marlene. "Challenging Sovereignty? The USA and the Establishment of the International Criminal Court." *Ethics and Global Politics* 2, no. 2 (2009): 83–108.

Winkler, Carol. "Encroachments on State Sovereignty: The Argumentation Strategies of the George W. Bush Administration." *Argumentation* 22, no. 4 (2008): 473–88.

Women's Caucus for Gender Justice. "About the Caucus." Accessed May 22, 2019. https://web.archive.org/web/20090108203343/http://www.iccwomen.addr.com/caucus/about.htm.

Women's Caucus for Gender Justice. "Clarification of Term 'Gender.'" Accessed May 22, 2019. http://web.archive.org/web/20150409235023/http://www.iccwomen.org/wigjdraft1/Archives/oldWCGJ/resources/gender.htm.

Women's Caucus for Gender Justice. "No More Compromises: Bring the Issues of Justice to a Vote." The Advocacy Project, July 13, 1998. https://web.archive.org/web/20081119150159/http://www.advocacynet.org/resource/375.

Women's Initiatives for Gender Justice. "Women's Initiatives for Gender Justice." Accessed May 22, 2019. http://4genderjustice.org.

World Family Policy Center. "About the World Family Policy Center." Accessed May 22, 2019. https://web.archive.org/web/20160820050512/http://www.law2.byu.edu/wfpc/about.htm.

Yale Law School. *Nuremberg Trial Proceedings Vol. 1: Charter of the International Military Tribunal*. Lillian Goldman Law Library, 1945. http://avalon.law.yale.edu/imt/imtconst.asp.

Yoneyama, Lisa. "Traveling Memories, Contagious Justice: Americanization of Japanese War Crimes at the End of the Post-Cold War." *Journal of Asian American Studies* 6, no. 1 (2003): 57–93.

Young, Hugo. "We Can't Allow US Tantrums to Scupper Global Justice." *Guardian*, July 2, 2002, p. 14.

Young, James E. *The Texture of Memory: Holocaust Memorials and Meaning*. New Haven, CT: Yale University Press, 1993.

Zarefsky, David. "Definitions." In *Argument in a Time of Change: Definitions, Frameworks, and Critiques*, edited by J. F. Klumpp, 1–11. Annandale, VA: National Communication Association, 1998.

Zarefsky, David. "Making the Case for War: Colin Powell at the United Nations." *Rhetoric and Public Affairs* 10, no. 2 (2007): 275–302.
Zelizer, Barbie. "Reading the Past against the Grain: The Shape of Memory Studies." *Critical Studies in Mass Communication* 12, no. 2 (1995): 214–39.
Zelizer, Barbie. *Remembering to Forget: Holocaust Memory through the Camera's Eye* (Chicago: University of Chicago Press, 1998).

Index

About the Author

Jennifer Biedendorf holds a PhD in communication arts and sciences from the Pennsylvania State University. A rhetorical theorist and critic by training, her research focuses on the rhetoric of public memory, international and intercultural communication, gender and LGBTQ studies, and social movement studies. She is a lecturer of communication studies at California State University, Stanislaus.

www.ingramcontent.com/pod-product-compliance
Ingram Content Group UK Ltd.
Pitfield, Milton Keynes, MK11 3LW, UK
UKHW041627031026
15587UKWH00001B/119

9 781683 931799